Population and Society

About the Author

Dr. A.K. Sharma is Professor of Sociology with Indian Institute of Technology, Kanpur. His areas of specialization are rural development, health and HIV/AIDS. He has authored six books including *Gandhian Perspectives on Population and Development* besides publishing more than one hundred research articles. He has been a consultant in various research projects of national importance and holds membership of many professional bodies including IUSSP and IASP.

Population and Society

A.K. Sharma

CONCEPT PUBLISHING COMPANY Pvt. Ltd.
NEW DELHI-110059

ISBN-13: 978-81-8069-818-7 (HB)
ISBN-13: 978-81-8069-819-4 (PB)

First Published 2012

Published and Printed by

Since 1974

Concept Publishing Company Pvt. Ltd.

Regd. Office:

A/15-16, Commercial Block, Mohan Garden,
New Delhi-110059 (INDIA)
Phones : 25351460, 25351794, *Fax* : 091-11-25357109
Email : publishing@conceptpub.com,
Website: www.conceptpub.com

Editorial Office:

H-13, Bali Nagar, New Delhi-110 015, India.

Cataloging in Publication Data--*Courtesy:* D.K. Agencies (P) Ltd. <docinfo@dkagencies.com>

Sharma, A. K., 1953-
Population and society / A.K. Sharma.
p. cm.
Includes bibliographical references (p.) and index.
ISBN 9788180698187

1. India—Population. 2. India—Social conditions. 3. India—Population policy. I. Title.

DDC 304.60954 23

Preface

There are very few departments in Indian universities and institutions which offer degree programmes in Population Studies or Demography as such. However, there are several of them which teach population as a paper in different disciplines like Sociology, Economics, Psychology, Geography, Mathematics, Medical Science and Engineering. The objective of this book is to make the students of Population familiar with important substantive concepts and technical tools of Population Studies. Thus the book is written keeping in view the needs of both categories of students, those who are studying Population as an independent subject, and those who are studying Population as part of some other discipline. The book would also be useful for researchers who are exploring demographic issues in the Indian socio-cultural context.

Special Features

- Sociological theories of population which are often missing in introductory books in population
- Sociological concepts relevant for study of population in India, drawn from writings of the Western and the Indian sociologists
- Demographic models presented in relation to substantive questions often raised in the field of Population Studies
- Emerging issues in population in India in relation to changing paradigms of development
- Review questions and activities for students

A.K. Sharma

Acknowledgements

I would like to thank Dr. T. Ravichandran and Dr. Satyaki Roy for coaxing me to develop this book on Population and Society for students of Population, pursuing degree programme in various departments, in different universities and institutions. This whole project would not have come into existence without the financial support and encouragement from NPTEL. Thanks are also due to Ms. Ritu Gupta who raised several questions about the organisation of chapters while working with the soft copies of the draft. I have been teaching undergraduate and postgraduate courses on Society and Population in IIT Kanpur for nearly thirty years and the book reflects the collective wisdom of me and my students on the subject of *Population and Development*. I have benefited immensely from the questions and comments raised by my brilliant students in the classroom.

I gratefully acknowledge the support of the staff of Concept Publishing Company for making the publication of this book possible.

A.K. Sharma

Contents

Contents

1

Population and Society

INTRODUCTION

Social processes are closely linked with human population. Therefore, for students of society it is important to study characteristics of population. According to the provisional population totals published by Census of India, 2001, the size of India's population on Ist March 2011 was 1,210.2 million. Imagine if the size of population of India were 120 million, i.e., one-tenth of the present population, what would be its impact on society. Would we have the same level of poverty and unemployment? Would we have the same level of conflicts and chaos? Would that affect the position of India in the international politics? Are there only good consequences of lower population or there are some harmful consequences too? Remember that today in India a city like Mumbai itself has more population than you are imagining for whole India. You will learn that the relationship between population and society is not one way. Not only population determines structure and processes of society but society also determines the population characteristics and dynamics. Is it not true that industrialization and development have reduced family size in all the Western countries? Is it not true that concern for children's education leads to use of contraception; and women's employment improves their decision making power in the family? It is hoped that after completing this book a student of sociology will be able to relate population trends and policies with society and social change.

This book aims at understanding of various linkages between population and society at various levels: national, regional, village, household and individual. An attempt has been made to present material in a manner that a graduate student of sociology can grasp the subject without difficulty. There is only one chapter that requires some familiarity with statistics and basic mathematics. This is Chapter 4 on models. All other chapters are devoted to substantive issues. Questions given at the end of each chapter would help the students in self-evaluation.

POPULATION STUDIES AS A BRANCH OF SOCIAL SCIENCES

Population studies is a branch of social sciences. Social sciences include sociology, economics, psychology, political science and anthropology. Not only sociologists but economists, psychologists, political scientists, anthropologists, and social historians have also contributed to development of theory of population. Table 1.1 shows some illustrative questions of interest to different social scientists working in the field of population studies.

Economists are interested in economic aspects of demographic phenomena. They may use cost-benefit approach to reproductive decision making or migration. Psychologists focus on individual differences. Political scientists explain everything in terms of power and forms of state. Anthropologists have been traditionally interested in culture of preliterate societies though these days they also study urban and industrial organizations and examine belief systems, symbolic communication, patterns of interaction and behaviour, and values. Social historians examine historical roots of population changes and rise and fall of death rate, migration and nuptiality (marriage). Sociologists claim that they study population variables in relation to social structure.

It may be said that in the field of population research sociologists are playing an increasing role. The reasons are:

- While other disciplines focus on one specific aspect of reality sociologists attempt to explain things in a holistic perspective.
- Sociologists have the advantage of freely borrowing concepts and methodologies from all other branches of social sciences.
- Sociologists are the first to venture into new areas as they are less constrained by disciplinary limitations.
- Sociologists who take whole society as the level of analysis are in a better position to explain differences between different societies and cultures.

However, the entry of sociologists in the field of population is relatively new. In the beginning population research was dominated by statisticians and economists. The stress was on estimation of rates and ratios from incomplete data. With improved data and survey, as the main method of research, sociologists are playing a more important role than others in confronting the challenging issues of our times.

BASIC CONCEPTS IN POPULATION STUDIES

In population studies scholars study size and composition of population. They also study various processes through which size and composition of population change. The processes are: nuptiality or marriages; reproduction or births; mortality or deaths; migration of people from one place to another (both within a country and between different countries); and social mobility leading to changes in social stratification (primarily caused by changes in education, work and occupation). Size, composition and processes of population affect society and social institutions directly or through economic and environmental factors.

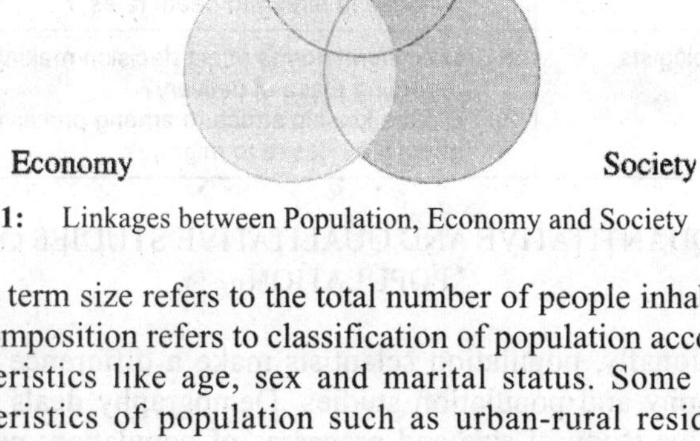

Figure 1.1: Linkages between Population, Economy and Society

The term size refers to the total number of people inhabiting an area. Composition refers to classification of population according to characteristics like age, sex and marital status. Some specific characteristics of population such as urban-rural residence or geographical divisions are studied under the aegis of population distribution.

Table 1.1: Important Questions in Population Studies

	Important questions
Sociology	1. Are there religious differentials in fertility in India? What are the causes behind them? 2. How does social stratification affect health inequality and quality of life? 3. What role did the industrial revolution play in promoting rural to urban migration?
Economics	1. What are the short term and long term effects of population growth on productivity and national income? 2. What are costs and benefits of children in different types of societies? 3. Will the falling birth rate improve unemployment rate? 4. How does one assess the impact of population growth in urban or rural areas?
Psychology	1. What are all the values of children? 2. What is the relationship between locus of control (i.e., attribution of successes and failures to oneself or environment) and fertility preferences? 3. What are social representations of health and illness among the tribal communities? 4. How does one measure stigma against HIV/AIDS?
Political scientists	1. How does empowerment of women help in reducing maternal mortality ratio? 2. Is there a relationship between political structures and demographic transition (i.e., changes in birth and death rates)?
Anthropologists	1. Do cultural norms affect decision making regarding place of delivery? 2. Did the kinship structure among primitive tribes affect their desire to migrate?

QUANTITATIVE AND QUALITATIVE STUDIES OF POPULATION

Conventionally, population scientists make a difference between demography and population studies. Demography deals with the quantitative study of size and processes of population; population studies deals with complex and qualitative relationships between socio-economic environment and population. In practice there is no separation between the two. In this book we will use them interchangeably. Demographers make their models in the light of substantive theories developed by sociologists and economists; and sociologists and economists employ demographic measures, data and models to explain the various links between population and society.

RELATIONSHIP BETWEEN SIZE, GROWTH, COMPOSITION AND DISTRIBUTION OF POPULATION

Size, growth, composition and distribution of population are interrelated. In a territory of a given size population cannot increase indefinitely. Therefore, as we will see later, size of population determines at what rate the population would be growing. Composition of population also affects the rate of growth of population. In turn, rate of growth affects the composition of population. Most of the rapidly growing populations are younger than the declining populations or populations growing at a very slow pace. Rate of growth also affects distribution directly and indirectly. One reason behind this is that all the regions and groups in a country do not grow at the same rate: while some regions and groups may grow at a fast pace others may grow only at a slow pace or even decline, leading to spatial and social class differences in growth rate of population. In most countries, therefore, the governments are not only concerned about overall growth rate of population they also take cognizance of and intervene in population growth differentials. No wonder, in many countries, the social classes are themselves raising concerns about social class differences in fertility, mortality and migration.

USES OF POPULATION STUDIES

Population studies is in great demand today. Poston *et al.* (2007) say that there are three specific demographic activities for which persons trained in population studies are employed:

- Demographers serve as advisors, witnesses, and technicians on matters of political apportionment and redistricting.
- They are frequently called to participate in multidisciplinary teams given the responsibility of developing a plan to halt the environmental damage.
- They are asked to provide the various types of forecasts in conjunction with community development.

In India, demography is taught in different university departments such as sociology, economics, geography and statistics. Preventive and social medicine departments of medical colleges too have demographers to teach demography and assist research students. Demographers, with their strong training in methodology, are recruited by Non-Government Organizations (NGOs) and research organizations working in diverse areas: health, sexuality, gender issues and development. They are consulted by civic bodies and governments for providing projections of urban and rural populations and different types of services. Sociologists with training in demography can look for jobs in universities, NGOs and research and consultancy organizations. Of late, engineers and environmentalists have included demographic variables in studies of impact of development projects on people. Lastly, it is notable that in plural societies, having presence of multiple ethnic and religious groups, political parties cannot afford not to pay heed to population matters. Differences in growth rate of population have been both political and emotive issues in India where people's groups have asked whether there are religious differences in practice of birth control methods, what are the causes of this, and what are the implications of this.

BASIC CONCEPTS AND MEASUREMENTS

Size

As said earlier, the term size refers to what is the total number of people inhabiting an area. The area may be the world as a whole, a nation, a region, a locality or a ward within a locality. The number includes both males and females and all age groups.

Growth Rate and Doubling Time

Growth rate shows percentage change in population of an area, and is expressed on per year basis. It is computed from quinquennial and decennial censuses of population. Suppose the population of a country is 100,345 in year 1991 and it has risen to 120,619 in year 2001. Then the decadal growth rate of the population is

$$[120{,}619-100{,}345)/100{,}345] \times 100$$

i.e., 20.20 per cent. On per year basis it may be defined as 2.02 per cent per year (average annual rate of growth).

In advanced technical discussions in place of simple growth rate exponential growth rate is preferred. This is computed by using the following formula:

$$P_t = P_0 e^{rt}$$

where P_t refers to population at time t, P_0 to population at time 0, r to rate of growth and t to time. For short time it does not matter much whether you use the decadal growth rate method or exponential growth rate method. The former assumes a discrete change in population size, the latter a continuous change.

The growth rate is often converted into doubling time which conveys that at a given rate of growth how much time would be required to double the population size.

Box 1.1: Doubling Time

Imagine that a population is growing exponentially at rate r, i.e.,

$$P_t = P_0 e^{rt}$$

where P_1 refers to population at time t, P_0 to initial population (at t=0), e to exponential function and r to rate of growth.

By taking natural logarithm on both the sides it can be shown that

$$t = \frac{1}{r} \log \frac{P_t}{P_0}$$

Putting $P_t = 2\,P_0$, one gets

$$t = .69/r$$

For approximate values of it, doubling time t is often expressed as 70/r in which r is expressed in percentage form. The following table gives the doubling time for different values of growth rate.

r (per year)	*Doubling time in years*
1 per cent	700
5 per cent	140
1 per cent	70
2 per cent	35
3 per cent	23.3
4 per cent	17.5
5 per cent	14

COMPOSITION OF POPULATION

Among various characteristics of population, age and sex composition are the most important ones. Sex composition of population is commonly studied by calculating sex ratio which is defined as the number of females per thousand males. Improvement in sex ratio is often seen as indicative of empowerment of women.

Sex ratio = (Number of females/number of males) *1,000

In India population scientists also calculate sex ratio for age group 0-6. This has special significance. Low sex ratio for the age group 0-6 suggests that either there is practice of female feticide or there is neglect of female babies due to which they have higher mortality than males. Percentage of young, aged less than 15 years, and percentage of old population, aged 65 and more, are of common interest to population scientists. Increase in percentage of population aged 65 and more leads to aging of population and it results mainly from declining fertility. Ratio of population of old to population of young, multiplied by 100 or 1,000 is called dependency ratio. Ratio of population aged 80+ to population 65+ indicates aging among the aged. Dependency ratio is closely related to labour force participation rate which expresses number of workers (including those looking for work) as a ratio of the total population.

Dependency ratio = (Population aged 65 years or more + population aged less than 15 years)/(Population aged 15–64 years)* 100

Labour force participation rate = (Number of workers/total population)*100

Labour force participation rate may be computed separately for males and females and for urban and rural areas.

Distribution

Distribution is a more general term than composition. It refers to any statistical classification of population according to a given characteristic. The most commonly used types of population distribution are urban-rural and spatial distributions of population.

They are obtained by calculating percentage of total population living in urban areas and in different geographical regions, respectively. Thus

Per cent urban	=	(Urban population/total population)*100
Per cent of population living in Uttar Pradesh State	=	(Population of the state/total population of India)*100

Changes in spatial distribution of population, i.e., per cent of population living in different states or regions may be caused by difference in fertility or mortality or the process of migration-movement of people from one state or region to another for education, employment, marriage or other reasons.

As above, you may study the following:

- Occupational and industrial distribution of population
- Income and wealth distributions of population
- Distribution of population by source of drinking water and possession of household amenities
- Distribution of population by place of birth and place of current residence

Population distribution, as defined above, can be compared between different countries/societies as it makes the numbers in any category of study free from the effect of size of total population.

Population Processes

Study of population processes requires separate measurements of nuptiality, fertility, mortality, migration and social mobility. Among them, nuptiality is measured in terms of mean age of marriage and proportion married in different age groups. Fertility is measured by birth rate, total number of children ever born, and total fertility rate.

Birth rate is defined as

(Number of births in a year/total population) * 1,000

If a measure of fertility is to be obtained from census or surveys average number of children ever born per woman may be computed for different age groups of women. Average number of children ever born among women in the age group 40-44 (sometimes 45-49) is of special significance. It is called the total fertility rate.

Likewise, mortality is measured by death rate. Death rate is defined as

(Number of deaths in a year/total population) *1,000

Birth and death rates are called crude rates as they are dependent not only on the rapidity of reproduction and mortality but also on age and sex composition of population. In many developed countries where people live longer than in the less developed countries death rates are higher because more of their population consists of old people. In less developed countries people live shorter than in the developed countries but more of their population consists of young people. Therefore their death rates are lower.

The most commonly used measure of fertility is total fertility rate. For computing it, one has to calculate Age-Specific-Fertility-Rates (ASFR) at different ages.

$ASFR_x$ = (No. of children born in a year to women aged x)/(No. of women aged x)

Sum of age-specific-fertility-rates over all ages (from 15 to 44 or 49) is called Total Fertility Rate (TFR). It is interpreted as the average number of children born per woman in the entire lifetime by a group of women who all start reproductive life (age 15) together and experience schedule of ASFRs as existing in a particular year. It is, however, a technical concept. It does not show actual fertility of any real group of population. Yet, it is widely used as a measure of fertility as it does not depend on age distribution of population.

As in case of fertility, mortality rates are also computed separately for different ages or age groups. Thus Age-Specific-Death-Rates (ASDRs) are defined as

$ASDR_x$ = (No. of deaths in a year among persons aged x)
(No. of persons aged x)

The most commonly used measure of mortality is life expectancy which refers to time in years for which a new born child is expected to live. Life expectancy at birth is calculated from Age-Specific-Death-Rates (ASDRs). Since there are gender differences in ASDRs, life expectancy is calculated separately for males and females.

Number of infant deaths, i.e., deaths of children in age group 0-1 year per thousand births is called Infant Mortality Rate (IMR). Likewise one can also define Child Mortality Rate (CMR) for children aged 0-5 years. IMR is considered to be an indicator of both development and health services.

Migration rate can be defined on the pattern of crude birth rate and crude death rate. However, in countries where migration records are not kept and migration data are collected from surveys or censuses some other measures are employed. These measures and measures of social mobility are beyond the scope of this book.

For calculating the above measures one needs data on size of population, age-and-sex composition of population and births and deaths by age.

The sources of data are: population census; vital registration system; sample registration system; national and regional surveys; and administrative data collected from routine records of various government departments. These sources of data will be discussed in Chapter 3 on methods.

PERSPECTIVES AND LINKAGES

Relationship between Population and Society: Sociological Approaches to Population

Sociology and population studies developed mostly in nineteenth and twentieth centuries. The founding fathers of sociology have little to say on population. In their time population was growing at a slow pace. In the nineteenth century social thinkers could see that in the developed countries death rates had begun to fall and as a result of that population had started growing. This growth of population started affecting society and economy. This produced interest in studying population. Population-society link became a hot subject in second part of the twentieth century when the population in the developing countries started growing at a fast rate. Among the founding fathers of sociology, Emile Durkheim, Max Weber and Karl Marx, it is mainly Marx who wrote on population, though only to illustrate the point that there is no universal law of population. Each historic mode of production has its own law of population. The law of reproduction valid for capitalist society is not the same as that was valid for feudal or ancient societies. Durkheim's views are given below. You will learn Marxist population theory in detail in Chapter 8 on theories. Weber was more concerned with the relationship between religion and capitalism and although he included population in the factors contributing to industrialization, he did not give much importance to this issue.

Emile Durkheim

Emile Durkheim believed that growth of population increases physical density of population, i.e., number of persons per square kilometre. This in turn increases the moral density of population, i.e., number of interactions between people. For example, if the number of people at a given time is n the number of one-to-one interactions is ${}^{n}C_{2}$. This implies that number of interactions increases faster than the size of population.

Subsequently, the increased moral density produces a high degree of competition and anomy (i.e. normlessness). In the Western, industrially advanced countries, society responded by producing division of labour. The division of labour saved society from falling into anarchy. Thus to follow Durkheim we may say that the population growth was primarily responsible for change over from mechanical to organic solidarity, i.e. social integration based on homogeneity to social integration based on interdependence between different industrial and occupational groups. It may be noted that Durkheim is known as much for his sociological theories as for his contribution to methods. His study of suicide shows how multivariate statistical reasoning can be used to draw inferences about social facts like suicide rates.

Pitirim Sorokin

Sorokin gave a serious thought to population processes. In *Contemporary Sociological Theories* Pitirim Sorokin (1978) has one full chapter devoted to demographic school in sociology. Though he is more known for his theory of cyclical change but his writings show a clear Durkheimian approach in which one social fact is explained in terms of other facts. He relates the fact of "size and density" of population to other facts:

- Birth and death rates

- Migration
- Revolution and war
- Economic prosperity
- Forms of ownership and possession
- Forms of social organization
- Political and social institutions
- Inventions and birth of men of genius
- Mores and customs
- Language, religion, mysticism, equalitarian ideology
- Progress and decay of societies

Sorokin reviewed literature on population and recognised the importance of sociological studies of population. Box 1.2 presents Sorokin's conclusion of the survey of literature of demographic school. To Sorokin size, density, heterogeneity and mobility are factors that affect ideas, institutions and history in complex ways.

Box 1.2: Sorokin on Findings of Demographic School in Sociology

Numerous investigators have succeeded in showing the importance and efficiency of demographic conditions in almost all fields of social phenomena. If we cannot say that all these attempts have been successful, or quite accurate, we have to admit that a considerable number of them are likely to be accurate, at least in part; and some of them are as near to reality as it is possible to arrive in the present stage of social science. The school has thrown light on a series of social phenomena. It has supplied us with a series of probable correlations. For those reasons the school has as much right to its existence as has any other sociological school. Putting away its mistakes and one-sidedness, we may gratefully take its valuable contributions to the science of social phenomena.

Kingsley Davis

Kingsley Davis linked population growth with development and migration. Kingsley Davis is famous for his theory of change and response (also called theory of multiphasic response) according to which economic and technological developments and subsequent fall in mortality led to various responses among people which resulted in low fertility. These responses include increasing use of birth control methods, increased celibacy, postponement of marriage, practice of abortion and emigration. Improvement in mortality in Japan and pre-transitional Europe increased family size and as time passed people could perceive the stress of increasing family size on family resources (Davis, 1963). In this context, people started exploring various ways of limiting family size. Davis is a functionalist and he shows how disturbance created by a factor of social change (e.g. mortality) leads to changes in individual behaviour (limiting family size) which eventually restores the equilibrium (zero population growth).

Kingsley Davis claims that this theory is reflexive and behavioural; reflexive as it explains individual level changes in terms of socio-economic changes, and behavioural as it explains individual behaviour. In the 20th century Davis has been the most known of all the sociologists for works in the broad field of population studies. He has also worked on the history, analysis and prediction of populations of India and Pakistan (1968). Davis has also made enormous contribution to measurement of urbanization and relationship between urbanization, industrialization and economic development.

Pierre Bourdieu

In the post-modern age, sociologists view that the world has become more complex, fragmented and uncertain. It is characterized by hyperdifferentiation (excessive fragmentation of society and people), hypercommodification (rise in consumerism) and hyperrationalization (disbelief in science and the idea of truth). It is not possible to have an essentialist theory of society any more. We can only talk about specific subjects and specific locales. Therefore, theory must deal with the problems facing the different vulnerable groups; to be valid it should be of use to them. Postmodernists are less interested in grand narratives of social change and transformation. They concentrate on piecemeal changes and emancipation of subjects, defined varyingly in different economic, social, political and cultural terms (little narratives). Postmodernism has been applied to studies of health, social stigma, feminism, constructions of sexuality, risk behaviour, environmental movements, anti-abortion movements, ethnicity, etc. where the focus of studies has been more on individual dispositions and behaviour rather than state policies. Postmodernism makes no truth claims about the world and postmodern sociologists have turned interpreters (Bauman, 1988).

Among the social theorists, who went beyond positivistic sociology of Durkheim, Sorokin and Davis, Pierre Bourdieu focuses on how individuals take an action such as arranging for marriage of children.

He says that their strategies are not to be seen in abstraction. They are part of the complex process of social reproduction through which power and privileges are passed on to new generation. For Bourdieu, individual's strategies are more important than rules governing society. This shifts sociologists' attention from positivism to dispositions to act, which are constructed through socialization and experiences. To theorize about strategies, he gave the concept of *habitus*:

> ...the practical mastery of a small number of implicit principles that have spawned an infinite number of practices and follow their own pattern, although they are not based on obedience to any formal rules. Hence, since these patterns emerge "spontaneously," it is unnecessary to make them explicit or to invoke or impose any rules. *Habitus* is thus the product of very structures it tends to produce. Predicated upon a "spontaneous" compliance with the established order and with the will of the guardians of that order, namely the elders, *habitus* is the principle that will generate the different solutions (such as the limitation of family size or the emigration or enforced celibacy of younger sons) which individuals, depending on their position in the social hierarchy, their place in the family's order of birth, their sex and so forth, can bring to the practical dilemmas created by the various systems of exigencies that are not necessarily mutually compatible.

For Bourdieu the constraints of rules surrounding every choice are infinite. The choices and practices too are infinite. It is not possible for any individual to deal with all the norms and make the choices consciously. Thus social conditions are like those of fencing and chess and decisions are like parries and moves.

Box 1.3: Bourdieu on Habitus

Bourdieu defines habitus as "systems, of durable, transposable dispositions, structured structures predisposed to operate as structuring structures, that is, as principles which generate and organize practices and representations that can be objectively adapted to their outcomes without presupposing a conscious aiming at ends or an express mastery of the operations necessary in order to attain them.

Quoted in Cockerham, 2005.

Postmodern sociology is more about emancipation of plural subjects and their choices rather than truth claims. It focuses on small groups, their risks and dispositions and supports their advocacy. In place of theorizing at the level of society it looks for practical solutions to problems of specific subjects (agency). For example, in case of health it says that the responsibility for one's health falls on oneself through healthy living (Cockerham, 2005). New sociologists of population are taking increasing interests in the emerging relationships between gender, race, class, religion, media, market and health.

In the new age, increasing number of sociologists favour qualitative approach, paradigmatic theories and counterstructural method. There is preference for understanding subjective meanings in place of positivistic explanation. And for this a particular theoretical orientation is chosen without any claim for universalization. Then an attempt is made to ensure that the findings of narratives of health and illness (or other issues pertaining to life) are in agreement with the subjects' understanding of them. In years to come, "population studies" is likely to take over "demography". Qualitative methods will take over modelling and theory of vulnerable and marginal groups will take over the mathematical and statistical studies of population and society. Students of population need to be prepared for this.

QUESTIONS AND EXERCISES

1. What is the subject matter of population studies? How does the subject of population studies differ from demography?
2. What is doubling time? If the rate of growth of India's population declines from 2 per cent to 1 per cent what will be its impact on doubling time?
3. Define total fertility rate. How is total fertility rate a better measure of fertility than birth rate?
4. What do the demographers do and where do they find employment?
5. Select five developed and five developing countries and find out birth rate, death rate, total fertility rate and life expectancy for each of them. Do you see a relationship between development and demographic characteristics?
6. Select a sample of five illiterate, married women and five graduate, married women of the same age from your town. Look at the following:

(a) At what age did they marry?
(b) How many children do they have?
(c) How many children do they plan to have in lifetime?
(d) Which women—illiterate or graduate—have more say in family in matters like how many children they should have?
(e) Are the graduate women working or have any plan to work?

7. Write short notes on the following:
(a) Durkheim's views on population growth
(b) Difference between dependency ratio and labour force participation rate
(c) Causes of low sex ratio in age group 0-6 years
(d) Bourdieu's concept of *Habitus.*

REFERENCES

Bauman, Zygmunt, 1988, Is There a Postmodern Sociology?. *Theory, Culture and Society*, Vol. 5: 217-37.

Bourdieu, Picrre, 2002, Pierre Bourdieu on Marriage Strategies. *Population and Development Review*, Vol. 28, No. 3: 549-558.

Cockerham, William C., 2005, Health Lifestyle Theory and the Convergence of Agency and Structure. *Journal of Health and Social Behaviour*, Vol. 46: 51-67.

Davis, Kingsley, 1963, The Theory of Change and Response in Modern Demographic History. *Population Index*, Vol. 29, Issue 4: 345-366.

Davis, Kingsley, 1968, *The Population of India and Pakistan*, New York: Russell and Russell.

Poston, Dudley L. Jr., Micklin, Michael and Baumle, Amanda K., Demography. In Bryant, Clifton D. and Peck, Dennis L. (eds.), *21st Century Sociology: A Reference Book*, Vol. 1. Thousand Oaks: Sage Publications, 2007, 508-517.

Sorokin, Pitirim, 1978, *Contemporary Sociological Theories*. Ludhiana: Kalyani Publishers.

2

Basic Characteristics of Indian Society

INTRODUCTION

Students of sociology are primarily interested in the study of social structure and change in it. Social structure refers to patterns of expected behaviour or sum total of social institutions. "For Radcliff Brown, Malinowski and Nadel, social structure is the 'order' of social relationships, roles and statuses which constitute the apparent reality and are outside human mind." (Singh, 1993). Structure is closely associated with the culture of society which refers to values and norms transmitted from one generation to another. Culture may be broadly divided into material culture and non-material culture. The former includes all the physical artefacts—tools, ornaments, material, utensils or any other object developed and used in a culture. The latter includes values and norms. Values are the standards of goodness, truth and beauty. Norms are the guidelines for behaviour. Members of society are expected to attain values by following prescribed norms (folkways, mores, laws, etc.) of society.

This chapter deals with society of India. It discusses the nature of Indian society, processes of change and development, their consequences for inequalities and the major demographic and health goals as envisioned by the Eleventh Five Year Plan.

CHARACTERISTICS OF INDIAN SOCIETY

Indian society is characterized by poverty, illiteracy, diversity, patriarchy, importance of caste, community and tribal identity, and weak governance even after 60 years of independence. The major complexity in theorisation of Indian society lies in the fact that India has had its own unique civilization, social structure and culture and contradictions and oppositional forces within and is also greatly influenced by the worldwide processes of change such as postmodernization and globalization.

Poverty

Poverty has the closest link with all demographic processes. Therefore, we need estimation of poverty by regions and social classes. According to Planning Commission (2008), 27.5 per cent population of the country is living below the poverty line—Rs. 356 monthly per capita consumption expenditure for rural areas and Rs. 539 for urban areas. The per cent poor are slightly higher in rural areas (28.3) than in urban areas (25.7). Planning Commission also notes that there is growing consensus that the poverty line in India is too low. If the poverty line was higher, the share of the population below the poverty line would be accordingly higher. Further, only about 15 per cent of the labour force is engaged in relatively high quality work in the organized sector, the rest is engaged in agriculture, self-employment, unorganized sector and informal work without regular salary or job protection.

Literacy

Literacy is an indicator of development, particularly social development. It is also correlated with all demographic characteristics and processes. Before the advent of the British, India had its own model of education in which education was provided to all boys through schools associated with temples and madrasas, girls at home. The British rule destroyed it first and then tried to build its own model of education. This created multiple forms of inequalities. The new system helped the metropolitan people in the developed regions, especially males and upper classes, and marginalised others.

According to Census of India 2001, the level of literacy in India was 64.8 per cent (Table 2.1). This means that out of 1000 persons aged 7 years and above there were only 648 who could both read and write with understanding in any language. (It is not necessary for a person to have received any formal education or passed any minimum educational standard for being treated as literate. People who were blind and could read in Braille are treated to be literates.) Separately among males and females the literacy rate was 75.3 per cent and 53.7 per cent, respectively. According to the provisional population totals provided by census of India, 2011, the overall literacy has risen to 74.04 per cent – 82.14 per cent among males and 65.46 per cent among females.

There are significant spatial differences in literacy and educational achievements too. Census 2001 showed that with 90.9 per cent literacy Kerala has the highest literacy rate and Bihar with 47.0 per cent literacy Bihar has the lowest literacy rate. Within Bihar, as in other states, there are great disparities between men and women. The literacy rate among women in Bihar is only 33.0 per cent. Overall, out of 593 districts in India 18 had female literacy below 25 per cent.

Table 2.1: Literacy Rate in India

		Persons	*Males*	*Females*
Total	No. of literates	560,687,797	336,533,716	224,154,081
	Literacy rate	64.8%	75.3%	53.7%
Rural	No. of literates	361,870,817	223,551,641	138,319,176
	Literacy rate	58.7%	70.7%	46.1%
Urban	No. of literates	198,816,980	112,982,075	85,834,905
	Literacy rate	79.9%	86.3%	72.9%

Literacy does not imply education. There are literates who have never formally gone to schools. A large number of them are primary pass. Only about half of all those who join school move beyond eighth standard. Others drop out. The proportion of those who go for higher education is still very low. Moreover, there are differences according to region, social class, gender and urban-rural residence. They are correlated with and are often the cause of other forms of hierarchies. In India education is closely correlated with spatial differences in demographic transition. Among women, it is associated with empowerment, domestic violence, fertility, maternal mortality, knowledge of RTI/STI including HIV and AIDS, migration and work.

What is more worrisome is that among persons of age 15-29 years only about 2 per cent are reported to have received formal vocational training and another 8 per cent are reported to have received non-formal vocational training. Eleventh Five Year Plan Draft says that the proportion of trained youth in India is one of the lowest in the world.

Spatial/Regional Variations

There are very significant regional variations in development. They manifest in the form of differences in demographic and economic characteristics of populations of different states. For example, while the state of Kerala has a literacy rate of 93.91 per cent, Bihar has a literacy rate of 63.82 only (Census of India, 2011). And while the states of Andhra Pradesh and Goa have as low a total fertility rate as 1.8 (i.e., below the replacement level), Bihar has a total fertility rate of 4.0 (IIPS and MI, 2008). We will come back to this issue in the third section of this chapter.

Major Social Groups

Social groups can be defined in many ways. In India they are customarily defined in terms of gender, caste and religious community. The Planning Commission recognizes that the economic growth in the post-independence period has not been sufficiently inclusive. Scheduled Castes (SCs), Scheduled Tribes (STs), and minorities have not benefited from development as much as others. SCs and STs are disadvantaged in terms of education, employment and income. Minorities also have lower level of income, lower participation in high quality jobs, and are more alienated, sometimes more alienated than SCs. Gender inequality also remains a pervasive problem. As a matter of fact certain types of developments have had an adverse effect on women. In the patriarchal and patrifocal society of India women suffer discrimination both at home and outside. At home they suffer from domestic violence—sexual, emotional and physical—and outside they suffer from discrimination in employment and wages. Illiterate, rural women, from minority groups in backward regions of the country suffer from multiple disadvantages.

People of India have primordial loyalties towards caste and community. At times they become source of violent conflicts. No wonder, certain sections suffer from discrimination. Thus from the beginning, the government of independent India adopted policy of affirmative action. This led to reservation in government jobs and seats in schools and colleges for Scheduled Castes (SC) and Scheduled

Tribes (ST), separately in proportion to their population. However, since caste was a local phenomenon no all-India standards could capture or do justice to complex reality of caste.

Right from the beginning there was a feeling that there are many castes/groups also which do not come under either SC or ST but are lagging behind and require special assistance. Eventually, in 1980 government accepted the reality of Other Backward Classes (OBC), and the recommendations of the Second Backward Classes Commission (Agrawal and Aggarwal, 1991). Then 27 per cent jobs in the Central services were reserved for the OBC. Some years later it was followed by reservation of seats in the colleges, universities and professional institutions.

In this backdrop, the Eleventh Five Year Plan went for the concept of inclusionary growth (Planning Commission, 2008). According to the Eleventh Five Year Plan the following groups/regions/sectors need special schemes for inclusion: social groups divided into four categories of Scheduled Castes, Scheduled Tribes, Other Backward Classes, and Others; minorities, particularly Muslims; eleven special category states comprising of seven North Eastern states, Jammu and Kashmir, Himachal Pradesh, and Uttarakhand; women and children; agriculture sector; old population; street children; physically challenged; and drug addicts. The plan aims at promotion of education and health among all the social groups, equal participation of all in the government jobs, meeting special needs of each group, and reducing inequalities. A serious reading of the draft shows that the concept of social groups has become most crucial to development plan. In this context, sociologists would like to study all population parameters according the social groups identified in the Plan. The different social groups in India are passing through different transitions. While some are passing through the first demographic transition, others are passing through the second demographic transition in which fertility declines rapidly to the below replacement level.

Thus for Indian demographers differences in size and growth rates between different social groups acquire paramount importance. At the same time the issue of social group inequality is not unaffected by the issue of regional imbalances. Certain groups, for example, may have higher fertility than others but there are also significant variations among the people belonging to the same group living in different regions. One may say that hyperdifferentiation of demographic trends is the present as well as the future of India. Migration will be a major factor in hyperdifferentiation. Migration is selective of caste and communities and by opening new opportunities to some it also affects the relative conditions of different communities, social relationships and belief systems. This is followed by hyperrationalization and further differentiation. At the same time, the new patterns are not non-independent of tradition and continuing class differences provide enough room for conventional analysis of inequality.

Religion

Indian society is a plural society. People belonging to all religions and faiths are found here. As per 2001 census, 72.2 per cent population of India lives in rural areas. The rural areas have the continuing influence of religious values. In urban areas also influence of religion and customs is quite strong though the situation is changing fast.

Census of India, 2001 provides data on religious composition of population of India. According to these data, 80.5 per cent of the population of India consists of Hindus. Next to them are Muslims who constitute 13.4 per cent of the entire population of the country (Table 2.2). Christians constitute 2.3 per cent. Sikhs constitute 1.9 per cent while other religions constitute less than one per cent each. It may be added here that the religious composition of population is not uniform across different states and regions. Thus there are states where the national minorities constitute the majority. Also, there are districts in Hindu majority states where other religions constitute the majority or a sizeable proportion of the overall population. There are also significant religious differentials in population growth rates. However, this is a matter of debate whether these differentials are due to religious ideas or socio-economic differences or a combination or both.

Table 2.2: Religious Composition of India

Religion	*Population*	*(%)*
Hindus	827,578,868	80.5
Muslims	138,188,240	13.4
Christians	24,080,016	2.3
Sikhs	19,215,730	1.9
Buddhists	7,955,207	0.8
Jains	4,225,053	0.4
Other Religions and Persuasions	6,639,626	0.6
Religion not stated	727,588	0.1
Total	**1,028,610,328**	**100.0**

Unity in Diversity

Vast differences in culture, religion, socio-economic levels, language and caste pose a big challenge to unity of India. This explains the partition of the country at the time of independence. This also explains why the country has had a long history of riots, secessionist movements, conflicts and demand for smaller states, which have continued after independence. Yet, despite differences and conflicts, there is a unity in diversity where democracy is firmly established.

To quote Sharma (2007):

> India can rightly be characterised as a society having unity in diversity and diversity in unity, as it is a plural society both in letter and spirit. Despite innumerable odds, India has maintained its unity. We find unity in India in all its historical and cultural facets. India is today a secular state. It has one Constitution and uniform rule of law for all its people living in different regions, speaking different languages, and believing in different religions and faiths. Today, Hindus, Jains, Muslims, Sikhs, Christians and people of other faiths participate together in administration, politics and public life. Ethnic, linguistic and religious diversities do not hinder the realization of the common national goals. The cultural heritage of India has been a living example of the synthesis of different cultures.

In sum, the demographic characteristics of India need to be analysed at various levels: national, state, district, block and village; social class and sub-classes. This requires collection of data at all these levels. At the moment we have data only at national and state level. Some data are available at the district level. Therefore, a need is felt to collect data going up to the block level. There is also a need for collection of reliable data for different social and religious groups and look for mechanism of demographic changes at the micro levels. Regional and social class diversities, when combined with economic and political diversities in the same direction, are disruptive. Therefore, for the unity of the nation it is important to promote demographic equality as well as economic equality.

The next section will focus on social change. It provides certain sociological concepts in terms of which we can analyse the processes of change and their consequences for demographic transition in the country. Three major ideas taken up for discussion are Sanskritization, Westernization and Globalization.

SOCIAL CHANGE IN INDIA

Change is a reality. Human society too experiences changes in different domains from time to time. However, all types of changes are not covered by the term of social change which has a definite meaning in sociology. Social change refers to change in social structure. Thus change in per capita income, if not accompanied by changes in social relationships, is not a part of social change.

Box 2.1

Ironically, despite our profession of socialistic pattern of society, our policies in social and economic fields have been most detrimental to the prosperity of the weaker sections of society, such as the dalits, the women, the scheduled castes, scheduled tribes, and the minorities. It is reflected also in the failure of our education policy. The mass illiteracy in the forty per cent of the population still persists. It is higher still in the case of women. There is a vicious circular relationship between poverty, susceptibility to fall a victim to exploitation, proneness to health morbidity, high fertility rate and illiteracy. Education is a single most effective factor which breaks this process of vicious cumulative causation. We find that wherever educational achievements, whether within a region or a social group are higher, the indicators of economic growth as also of the quality of life are higher. ...Our failure in the field of removal of illiteracy, and universalization of education is indeed at the root of the most facets of our "crisis of failures".

From: Singh, Yogendra, 1993, *Social Change in India: Crisis and Resilience*. New Delhi: Har-Anand Publications, p.15.

Sociologists have developed several concepts to study social change in India: development, modernization, Westenization, universalization, social development, great and little traditions are some of them. For a long time sociologists and anthropologists in India used the concepts of parochialization and universalization, and great and little traditions which were developed by McKim Marriot and Robert Redfield in studies of Indian and Mexican villages. Among them two most popular concepts are: Sanskritization and Westernization. They hold a special significance.

Sanskritization

The concept of Sanskritization has been used to explain the processes of cultural change in caste ridden society of India. It is a truism that social change is caused by both endogenous (internal) and exogenous (external) factors. Sanskritization concept was developed to show the processes of change which arise due to endogenous causes. However, it must be noted that social change occurs due to a large number of known and unknown factors and their effects are mixed and confounded. It is not possible to attribute any one type of change to any one specific factor. Now let us look at the concept of Sanskritization more closely.

The concept of Sanskritization is given by M.N. Srinivas. According to him, Sanskritization had been occurring throughout the Indian history. It may be viewed as the model of social mobility in India. To understand this concept it is important to distinguish between two related concepts of Varna and caste. Varna is an all-India framework and in this framework human society is divided into four hierarchical groups (Varnas). They are Brahmin, Kshatriya, Vaisya and Shudra. Untouchables are outside the Varna system. On the other hand caste refers to hereditary, endogamous groups which form a hierarchy, each having a traditional association with one or two occupations. Castes groups maintained relations in terms of purity and pollution. There were many castes which were only regional in character. Regarding hierarchy, in each region there are certain castes which are considered to be at the top and certain other castes are considered to be at the bottom. An interesting aspect of the caste system has been that the claims to position are contested and there is no general agreement regarding hierarchy, at least at the middle level.

Further, through Sanskritization, i.e., by changing customs, rituals, ideology and way of life towards upper castes people belonging to a particular caste claim a superior status on the caste hierarchy. This may or may not be granted by others and sometimes the matter reached the king who gave the final verdict. At times castes would fight violently till a status claimed by them is granted to them. Srinivas maintained that Sanskritization, however, led only to positional change but not structural change. This means that the perceived positions of different castes may change but it would not affect the Hindu belief in caste hierarchy. To be Hindu is to belong to a caste with a relative place in the hierarchical division.

Srinivas agrees that Sanskritization was only one source of mobility in Hindu society. Initially, he observed that Sanskritization means emulating the lifestyles of Brahmins. In his later works, however, he maintained that Indian culture being highly varied and the beliefs about status of a Varna being dependent on local culture, there were several models of Sanskritization: Brahmin model, Kshatriya model, Vaisya model; and Shudra model. Thus Brahmin model was only one of them. The concept of dominant caste supplemented the concept of Sanskritization in some way. At some places if the tribal groups were dominant, the other groups followed the tribal customs and thus one can also speak of a tribal model of Sanskritization.

Box 2.2: Sanskritization

Sanskritization is a process by which a "low" Hindu caste, or tribal or other group, changes its customs, ritual, ideology, and way of life in the direction of a high, and frequently, a "twice" born caste. It is followed by a claim to a higher position in the caste hierarchy than traditionally concealed to the claimant caste by the local community. Such claims are made over a period of time, sometime a generation or two before they are conceded (Srinivas, 1966).

The following example shows the process. Imagine that an outsider or an untouchable group decides to enter the caste society. By accumulating power they can enter the caste hierarchy at the level of Kshatriyas. Then the people belonging to caste of genealogists and bards create genealogical links and myths about them. Subsequently the outside or untouchable groups acquire the high· Kshatriya status. Secular power influences ritual ranking.

For a long time Sanskritization worked well. The major factors in Sanskritization were:

- Fluidity of political system with bardic caste having the special privilege of legitimization of the origin of different castes and Varnas
- Position of the dominant caste
- Pilgrimage
- Migration of values and beliefs from great tradition to little tradition
- Secular factors in determining the position of caste (in addition to pollution and purity)
- Migration to new areas
- Bhakti movement that established the idea of equality before

God and thus the idea of equality among different groups and castes.

After independence of the country, the issue of social mobility became more complex and cases of Sanskritization, de-Sanskritization as well as re-Sanskritization (Singh, 1974) were observed. Due to the policy of positive discrimination adopted by Indian Government now an increasing number of groups laid claim to backward status rather than high status. Some of them claim a backward status in state matters and a forward status in society.

Westernization

Different people defined the term Westernization in different ways. Srinivas used this term for all those changes that affected all Indians during British rule (after establishment of Pax Britannica) and which accelerated later. Thus it refers to "the change brought about in Indian society and culture as a result of over 150 years of British rule, the term subsuming changes occurring at different levels…technology, institutions, knowledge, and values." Westernization changed the society and culture of India significantly. It produced:

- Humanitarianism
- Secularism
- Equalitarianism
- Rationality
- Attack on untouchability

Rationality and humanitarianism may be called the hallmark of Westernization. Srinivas recognizes the importance of local culture in determining the nature of Weternization. For many people it produced "cultural schizophrenia" (in a non-pathological sense) which means that people who became Westernized in some domains of life (mostly in office) maintained tradition in other domains (for example at home). It must be noted that there were different Western influences on different people of India because different people in India came in contact of different types of British people: administrators, army men, traders, and Christian Missionaries. Srinivas also showed that the movement from tradition to Westernization was not linear: Westernization also produced revivalism, nationalism, communalism, casteism (vertical and horizontal solidarity), heightened linguistic consciousness, regionalism and passionate xenophobia (among Muslims). In some contexts Westernization led to rejection of the tradition while in others it led to mixing or combination of traditions and Western influences.

Globalization and Glocalization

In 20th century India both society and population have changed. India is experiencing several processes of change, such as demographic transition, industrialization and urbanization, skill development, social mobility, legal changes and greater assertion of autonomy. Among them effects of glocalization and globalization are very significant and far reaching. Globalization is economic and glocalization is cultural. The former concept refers to free flow of labour and capital across international borders, and the latter refers to spread of the culture of globalization through local cultures. Glocalization has given rise to new meanings of tradition and modern. Although Lee (1994, a) defined glocalization as the simulation of modernity for the spread of commodity forms in local cultures, it cannot be isolated from the replacement of thought categories in the process of commodity globalization.

These processes of change have both functions and dysfunctions. Among the positive developments are: opening of demographic window (due to declining birth rate, lower life expectancy in old age, and progression of baby boom children); improvement in literacy rate; rapid expansion of education at all levels; greater flow of labour, capital and technology across international borders with emigrants sending a significant part of remittances; increased productivity of service and industrial sectors; infrastructure development; promotion of tourism; new opportunities abroad due to aging of industrialized economies; some empowerment of women; and new ideas of equality and justice. Among the dysfunctions are: environmental degradation; increasing marginalization among the agricultural labourers and artisans; rising disparities; religious and community bigotry promoted by leaders, media and market; trafficking of women and children; a large number of cases of female feticide; violence against women; and at the root of many other dysfunctions, *an idea that all the emergent problems of the country are due to history.*

Sociologists have focused on social change and demographers

on demographic changes. There is a need to understand the link between the social and demographic changes.

Box 2.3: Globalization and Glocalization

From Lee (1994b):

1. Under contemporary conditions of globalization that are characterized by a dissemination of Western knowledge and technology, the notion of culture seems to be losing its underlying exclusiveness that once defined disparate identities and symbolic variances of peoplehood. The commodification of culture and the global spread of the culture industry have apparently contributed to this leveling process.
2. The crisis of modernity and representation in the West is generally a cultural crisis that reveals a recognition of and despondency over the dark side of the Enlightenment. The irony is that the jaded promises of the Enlightenment have been globalized and have found niches in the developing world under the sign of a simulated modernity.
3. The simulation of modernity is however a complicated process that hinges on globalization where the global is tailored to the local and *vice versa*. The outcome is not a simple local adaptation of the modernity paradigm, but possibly a revivification of traditional lifeworlds to alter modernity beyond its original image. Although the simulation of Western modernity, the power of traditionalisms in the developing world suggests that there can be no one modernity and thereby exposes the falsity of a Third World modernization.

SOCIETY AND DEVELOPMENT: THE MODEL OF INCLUSIVE GROWTH

Inclusive Growth

India is a developing country. In terms of indicators of development such as per capita income, literacy, life expectancy, level of urbanization and per capita energy consumption, it is far behind the developed countries. According to UNDP's Human Development Index, among 182 countries of the world included in the study India stands at 134th position. UNDP's *Human Development Report 2009* has divided 182 countries into four categories: very high human development (1-38), high human development (39-83), medium human development (84-158), and low human development (159-182). India with 134th position falls in the medium human development category (UNDP, 2009). According to the Planning Commission however the Indian economy has had the impressive record of growth in the Tenth Plan period. But this has helped only a small section of society. To quote:

> These positive factors notwithstanding, a major weakness in the economy is that the growth is not perceived as being sufficiently inclusive for many groups, especially Scheduled Castes (SCs), Scheduled Tribes (STs), and minorities. Gender inequality also remains a pervasive problem and some of the structural changes taking place have an adverse effect on women. The lack of inclusiveness is borne out by data on several dimensions of performance (Planning Commission, 2008).

In this backdrop the Eleventh Five Year Plan has came up with the paradigm of inclusive growth. This is a pattern of growth in which all social groups, i.e., SCs, STs, OBCs and others are equal beneficiaries (also the minorities, women, rural areas, backward regions, street children, drug addicts, disabled, and old people).

The Eleventh Plan examines the issue of poverty and development by social group at great length. Chapter 6 of Volume 2 is devoted to Social Justice. It looks explicitly at the economic, social, legal and other issues pertaining to development of Scheduled Castes, Scheduled Tribes, Other Backward Classes, Minorities, and Other Vulnerable Groups.

Condition of Minorities

In sociology minorities are defined in different ways. Theoretically, the term carries the notion of being outside the mainstream or power. But in India minorities are defined demographically as religious and linguistic minorities. However, in political sociology as well as in development discourse most often minorities refer exclusively to Muslims. The reason is that for various historical reasons in contemporary India Muslims have been lagging behind. This was not always the case. Other religious minorities such as Jains and Sikhs are quite prosperous.

Box 2.4 shows the condition of Muslims in India. It clearly exhibits that the condition of minorities is not good and this may be one reason why they often tend to fall back on tradition and communitarian ideologies and resist modernization. There is a need to uplift them and bring at par with the majority. At the same time, as said earlier, it has to be emphasised that the Muslims do not constitute a monolithic community. Among them there are rich and poor, educated and uneducated, modern and traditional, and highly Westernized and highly alienated. Thus they too require a differentiated approach to solve the socio-economic and demographic problems.

Box 2.4: On Condition of Muslims
(From the Eleventh Five Year Plan)

Muslims have the highest rate of stunting and second-highest rate of underweight children.

- 25 per cent Muslim children in the 6-14 years age group have either never attended school or have dropped out.
- Only one out of every 25 undergraduate and 50 postgraduate students in premier colleges is a Muslim.
- NCAER figures show that only about 4 per cent of all Muslim students are enrolled in madarsas.
- Workforce participation rate among Muslim women is only 25 per cent. In rural areas, 29 per cent of Muslim women participate in the workforce as compared to 70 per cent of Hindu women.
- 61 per cent of the total Muslim workers are self-employed as against 55 per cent of Hindu workers. 73 per cent of Muslim women are self-employed as compared to 60 per cent for Hindus.
- Only about 27 per cent of the Muslim workers in urban areas are engaged in regular work as compared to 40 per cent SC/ST, 36 per cent OBC and 49 per cent Hindu upper caste workers.
- Less than 24 per cent of Muslim regular workers are employed in the public sector or in government jobs as compared to 39 per cent regular SC/ST workers, 37 per cent Hindu upper caste and 30 per cent OBC workers.
- The share of Muslim male workers engaged in street vending (especially without any fixed location) is 12 per cent as against the national average of less than 8 per cent.
- The share of Muslims in Public Order and Safety Activities at the Central Government level is only about 6 per cent. Hindu upper caste workers have a share of 42 per cent and both SCs/STs and OBCs have 23 per cent share each.
- The share of Muslims among defence workers is only 4 per cent.
- Compared to other regular workers, a much larger proportion of Muslim regular workers have no written contract (73%, against 52% for Hindu upper caste and 63% each for Hindu-OBCs and SCs/STs) and no social security benefit (71% against the national average of 55%).

HEALTH GOALS IN THE FRAMEWORK OF INCLUSIVE GROWTH

Health connects society with population studies. Health is both the cause and consequence of social development. For the first time, the chapter on Health and Family Welfare and AYUSH in the Eleventh Five Year Plan of India, presents time bound goals in a social framework. The goals are:

- Reducing Maternal Mortality Ratio (MMR) to 1 per 1000 live births.
- Reducing Infant Mortality Rate (IMR) to 28 per 1000 live births.
- Reducing Total Fertility Rate (TFR) to 2.1.
- Providing clean drinking water for all by 2009 and ensuring no slip-backs.
- Reducing malnutrition among children of age group 0-3 to half its present level.
- Reducing anaemia among women and girls by 50 per cent.
- Raising the sex ratio for age group 0-6 to 935 by 2011-12 and 950 by 2016-17.

The above goals assume that health and family welfare are closely associated with women's place in society. In the patriarchal structure of India women are associated with reproduction. As they have low literacy, low awareness, lower entitlements and low decision making power they produce more children than they want, suffer from malnutrition and anaemia, and face high maternal mortality caused by home delivery and postpartum hemorrhage. In such a society a girl child is a burden on parents. Therefore, the family forces the pregnant women to go for sex determination test and abort the baby if the baby yet to be born is female. This results in low sex ratio in the age group 0-6. All these problems will have to be tackled jointly. They cannot be solved in isolation (Figure 2.1).

As said earlier, women's issues are connected with region. In general, status of women in the southern states (i.e., on the southern side of Vindhyal range of mountains) is better than in the northern states. This divide is reflected well in all the health and demographic parameters. This means that health issues, women's issues and regional issues are to be handled simultaneously.

The next section deals with the spatial inequalities in development.

Spatial Inequalities

Inclusive growth framework gives special importance to regional inequalities. Box 2.5 shows the differences in Human Development Index of different states. The box exhibits that in terms of HDI Kerala is at the top among Indian states and Madhya Pradesh is at the bottom. Further, there are both high and low HDI areas (districts) in each state. Interestingly, Kerala has the least inter-district variation in HDI meaning thereby that all the districts of Kerala have uniformly benefited from development. On the other hand Maharashtra has the highest inter-district diversity: it has one district with perfect value of HDI but also a district where HDI is lower than that for any other district in the country. This high regional diversity in development has serious social and political implications for the country.

Box 2.5: Disparities in the State HDIs

S. No	*State*	*No. of Districts in the States*	*State HDI*	*Highest HDI for a District in the State*	*Lowest HDI for a District in the State*	*Coefficient of Variation %*
1.	Arunachal Pradesh	17	0.515	0.660	0.362	18.36
2.	Assam	23	0.407	0.650	0.214	27.99
3.	Chhattisgarh	16	0.471	0.625	0.264	21.16
4.	Gujarat	25	0.479	0.582	0.309	16.14
5.	Himachal Pradesh	12	0.433	0.534	0.390	11.14
6.	Karnataka	27	0.633	0.753	0.547	7.62
7.	Kerala	14	0.773	0.801	0.749	2.37*
8.	Madhya Pradesh	45	0.394	0.694	0.372	11.37
9.	Maharashtra	34	0.580	1.000	0.210	36.55
10.	Nagaland	8	0.620	0.733	0.450	15.89
11	Orissa	30	0.404	0.736	0.389	16.94
12.	Punjab	17	0.537	0.761	0.633	4.93
13.	Rajasthan	32	0.424	0.656	0.456	8.88
14.	Sikkim	4	0.454	0.501	0.391	8.92
15.	Tamil Nadu	29	0.657	0.757	0.584	5.97
16.	Uttar Pradesh	70	0.532	0.710	0.366	11.59
17.	West Bengal	18	0.610	0.780	0.440	16.68

Source: SHDRs.

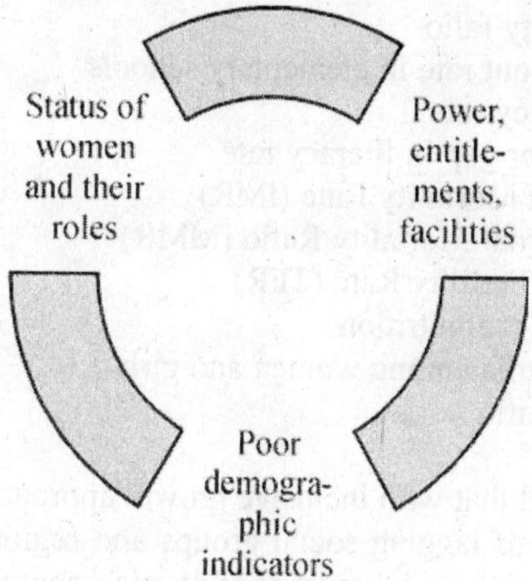

Figure 2.1: Patriarchy and Health

For development planning the Planning Commission has divided all the states of India into two categories:

1. Special Category States
    - North-Eastern States (Arunachal Pradesh, Assam, Manipur, Meghalaya, Mizoram, Nagaland, Sikkim and Tripura)
    - Himachal Pradesh
    - Jammu and Kashmir
    - Uttarakhand
2. Non-Special Category States (all other states)

Among the second category states there is very large variation in development. Among them Bihar is the poorest state. Punjab and Maharashtra are the richest states with ratio of per capita income above 20. Uttar Pradesh, Rajasthan, Orissa, and Madhya Pradesh are a few other backward states of India.

In the Eleventh Plan the following 13 targets are planned to be monitored for individual states:

(i) GDP growth rate
(ii) Agricultural growth rate
(iii) New work opportunities

(iv) Poverty ratio
(v) Drop out rate in elementary schools
(vi) Literacy rate
(vii) Gender gap in literacy rate
(viii) Infant Mortality Rate (IMR)
(ix) Maternal Mortality Ratio (MMR)
(x) Total Fertility Rate (TFR)
(xi) Child malnutrition
(xii) Anaemia among women and girls
(xiii) Sex-ratio

It is hoped that with inclusive growth approach (that focuses on the condition of lagging social groups and regions) Indian society will move towards a higher level of development with all sections of society benefiting from this.

CONCLUSION

This chapter shows that Indian society is high diversified. The processes of change have further divided society horizontally and vertically. There is a need to follow a differentiated approach to demographic problems of different sections and sub-sections of population which can be done by following an area and social class specific approach to fertility and health. To put it differently, the problems of India can be solved only by focusing on the most disadvantaged sections in most backward states. If the demographic diversity persists and is confounded with socio-economic and political disparities it can ruin the democratic fabric of the country and lead to political disintegration. In that situation we will certainly not be able to achieve the goal of inclusive growth.

QUESTIONS AND EXERCISES

1. What is the difference between values and norms?
2. Define the concepts of Sanskritization and Westernization.
3. What is the effect of policy of protective discrimination on Sanskritization?
4. What is globalization? How does it affect society of India?
5. What is the concept of inclusive growth? Why does India

need this concept? Enumerate the major health goals of India which are developed in the framework of inclusive growth?

6. Collect data on sex ratio in the age group 0-6 years for major states of India. Are there significant differences? What do they tell about social institutions and processes?
7. Review the skill development policy of India as presented by the Eleventh Five Year Plan?
8. Develop an alternative concept of social class and argue that for the policy of protective discrimination your concept is more useful than the Planning Commission's concepts.
9. What are the sources of weakness and resilience of Indian society?
10. Write a short note on regional inequalities in India and their implications for demographic diversity.

REFERENCES

Agrawal, S.P., and J.C. Aggarwal, *Educational and Social Uplift of Backward Classes: At What Cost and How? Mandal Commission and After*, New Delhi: Concept Publishing Company, 1991.

Census of India, 2001, http://censusindia.gov.in/Census Data 20001/India at glance/religion. aspx [accessed on 22nd November, 2009].

International Institute for Population Sciences (IIPS) and Macro International, 2008. *National Family Health Survey (NFHS-3), India, 2005-06*. Mumbai: IIPS.

Lee, Raymond L.M., 1994a, Modernization, Postmodernism and the Third World. *Current Sociology*, 42(2).

Lee, Raymond L.M., 1994b, Globalization and Cultural Change. *Current Sociology*, 42(2).

Planning Commission (Government of India), *Eleventh Five Year Plan, 2007-12*. New Delhi: Oxford University Press, 2008.

Sharma, K.L, 2007, *Indian Social Structure and Change*. Jaipur: Rawat Publications, p.24.

Singh, Yogendra, 1974, *Modernization of Indian Tradition: A Systematic Study of Social Change*. New Delhi: Thomson Press.

Singh, Yogendra, 1993, *Social Change in India: Crisis and Resilience*. New Delhi: Har-Anand Publications.

Srinivas, M.N., 1966, *Social Change in Modern India*. Berkeley: California University Press, 1966.

UNDP, 2009. http://hdr.undp.org/en/statistics/[accessed on 26 November, 2009].

3

Research Methods in Population Studies

METHODOLOGY AND METHODS

This chapter introduces different methodologies and methods used in population research. However, only some broad issues are covered; advanced techniques of research distinctively applied in population studies are beyond the scope of this chapter. At the end, an attempt is made to introduce various sources of data in India that are commonly used by demographers and sociologists working on population issues.

Positivism and Phenomenology

Methodology refers to philosophy and logic of methods, methods to specific tools and techniques of research. Broadly speaking there are two methodologies in sociology: positivist and phenomenological. Positivists assume that the social phenomena can be studied using tools and techniques of science. For them objectivity and value neutrality are the hallmarks of science. Phenomenologists reject positivism and claim that human behaviour is not amenable to scientific treatment. In order to understand human behaviour sociologists must study subjective meanings, and qualitative methodology is more suited for this.

In the past social scientists working in the field of population studies in general and morbidity and mortality in particular placed greater importance on quantitative methods such as survey and analytical methods. The shift in attention to AIDS epidemic, sexuality and empowerment has led to major changes in methodology. The reason is that researchers working on HIV/AIDS have to deal not only with estimation of incidence and prevalence rates but they also must explore the social representations of the virus, phenomenological issues in counselling, testing and care, effective intervention strategies and related policy issues.

The Debate between Quantitative and Qualitative Methods

As explained in Chapter 1, demographers are frequent users of statistical modelling and advanced statistical methods. They use latest versions of regression analysis, factor analysis and multidimensional scaling. In the recent times, however, there is a greater appreciation of qualitative methods. Today in population studies, as in other social sciences, qualitative methods such as participatory rapid (or relaxed) appraisal, discourse analysis, narratives, case history methods, and biographical methods are more in demand than the advance statistical techniques. Importance of qualitative methods is derived from greater appreciation of multiparadigmatic and shifting paradigmatic stances in various fields of social sciences, metatheoretical commitments, and growing popularity of postmodernism. All this also implies popular distrust of experts, importance of subjective and social representations, historical research, and empowerment. Social constructionists have diverted attention of researchers from exploring the causal connections to understanding of the knowledge which is taken for granted.

Yet, for a long time sociologists favoured one of the two approaches—statistical and qualitative—and took a rigid stand on the matter. A polarity between the quantitative and qualitative methods has emerged very clearly in the disciplines of sociology and psychology. While a large number of researchers, for example, believe that meaningful research cannot be carried out without employing statistical tools, an equally strong number of researchers seem to be absolutely dissatisfied with this approach. Historically, sociologists have always endeavoured to bring sociology at par with pure sciences. This is true for both those who used methodological structuralism and those who used methodological individualism. However, for several years now social scientists have been critical of such an approach and view it as a major source of narrowness in research. A considered view would be that no particular method is essential to social science research in all circumstances. Which method should be used and whether several methods should be used in combination depends on the purpose and approach of the study. It may be argued that the differences between statistical methods and phenomenological methods are not on a continuum between extreme polls. They may be combined at various levels.

Strength of Statistical Methods

Statistical methods are useful for a variety of purposes. They are used for constructing scales, designing studies, describing data, exploring patterns, revealing dimensionality, and predicting social phenomena. They may also be combined with qualitative methodology. Traditionally, sociologists have always tried to be in line with the principles of natural sciences and have favoured exact and standardized scientific methodology. They have considered quantitative methods as the only statistically valid and reliable methods of research. Using a deductive approach quantitative research yields statistically reliable results. The process of quantitative research is best suited for testing hypotheses. The statistical inferences are utilized for establishing causal relationships and making predictions.

Quantitative research methods can be broadly classified under the following three major categories:

- Descriptive or survey research,
- Correlational and causal research,
- Experimental research.

The above methods are discussed at length in the next section. Here it may be said that the positivists consider qualitative data as unreliable, ambiguous and doubtful, and despite criticism and attack, the quantitative approach dominates population studies. As late as in 2009, Cole and Gramajo have used a statistical model to explain the causes of homicide rates in different cultures. Although not acknowledged by them, they have precisely used the same methodology as used by Durkheim in explaining suicide rate. The only difference is their use of logistic regression which was not known to Durkheim.

Positivists aver that scientific observation is the keystone of social scientific research. In absence of objective observation and definition, verifiability of research findings is jeopardized. Social scientific theories and concepts can be studied meaningfully only through standardized measurement procedures. Therefore, it appears that social sciences cannot exist without objective measurement of variables. Such measurement provides the advantage of quantification of constructs and concepts which in turn provides a basis for using statistical and mathematical tools of analysis. Standardized measures are important for scientific communication. Objectivity and quantification enhance communication within the scientific community. Subjective evaluations of findings are far more difficult to codify and communicate as compared to results obtained through statistical analysis of standardized measures.

Economy of time, money and scientific resources, such as use of biomarkers in modern health research to measure factors like HIV status and anaemia, is another reason that justifies the use of standardized statistical procedures. This is especially true when one has to study a large sample. Large samples cannot be studied through qualitative methods. Qualitative methods of data-collection such as in-depth interviews and participant observation might prove to be unwieldy and cumbersome in dealing with a large number of participants. Even if data is somehow collected from a large group at the expense of economy, it is rather difficult to handle the data without employing statistical procedures for a meaningful analysis.

Scope of Statistical Methods

The above arguments bring this debate to a point where it is important to take note of the scope of quantitative procedures. In population research quantitative methods are particularly useful in:

- Estimation of size of national and sub-national populations
- Estimation of demographic rates, and incidence and prevalence rates of various diseases
- Causal analysis of concurrent and sequential variations in vulnerability to various risks
- Operations research in which one wants to know whether a programme has been effective in achieving the desired goal (such as promoting safe sex practices, reducing sigma against HIV and rehabilitation of people living with AIDS)
- Descriptive studies of knowledge, attitudes and practices of something like family planning methods

- Rapid situation analysis and benchmarking.

Quantitative survey research seems to be best suited for obtaining hard facts and factual descriptive information that is the keystone for most social scientific research. Qualitative research is not amenable to study many important research issues such as measurement of attitudes in various domains and for different purposes, study of demographic patterns, behaviour patterns pertaining to health and illness, evaluation of community intervention programmes, religious beliefs and their causal influence on social behaviour, etc. to mention only a few. Most research problems involve intricate relationships among variables. Such relationships involve various complex formats and structures. Tacq (1997) provides a comprehensive discussion of such structures and corresponding multivariate statistical techniques of analysis. The format of multivariate analysis techniques may involve convergent causal structure, interactive structure, spurious or indirect causality, discriminate structure, canonical structure and latent structure among others. The complex reality of social scientific problems is thus dealt with to a great extent by multivariate techniques.

However, critics of positivism believe that social scientists deal with complex phenomena and study contexts that are characterized by multiplicity of meanings. Complex social reality is not amenable to quantitative approach. One major criticism of the traditional statistical approach in social sciences is that it emphasizes objectivity at the cost of tampering with reality. This lends support to qualitative methodology and qualitative methods.

Qualitative Methods

Social scientists have produced a variety of qualitative methods. They include biographic theory, phenomenology, grounded theory, ethnography and case studies. Qualitative methods are particularly useful when the purpose is to explore new problems, when it is important to understand the people's perspectives, when one is dealing with unstructured issues or when standard measurements will be misleading. In population research one often confronts the additional problem of collecting reliable data which is of intimate and confidential nature (such as multipartner sex). Qualitative methods can help a lot in the initial phases and often produce useful results to design quantitative studies. In general, qualitative methods have been used in the following types of studies:

- Subjective meanings in reproductive decisions
- Why some couples who do not want additional child do not use contraceptive methods either (studies of unmet needs)?
- Community norms including gender norms regarding sexual behaviour and drug use
- Lived experiences of women kidnapped or tricked into being trafficked (Kristof and WuDunn, 2009)
- Social and cultural dimensions of diseases
- Community responses to various risks including risk of HIV
- Sexual and drug use networks
- Subjective understanding of needle exchange among drug users
- Phenomenological understanding of unsafe practices

One of the most significant aspects of the qualitative research is that it enables researchers to use counterstructural method whereby they can verify if the subjects agree with their findings. This also reduces the power gap between the research and the subjects and de-emphasizes the distinction between expert knowledge and lay perceptions (Wilson, 1983). Qualitative methods are also favored by those who use sumbolic interactionism or structural symbolic interactionism in studies of labeling or stigma. The next section argues that as compared to exclusive use of one methodology or methods it may often be very useful to mix them.

COMBINING METHODS AND DATA

Combining Methods

One can prevent indiscriminate application of one or the other type of methods by spreading knowledge about the nature and limitations of each of them. At the moment there is very little critical understanding of quantitative methods among sociologists in India. Statistical methods are often misused (due to avoidance of assumptions, fallacious use of small samples for 'show-biz', deliberate concealment of facts, easy availability of computing equipment, and lack of comprehensive knowledge of appropriate techniques). This charge, however, applies equally to qualitative methods. It is important to note that the problem actually does not lie with the statistical methods or the qualitative methods *per se*. The actual problem may arise due to misuse of any particular approach. The misuse might occur due to lack of knowledge and ritualistic usage of a method, whether quantitative or qualitative. Statistical methods such as chi-square may be used or abused. The mindful and creative use of statistics may rest some of the criticisms of the positivistic paradigm. Qualitative approach on the other hand has to be evaluated in terms of its quality and reliability. Most of the criticisms of qualitative methods are directed towards the question of validity and reliability.

The aforementioned discussion makes it clear that both the approaches have their strengths and weaknesses. In practice, the distinction between the two is more or less spurious, superficial and not well grounded. What should then be the answer to this debate? A complementary relationship between the two is a good idea, i.e., the idea of triangulation or method-mix or employing multi-method approach is very useful. Operations researchers commonly advocate use of combining different methods, such as questionnaires, interviews, check-lists, content analysis etc., to study the various components of a complex phenomenon. They suggest collapsing the construct into its components (values, ideas, images etc.) and using different methods to study each component.

Today most practical researchers would favour methodological pluralism. The best way is to use the two seemingly different approaches as complementary. Since complementary methods are those that do not share the same limitations, triangulation by application of multiple, complementary methods may provide a firm basis for eliminating methodological limitations. Complementary methods can be used for the purpose of verification, estimation of error, monitoring of data collection process, and testing out the meaning of data.

The above discussion provides a basis for arguing in favour of mixing qualitative and quantitative approaches for maximum gain. It must be emphasized that much of contemporary research in population deals with risk behaviour and its psychological correlates necessitating explorations of social representations of risk and risk behaviour. HIV/AIDS epidemic has led to new issues and new definitions. This involves change in the meanings of sexuality and condoms, place of women in society, debate on certain religious practices and greater acceptance of sub-cultures within a culture. The complex and multi-faceted nature of social representations of HIV/AIDS is evident from the field studies. Since the HIV/AIDS research is about complex social representations, such as sexuality, homophobia, process of coming out, and meanings of life and death, it cannot be captured by any one approach: quantitative or qualitative.

Qualitative methods provide a detailed exploration of meanings in a research context whereas quantitative methods provide rigour and form. Qualitative methods may be used successfully in combination with Multi-dimensional Scaling (MDS), regression analysis, cluster analysis and qualitative content analysis. MDS and cluster analysis are used as complementary methods to analyze proximity data. Content analysis is used to draw inferences from qualitative data—written and verbal.

On the basis of the arguments and evidence presented in this section it can be concluded that combinations of qualitative and quantitative methods can be very fruitful because they offer an opportunity for validating research findings and make it possible to gain required information using suitable methods.

Primary and Secondary Data

Population research requires diverse kinds of data. They may broadly be divided into two categories of data: primary and secondary. Primary data are those data which are collected by the researchers themselves. Thus the data collected from key informants, survey data, Focus Group Discussions (FGDs), and experimental data—frequently used in action research—are all the types of primary data. Secondary data refer to pre-existing data, collected by other researchers in the past for the similar or different objectives. For example, in situation analysis of HIV/AIDS, results of national and sub-national surveys on issues pertaining to reproduction, STI/RTI, mortality and morbidity, administrative records from police and health departments, development data from District Rural Development Authorities (DRDAs), education data from Basic Education Officers, etc. are secondary data. They present a broad scenario of development and HIV/AIDS in the study area.

The secondary data can be of immense use but the problem with secondary data is that those who collected them may have used other definitions of study variables than used by the researcher. One must know these definitions before using the data. One must also examine the limitations and various kinds of errors that may be present in the data. If you are using census or NSSO data on work and employment you must study the definition of employment and unemployment used by them so that data can be interpreted appropriately. Secondary data has the attraction of being natural, unbiased and non-obtrusive. In sociology class many of my Muslim students claimed that Muslims did not believe in the caste system and the data collected by sociologists of caste, among Muslims, is biased and distorted. I told them to look at matrimonial pages (newspapers and net), and treat them as the secondary source of data. They are written by Muslims themselves and they show that common Muslims (or their parents) are looking for brides and grooms in the same caste. If they are liberal they write "caste no bar". This shows that caste among Muslims is a social reality.

Among Indian researchers there has been a preference for primary data. Today we have very rich data on population and related issues, produced by censuses, national and sub-national surveys and Sample Registration Scheme (SRS). One can do good research by analysing these data through innovative conceptual schemes and advanced statistical techniques.

Ethical Issues in Data Collection

Research on human subjects presents several dilemmas and conflicts as the researchers have to develop a set of ethical guidelines for all those people involved in the research process at any stage. Ethical considerations demand that the researchers respect the subjects and do not do anything which can harm them in any way. The subjects should be properly informed about the nature of research and its possible uses. In other words, the research has to adopt a "no harm policy." When field workers approach the individuals and groups with whom they need to talk in an opportunistic manner, they must respect the needs and wishes of people with regard to privacy. The subjects who are asked to share information during the fieldwork should not be put to any kind of risk during the process, nor should participation in the process lead to any kind of loss. The purpose of research and the methods involved should be explained to all subjects approached by the research team. On the basis of information respondents may give their consent (written or oral) to participate in the research or not.

Respondents are informed that session will last about one hour (or whatever is the expected time for interview or experiment), and they are not obligated to stay till the end if they do not wish to. They are told where the session will be held, how the information they share will be kept secure, and that their participation in the study will remain anonymous. The ethical issues acquire great significance while dealing with vulnerable populations, such as commercial sex workers, truckers, the marginal communities and others who come from disadvantaged sections of society. With them an attitude of equality and sharing should be maintained. This requires that before the actual work is taken up the research proposal is cleared by a duly constituted ethical committee.

It may be noted that in "no harm policy" harm has to be defined in a broader sense. It covers not only loss of income or clientele it also covers embarrassment or shame. Imagine that a male investigator is interviewing a female respondent on sexuality, childbirth practices or RTI/STI in an Indian village. Will the respondent feel comfortable? If you are a woman, would you like to be a respondent in such a study? If the answer is no, it means that even if permitted by donors, such a research practice is unethical. Male respondents must be interviewed by males and female respondents by females. However, if the topic of research is poverty or one is collecting data on education and work, topics which have no connection with sexuality, then it may be accepted that male investigator collects data from both male and female subjects.

INTERVIEW, EXPERIMENT, FOCUS GROUP DISCUSSION AND OBSERVATION

In this section we will discuss the various methods used by researchers to collect data. As such, these methods are not unique to population research. Population researchers use all those methods which are developed and used by anybody in social research.

Survey

Population surveys produce objective data from a sample of respondents on biographic details of the respondents, concepts of health, knowledge and misconceptions, attitudes and beliefs, practices, fertility, mortality, migration, health seeking behaviour, and affordability of treatment, etc. To conduct a survey one has to define:

- Purpose of the study
- Specific objectives of the study
- Hypotheses
- Sampling methodology
- Interview schedules, i.e., exact questions to be asked in the interviews with fixed wordings and order
- Field operations
- Analysis plan
- The structure of the report

Since it is not always possible to collect data from the entire universe, researchers have to depend on sampling. They are, however, aware that the results of the sampling survey are subject to sampling fluctuations. Therefore, along with means, proportions and other advanced statistics such as regression coefficients, estimates of standard error and confidence interval of these statistics should also be given. This tells them how reliable their statistical findings are.

The main advantage of the surveys is their objectivity. Here an attempt is made to make all steps of research independent of the understanding of researcher. For example, simple random sampling is preferred over purposive sampling so that the decision to identify sampling units is taken on unbiased basis.

In analysis plan, the researcher must decide in advance what statistics, graphs, charts and models would be required to interpret data so that the objectives of the study are achieved. We have found that this has often helped us even in adding some items to interview schedule or deleting some from there. Interview schedules with all close ended questions are called structured interview schedules and those with some close ended and some open ended questions are called semi-structured interview schedules. Lastly, deciding about the organization of the report in advance also helps. The report must be divided into a number of chapters. The first chapter presents the statement of the problem. It may also cover the review of literature, conceptual framework of the study, objectives and hypotheses. The second chapter may present the methodology and methods. The third chapter may present the characteristics of the sample. This is followed by two or three chapters of major findings. The last chapter is devoted to discussion. It should include the limitations of the study and suggest some problems for future research.

Key Respondents Interview

There are some people in the field who know a lot about subjects relevant for the study. They may be defined as key respondents and they may be contacted to learn more about the subject. For example, police officials can tell a lot about cases of domestic violence, rape and other crimes against women in the area and also relate them to social structure and value system of the region. Doctors can tell a lot about pockets of vulnerability under their jurisdiction, causes of RTI/STI and HIV/AIDS, general health beliefs, and social class variations in risk. School teachers can tell a lot about variations in and causes of school drop out. Migrant workers can tell about the causes of migration, routes that migrants follow, and life and risks at places of destination.

We conducted a study of post-partum haemorrhage among women (a risk that may lead to maternal death in some cases). Our key respondents were: ASHA workers, anganwadi workers, NGO functionaries working in the field of health, medical officers working in health facilities from block level to district hospitals, in-charges of reproductive and child health programmes, and block level programme managers. These people know a lot about the causes of maternal deaths in the field and also about what all needs to be done to improve the situation covering larger issues such as strengthening medical facilities, improving access to transportation, women's education, strengthening community support and introduction of new drugs like Mag Sulf in the programme. This helped in identifying several intervention variables.

Experimental Method

Experimental data can be used for testing specific hypotheses regarding policy initiatives. Usually this implies:

- comparison of control and experimental groups; or
- comparison of base line and end line data

The idea is to test whether something (experiment or intervention) has an effect. If the data are collected using appropriate scales one may also use the analysis of variance and covariance techniques for analysing data.

The logic of having control and experimental groups is simple. Sometimes the outcome may actually not be due to the intervention or independent variable. It may be due to historical and environmental factors, biographic characteristics of the subjects or other factors. Therefore to ensure that the dependent variable is explained by the independent variables only we need to compare results of intervention in experimental group with changes in the dependent variable in one another group which is similar to the experimental group in all respects except that intervention is not made there.

Focus Group Discussion

Focus Group Discussion (FGDs) comes under qualitative methods. In this method the researcher forms groups of 8-10 people and discusses with them the issues of research interest. It may help if two researchers conduct FGD. One of them would ask questions and the other person would note down the answers. Care must be taken that no single person in the group dominates the discussion. FGD differs from group interview in the sense that in FGD we do not ask direct questions as we do in group interview. We raise certain issues and the group discusses them. Here both the outcome of discussion and the way the group arrives at the outcome are important. This method is of great help in developing narratives. Sometimes researchers fail to see the distinction between survey questions and checklists prepared for the focus groups. Survey questions have a degree of fixity about them. However, checklists are only guides and are flexible. Moreover, while in survey questions are normally directed to elicit life and views of respondents, in FGDs checklists are prepared to develop themes and hypotheses. As far as possible, in FGDs direct and personal questions should be avoided. Efforts should be made to understand the cultural context and patterns of behaviour and social representations.

I benefited immensely from use of FGD in training needs assessment of Elected Representatives (ERs) of gram panchayats and panchayat secretaries/sahayaks (PSs) in Himachal Pradesh. I called the ERs at a particular level—district, block and village—to sit in groups and discuss among them what all competencies are required to function effectively as ER, what importance they attach to various activities and tasks, and how competent they feel to carry out these activities and tasks. Their meetings were arranged by the administration at district and block levels. I could identify various needs of the ERs and PSs and develop a training programme and a training module on that basis. I also made recommendations about the composition of trainees etc. which were found to be quite useful by the government. Obviously, there were several challenges.

The biggest challenge in this work was how to make participants feel that we are not evaluating their individual competence or performance. We had to convince them first that that the purpose of FGDs is not to judge them, whether they are working effectively and efficiently or not, but to understand their problems in working as ER or PS. They were told that we were not there on behalf of government or any NGO to sanction any reward or punishment to their district/block/village or to them. We want to help ERs and PSs to work better and, therefore, we want to know what problems they face in performing different activities and tasks. We also want to understand that in the field out of all the activities and tasks assigned to them which ones are more important to them.

Soon we realized that members of ZP and Block Panchayat are very frustrated people. They did not cooperate initially, certainly not so much as the members or GP. We have to involve them, listen to their woes, and give them time to express their frustrations. When they fought the election they thought that they are fighting for a post higher than gram pradhan. After getting elected they found that there is no role for them. They have no power to intervene in the programmes anywhere and they are not even respected by the gram pradhans. Once you listen to them they get ready to participate in the study. We also learnt that at the district and block level, you have more problems working with men. Women have the same power and funds but they look more enthusiastic than their men counterparts. This was because most of them have come out in the field first time and even small role for them in society makes them more enthusiastic and confident. They are less complaining, more confident and more cooperative.

In FGDs it is very important to tell the participants what is the usefulness of FGDs and how discussions will help the community.

We have to convince them that this exercise is being done because this is useful to them in some way, for example through its influence on the state policy. In the above case it was told that government wants to help the ERs and PSs through better training. Government wants their suggestions regarding nature of training, place of training, content of training and related issues. Thus we are not doing only an academic exercise; what we learn in the sessions will be communicated to the government and appropriate action will be taken to help the ERs and PSs.

Experience shows that once people understand the purpose of the research and that research will help them directly or indirectly, in short run or long run, they cooperate. Participation in interviews and FGDs also provides them an opportunity to express their feelings that they have long wanted to share with someone.

Observations

Observation method also comes under qualitative methods. It is common to divide observations into two broad types: participant observations and non-participant observations. The latter differ from the former in the sense that in the former the researcher takes part in the community life, lives for substantial period of time in the field, mixes with people, becomes one of them, and then writes about their practices and ideas. In non-participant observation method researcher simply observes their behaviour and ideas as outsider.

There is no simple way to decide which method should be used in a particular study. The choice depends on a number of factors: objectives of the study; past traditions; preferences and competence of researchers; current methodological fashions in the community of researchers; time, money and other resources at the disposal of the researcher; and facilities (such as computing facilities) available. It is always good to discuss your research design with experts in the field. They may give you suggestions some of which may be quite useful. In general, however, if the purpose is to test a hypothesis we go for quantitative methods (experimental method or survey) and if the purpose is to collect in-depth and rich data we go for qualitative methods. Some people suggest that in exploratory (first time) studies qualitative methods may be preferred. This will help in generating hypotheses which may later be tested in quantitative studies.

INTRODUCTION TO CENSUS, SAMPLE REGISTRATION SYSTEM, AND OTHER NATIONAL SURVEYS

Census

Population census is one of the most reliable and most common sources of data on size, growth and composition of population. In India, the first population census was conducted in early 1870s. It was conducted over a number of years. The second census was conducted on a fixed date in 1881. After that India has had a record of conducting census every ten years uninterruptedly. The last census was conducted in 2011 and the next census will be conducted in 2021. The main purpose of the census is to provide data on size and composition of population of India and its geographic divisions, i.e., population of different states and union territories, districts, blocks and villages. Census collects data from all households, and all individuals living in the country on a number of items such as age, sex, urban-rural residence, marital status, religion, literacy and education, SC/ST community, work status, and migration status. The recent censuses have also provided data on total number of children ever born, children born last year and children surviving which are collected from all ever married women (Census of India, 2009). In certain censuses data were also collected on ex-defence personnel and disabled population by type of disability. Census data are used for demographic estimates, projections of populations, and various planning purposes. They are also used to provide sampling frame for national and sub-national surveys. Census data on household characteristics and village infrastructure are very useful for research and planning.

Census data on size is considered to be quite reliable. In the past, post-enumeration checks have shown that the size of India's population was underestimated not by more than two per cent. Yet, some other data, for example, the data on fertility suffer from considerable errors. Demographers have, therefore, developed various techniques for study of errors in census data. When census data are used for population predictions, they have to be adjusted for all types of errors known to be present in age data as well as in overall size of population. Errors due to preference and avoidance of figures ending in certain digits, and deliberate under and over reporting of ages are common to census data.

Vital Registration System

Censuses produce data mainly on size and composition of population. Demographers need data on fertility and mortality also. These data come from vital registration system in which all vital events—births and deaths—along with certain characteristics of the parents (in case of births) and the deceased (in case of deaths) are recorded, wherever they occur. These data are collected and maintained on a continuous basis. In India, we are legally bound to report occurrence of births and deaths to local Registrar—village head in rural areas and a Municipal Registrar in urban areas as registration of birth and deaths is done under the legal provisions of the Registration of Births and Deaths (RBD) Act, 1969. The Registrar General, India, appointed by the Central Government under the Act, coordinates and unifies the activities of the State Governments in respect of registration of births and deaths (Government of Karnataka, 2009). Under the Act, the head of the household is responsible to provide information within the prescribed period of 21 days; the institutional events are to be reported by the in-charge of the institution. However, the vital registration data are not complete and correct. They do not produce accurate estimate of birth and death rates.

National Sample Survey

In India national sample surveys conducted by National Sample Survey Organization (NSSO) which comes under Ministry of Statistics and Programme Implementation (Government of India, 2009) has produced data on different characteristics of population including employment, migration, health and poverty. They have also produced data on vital events. NSSO has been known worldwide for highly sophisticated sample design and a quick processing of results. Yet, unlike the vital registration scheme that can produce data on continuous basis, survey can produce data on discrete time points only (say at the gap of five years). They also suffer from various sampling and non-sampling errors

Sample Registration System (SRS)

Sample registration system was developed in India due to lack of reliable registration data. It is also called a dual record system as it combines the methods of vital registration and survey.

As aptly described by the Registrar General of India (2009):

> The Sample Registration System (SRS) is a large-scale demographic survey for providing reliable annual estimates of birth rate, death rate and other fertility and mortality indicators at the national and sub-national levels. Initiated on a pilot basis by the Office of the Registrar General, India in a few selected states in 1964-65, it became fully operational during 1969-70 with about 3700 sample units. The field investigation consists of continuous enumeration of births and deaths in selected sample units by resident part time enumerators, generally anganwadi workers and teachers, and an independent survey every six months by SRS supervisors. The data obtained by these two independent functionaries are matched. The unmatched and partially matched events are re-verified in the field and thereafter an unduplicated count of births and deaths is obtained. The sample unit in rural areas is a village or a segment of it, if the village population is 2000 or more. In urban areas, the sampling unit is a census enumeration block with population ranging from 750 to 1000. The SRS sample is replaced every ten years based on the latest census frame. It had been a practice to stagger the replacement process over 2-3 years. However, the latest replacement has been carried out in one go. Effective from January 2004, this sample is based on the 2001 Census frame. At present, SRS is operational in 7,597 sample units (4,433 rural and 3,164 urban) spread across all States and Union territories and covers about 1.5 million households and 7.10 million population.

Other Surveys

Demographers and sociologists engaged in academic and consultancy research generate data on demographic variables. Many of them are now using data collected by national and sub-national surveys, such as Demographic and Health Surveys (DHS), National Family Health Surveys (NFHS), Reproductive, Child Health Surveys (RCHS), and youth surveys. Several private research organizations and NGOs are involved in consultancy and operations research. They generate their own data to help the planners in testing strategies and schemes. This section provides a brief introduction to NFHS and RCHS.

National Family Health Surveys

National Family Health Survey (NFHS)–1 was initiated in 1991. This was an important component of the Project to Strengthen the Survey Research Capabilities of the Population Research Centres in India. NFHS was launched by Ministry of Health and Family Welfare (MHFW) which designated International Institute for Population Sciences as the nodal agency. It was followed by two more national family health surveys, called NFHS-2 and NFHS-3. These surveys have produced national and state level estimates of fertility, infant and child mortality, the practice of family planning, maternal and child health care and the utilization of services provided for mothers and children. NFHS-3 has also provided data on reproductive and child health indicators including Reproductive Tract Infection (RTI) and Sexually Transmitted Infections (STI). NFHS-3, for the first time, made use of biomarkers and produced data on anemia and prevalence of HIV. NFHS-3 provides data for the reference period, 2005-06

Reproductive and Child Health Surveys

The Reproductive and Child Health Survey (RCH)–1, was conducted to generate district level data on fertility and family planning, utilization of services provided by the government health facilities and people's perception on quality of these services. About 50 per cent districts were covered in the first phase in 1998 and the remaining 50 per cent were covered in the second phase in 1999. The survey was conducted by various regional agencies and coordinated by the International Institute for Population Sciences (IIPS), Mumbai. Among other things RCH surveys have produced data on the following indicators: girls marrying below age 18, births of order 3 and above, women age 15-44 knowing all modern methods of family planning, married women using any modern method of family planning, married women having unmet need for family planning, women who receive Ante Natal Care (ANC), women having institutional delivery, women having safe delivery, children receiving complete vaccination, women who reported knowledge of HIV/AIDS, women who had any symptoms of RTI/STI, men who reported knowledge of HIV/AIDS, men who had any symptoms of RTI/STI, and rural women who were visited by ANM during three months prior to survey The last of the RCH survey, more known as DLHs–3 provided data for the reference period 2007-08.

RCH report produced data on the above variables for states and union territories and districts. It also produced bi-variate tables linking the above variables to urban-rural residence, caste (SC/ST and others), education (illiterate, 0-9 years and 10 and above) and type of house (kachcha, semi-pucca and pucca).

QUESTIONS AND EXERCISES

1. What is the difference between positivism and phenomenology?
2. Select a national level study of fertility (you may use internet material) and critically examine its methodology and analysis plans.
3. What is the difference between interview and observation methods?
4. Suppose you are to conduct a sample survey of child mortality in UP. Develop a research design for this and identify major steps of research.
5. What is the difference between primary and secondary data? What secondary data you would use if you are to study causes of school drop out in rural areas in a few districts of Bihar?
6. What are major sources of demographic data in India? Which sources provide data on fertility and mortality?
7. Suppose you are to conduct FGD of rural youths to explore factors that expose them to risk of HIV. What steps you would follow?
8. Write short notes on the following:
   a. Quantitative methods
   b. Limitations of observation methods
   c. Census data in India
   d. Experimental methods
   e. RCH surveys.

REFERENCES

Census of India, Census Data Finder, 2009http://censusindia.gov.in/Census_Data_2001/Census_data_finder/Census_Data_Finder.aspx, Office of the Registrar General and Census Commissioner India [accessed on 13th December, 2009].

Cole, Julio and Gramajo, 2009, Homicide Rates in a Cross-section of Countries: Evidence and Interpretations. *Population and Development Review*, Vol. 35, No. 4: 721-748.

Government of India, 2009, http://mosps.gov.in/nssonang2008 web/nsso.htm.[accessed on 22nd December, 2009].

Government of Karnataka, 2009, http://des.kar.nic.in/arc/cnl%20division/pdf [accessed on 22, December, 2009].

International Institute for Population Sciences (IIPS) and Macro International, 2008. *National Family Health Survey (NFHS-3), India: Uttar Pradesh, 2005-06*. Mumbai: IIPS.

International Institute for Population Sciences (IIPS), 2001. Reproductive and Child Project: Rapid Household Survey (Phases I and II1998-1999. Mumbai: IIPS.

Kristof, Nicholas D. and WuDunn, Sheryl, 2009, *Half the Sky: Turning Oppression into Opportunity for Women Worldwide*. New York: Knopf.

Registrar General, India, 2009, *SRS Bulletin, October, 2009*. New Delhi: Vital Statistics Division, Registrar General India.

Wilson, H.T., 1983, Anti-method as a Counterstructure in Social Research Practice. In Morgan, Gareth, *Beyond Method: Strategies for Social Research*, Beverly Hills, Sage Publications, 247-259.

4

Demographic Models

MODELLING POPULATION PHENOMENA

As discussed in Chapter 1, population research deals with quantitative and qualitative studies of five demographic processes: fertility, mortality, migration, mobility and marriage. It uses both primary and secondary data. The data collected by the researcher is called primary data and the data that already exists in the form of census reports, publications of National Sample Survey (NSS), administrative statistics collected by different government departments, hospital records, etc. is called secondary data. For those who use quantitative methodology (also considered to be scientific methodology by them) the methods of data collection include sample survey and experiments. For those who use qualitative methodology the methods include fieldwork, observation, ethnographic methods, unstructured and in-depth interviews, and participatory rapid appraisal methods. Quantitative methods are more suited to hypothesis testing while the qualitative methods generate hypothesis and provide subjective meanings.

Among those who prefer quantitative methodology, mathematical models are used quite frequently for estimation, policy experimentation and theory building. They are also used for description of demographic phenomena, interpretation of data, and often to smooth questionable data (Halli and Rao, 1992). They provide answers to many questions which cannot be answered otherwise due to lack of data or observations. For example they can answer:

- How many people have ever lived on earth?
- In a country having a life expectancy of 70 years what proportion of people are likely to survive till the age of 65?
- If the present schedule of fertility (i.e., the set of age-specific-fertility rates) remains unchanged how many children a woman will produce in her lifetime?
- If the prevalence rate of HIV is reduced to half what will be its impact on life expectancy?
- If all couples follow a stopping rule of α sons and β daughters what will be its effect on the sex ratio of the population (Keyfitz, 1968)?
- Are there errors in census age data? What corrections in age data need to be made before using them for prediction of India's population?
- If the data is available on proportion married by age, how can one calculate average age of marriage?

Mathematical and Statistical Models

Models are mathematical and/or statistical expressions of relationships between variables describing some major, chosen aspects of a phenomenon. In population studies they are often used to explore relationship between different components of demographic systems, and to explore relationship between demographic variables and socio-economic and cultural variables. Mathematical models are expressions of real world relationships expressed in mathematical form of some kind. Exponential growth model of population (such as $P_{t=} P_0$ Exp (r.t)) is an example of a simple mathematical model which states that population growth follows the exponential model. When the relationships are developed using statistical methods such as regression analysis they are called statistical models. They contain an element of uncertainty. Statistical models have been developed for studying growth of population as a stochastic process, i.e., a process which can be described only in terms of probability distributions (Kendall, 1949). Thus statistical models are closer to reality than mathematical models. They are particularly suited for the studies of random errors. Models which use probability distributions, Monte Carlo computer simulation methods (because of their reliance on repeated computation of random or pseudo-random numbers), regression analysis, discriminant analysis, and factor analysis are statistical models.

History of Mathematical Models

For long, scholars from different fields have looked for ways of representing social and scientific phenomena in the form of abstract laws, principles and mathematical forms. Population studies is no exception to this. One of the earliest and most forceful argument in favour of modelling was, however, given by Keyfitz. In the first volume of *Population and Development Review* Keyfitz (1975) published an article entitled "How do we know the facts of demography?" He argued that the empirical relationships based on regression analysis can be misleading as they depend heavily on the cases for which data are available. Without modelling questions regarding cause and effect, multiple causation, and nature of relationship cannot be answered. In this article he showed that the empirical relationship between per cent aged 65 and over and growth rate of population was dependent on: (a) number of countries for which data are available; and (b) homogeneity among the countries. In such situations analytical and mathematical models can provide a better understanding of the relationship.

The most important of all the demographic models is the stable population model (Smith and Keyfitz, 1977; Keyfitz, 2005). It says that if individuals are born at a constant rate of 1 person per unit of time, and the survival probability of a person aged x is $p(x)$, then at any time the expected size of the population is given by

$$E\,[x] = \int_0^{\alpha} p(t)\,dt$$

where E[x] refers to the expected size of population at age x, $p(t)$ refers to chance of survival from birth to age t, and α refers to the upper limit of the age distribution.

It may be noted that the stable population model is a deterministic model and population following the stable model always results in a population in which the proportion of persons at any age (x) does not change with time. Further, suppose the individuals are born at rate $Be^{\rho t}$ where ρ is a constant and t is time. Then the size of population at time t, or

$$V(t) = Be^{\alpha t}\int_0^{\infty} e^{-\rho x}\,p(x)\,dx$$

This population grows or declines at rate ρ, and its age distribution, i.e., proportion surviving to age x is proportional to $e^{-\rho x}p(x)$. Using the property of stable populations that age distributions of two stable populations never cross each other, census growth rate and proportion of population up to a certain age (normally 35 years) demographers have estimated birth and death rates for those populations which lacked reliable and complete data on them. Development of model populations, showing probability of surviving from birth to different ages at different levels of life expectancy, for different regions of the world helped the demographers working on the populations of developing countries immensely (UN, 1983). Subsequently, the stable population theory was modified to accommodate for changes in mortality or fertility or both. Nath and Kalita (1989) developed a two-sex quasi-stable population in the presence of immigration.

Stable populations with zero rate of growth are of special interest to demographers. In such types of stable populations, the number of persons at any age x as well as total population are fixed. The number of births is same as the number of deaths. They are called stationary populations. Models based on following assumptions produce stationary population: (a) the whole population consists of one sex; (b) the population is closed to migration; (c) a fixed number of children are born every year; (d) all of them die at various ages according to a given schedule of mortality; (e) at any age x deaths are evenly distributed. This model is used to prepare life tables and compute life expectancy at birth.

ISSUES IN MODELLING

The major issues in population studies are as follows:

- growth of population;
- changes in composition of population; and
- demographic processes such as nuptiality (i.e., marriage), fertility, mortality and migration.

Mathematical and statistical models have been used in studies of all the above issues. Among them as compared to nuptiality more attention has been paid to modelling of fertility and mortality.

Predicting Growth of Populations and Sub-populations

Mathematical models have been used commonly to predict the size and composition of population of a country or a geographical region. For this purpose, various functions such as linear function, geometric or exponential growth function, modified exponential function, logistic curve, Makeham curve, Gompertz curve, polynomials, hyperbolic functions and autoregressive series have been used (Misra, 1980). Among them logistic curve has found more support than any other function on empirical grounds as well as the logic that the "population increase is proportional to the absolute population size already attained and the amount still left until the maximum, where the population becomes stationary" (UN, 1973).

Logistic Model

Among all the growth models existing in literature logistic model is most widely used model of population growth. The model and its assumptions are discussed below.

Assuming that r is the maximum rate of increase of the population,

$$\frac{K-N}{K}$$

the fraction by which the actual population (N) remains below the maximum (K), then the increase of population per unit of time is

$$\frac{dN}{dT}=rN\frac{K-N}{K}$$

The total population will then be

$$N=\frac{K}{1+be^{-rt}}$$

Figure 4.1 shows the various forms of logistic growth curve for different values of t and r (Weisstein, 2009). In a typical logistic growth model, showing growth of population, N increases continuously from zero to a saturating level in a certain manner: initially when N is small the growth rate is also small but it continues to increase till a maximum point of growth rate is reached after which although N continues to rise but the rate of growth becomes smaller and smaller, ultimately reaching zero. Is this not a realistic assumption for population growth? Almost same thing can be said about degree of urbanization, spread of literacy and many other things in population studies. All these processes can be modelled using logistic curve.

Logistic regression is a type of regression model in which log of odds ratio of a binary/qualitative dependent variable is expressed as a linear function of a number of qualitative as well as quantitative variables. During last fifty years logistic regression has completely replaced the simple multiple regression analysis in sociology.

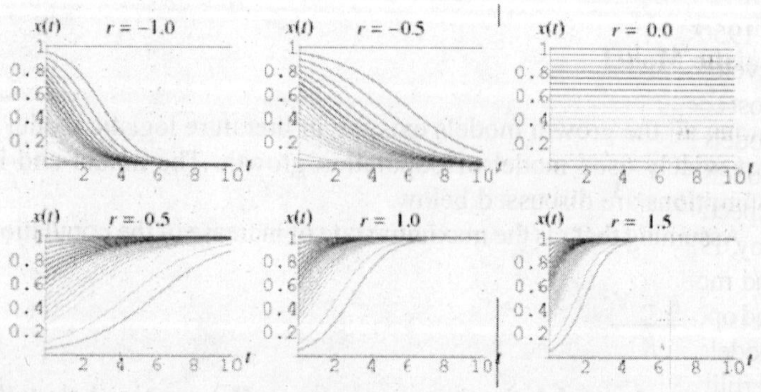

Figure 4.1: Forms of Logistic Growth Curve

In the above equation r is also called the Malthusian parameter (being rate of maximum population growth) and K is called the carrying capacity (i.e., the maximum sustainable population). Dividing both sides by K and defining N/K as *x* gives the differential equation

$$\frac{dx}{dt} \quad rx\ 1\quad x$$

Growth rate of a population following logistic curve has a definite pattern: rising from an extremely low level to a maximum level sometimes and declining after that, gradually reaching zero. Logistic model has also been found to be of immense use in predicting sub-populations (Leach, 1981) because it provides a working model of the "mechanism of self-correction". UN Manual XIII (UN, 1974) showed that a constant Urban-Rural Growth Difference (URGD) leads to logistic growth of the degree of urbanization (i.e., per cent urban).

Subsequently, URGD method was used for projections of ratio of urban population to total population, and even other types of ratios such as ratios of populations of cities to total urban population, ratios of labour force to total population and school enrolment rates. Thus urban population can be predicted by multiplying projections of total population by projected ratios of urban population to total population. Projections of total population are obtained using component method (Smith, 1992).

Estimation of Mortality and Fertility

In 1950's when the studies of population started in both developed and developing countries lack of data on the vital rates was a big problem for most countries. This was the best period for development of mathematical models in population studies. Mathematicians and statisticians developed models to estimate birth rate, death rate, total fertility rate and life expectancy using incomplete and unreliable data (Shryock *et al.*, 1971; Roy, 1987). The main issue was: can we get working estimates of fertility and mortality using census growth rate, age distribution of population, and open and closed birth intervals found from survey data? Mathematical models helped in this greatly. For example, when reliable data on Total Fertility Rate (TFR) did not exist but data on parity by age was available from surveys, using an empirical relationship Coale and Demeny suggested the following approximate formula:

$$TFR = \frac{P_3^2}{P_2}$$

where P_2 and P_3 refer to average parity of women in the age groups 20-24 and 25-29 years respectively.

Gompertz Model

Brass showed that if the fertility pattern can be described by a Gompertz function of the proportion experienced by each age, then the following is a better estimate of TFR than the above (Brass, 1979).

$$P_2\left(\frac{P_4}{P_3}\right)^4$$

where P_4 refers to average parity of women in the age group 30-34 years.

With improvement in data sources and development of new sources such as Sample Registration Scheme need for such models declined.

Knud (1983) compared cancer mortality between sexes, cohorts and cities by using Poisson distribution for number of deaths at a particular age and the mortality rate (defined as chance of survival to age *x*) as follows:

$$1_x = b^{x^k}$$

b and *k* are two parameters for which maximum likelihood estimates were obtained.

Gompertz model has been commonly applied for studying mortality. Using an age-dependent shape parameter, Weon (2004) used a Weibull model for mortality rate μ(t), i.e., ratio of density (f(t)) and survival functions (S(t) = 1–F(t)) for estimating maximum longevity, as follows:

$$S(t)=\exp\left(-t/\alpha\right)^{\beta(t)})$$

$$\mu(t)=(t/\alpha)^{\beta(t)} \times \left[\frac{\beta(t)}{t}+In(t/\alpha)\times\frac{d\beta(t)}{dt}\right]$$

He assumed that the typical human survival curves shows a rapid decrease in survival in the first few years of life, followed by a relatively steady decrease, and then an abrupt decrease near death.

In absence of data on measures of fertility they were derived from surveys. In India demographers derived parity progression ratios from survey data and used exponential model, displaced exponential model, Poisson model and life table approach for birth intervals (Pathak, 1989; Krishnamoorthy, 1989; Pathak and Ram, 1989) for this.

Prediction and Estimation of Migration

Studies of migration aim at estimation, prediction and explanation of migration. In this context, for the first time Ravenstein published an article in *Journal of the Statistical Society* in 1885 in which he showed that, as believed by William Farr and many others, migration is not without laws. He developed some well known laws of migration, such as follows, which are still difficult to refute:

- The great body of migrants travel short distances.
- Women outnumber men in short distance migration.
- Migrants move from agricultural areas (places of dispersion) to industrial cities (places of absorption) followed by migration from centres of industrial cities to suburban areas and from remote areas to places of dispersion.
- Each migration current has a counter current with similar characteristics.
- The major causes of migration are economic.

Four years later in 1889 Ravenstein published another article in the *Journal of Royal Statistical Society*. This article was based on the experience of North America and Europe (the first article was based on the experience of UK). In this article he said that people travel long distances to occupy unsettled land. Nearly 100 years later, in 1940 Samuel A. Stouffer published an article in *American Sociological Review*. He showed that the number of migrants from place i to place j is inversely proportional to intervening opportunities. The model was confirmed in 1975 by Wadycki who found it to be quite an accurate description of migration. Zipf (1946) developed and validated a gravity model to represent that volume of migration between two cities (M_{ij}) is directly proportion to populations of the cities (P_i and P_j) and inversely proportional to distance separating the two cities (d_{ij}) He assumed that income and unemployment are uniformly distributed over the areas.

$$M_{ij} = K\,(P_i \times P_j)/d_{ij}$$

where K is a constant to be found out from the empirical data. To some sociologists the model may look funny or absurd, but Zipf found that the model fitted very well for all modes of transportation. After all, if the logic used in the model is sound and accurate data are available why would mathematical equations not produce a good fit to empirical data?

In 1975 Using a similar argument Dorigo and Tobler (1983) expressed:

$$M_{ij} = k\left(U_i W_i / U_j W_j\right) L_i L_j / d_{ij}$$

Also

$$R_i - E_j = k\left(U_i W_j / U_j W_i\right) L_i L_j$$

where M_{ij} refers to migration from place i to place j. R refers to rejecting, repelling, or repulsing, "push" away factors. E refers to enticing or "pull" toward factors. U, W and L refer to unemployment rate, wage rate and number of people in the labour market.

One can change the variables in the model, delete or add some, transform variables to mathematical or trigonometric form, but as long as the logic developed by Zipf in suggesting gravity models is correct the above types of models would remain relevant.

Economic-Demographic Models

Coale and Hoover (1958) pioneered the modelling of demographic and economic variables through which they showed what the short term and long term effects of population growth on economic development are. Their model paved the way for large scale computer simulation models in population and development (Arthur and McNicoll, 1975). These models are developed on the basis of certain axioms, empirical relationships and theoretical understanding of the issues involved. The variables of the system are connected through mathematical equations and the parameters of the equations are estimated using available data and appropriate estimation techniques. Predictions based on these models are correct to the extent we have correct assumptions, accurate data, and appropriate estimation procedures. Error at any level may lead to error of unknown magnitude in the results.

CONTEMPORARY ISSUES IN MODELLING

With improved data on demographic processes the need for certain types of mathematical models has diminished gradually. Population censuses, improved vital registration systems, new data sources as Sample Registration Scheme in India, demographic health surveys, national surveys such as National Family Health Surveys in India (NFHS), child and reproductive health survey have provided quite reliable estimates of various demographic measures along with social class and urban-rural differences. Moreover, demographic transition from high to low death and birth rates is occurring in all countries of the world. Now the issues are not the estimation and prediction of demographic rates and ratios but the explanation of trends in them. There are also some new issues: aging and health at the older ages (Crimmins, 2005; Turra, *et al.*, 2005; Lutz and Scherbov, 2005; Bongaarts, 2006; Jansen and Kunst, 2007), timing of the end of world population growth (Lutz *et al.*, 2003, sexuality (Mensch, 2006, Gabrielli, 2007), determinants of neonatal mortality (Vandresse, 2008), and trends in HIV/AIDS (Bongaarts, 2008).

It may be said that models can be used in any field of demographic interest. What one needs to apply modelling is to have:

- Clarity of objectives
- Appropriate measurement of the variables of the system
- Theory that links the various variables—directly or indirectly
- Mathematical equations to describe the above relationships
- Adequate data of high reliability
- Adequate computing facilities
- Instruments to measure the fitness of the model to real world data

As time passed and demographers took interest in new areas several new domains of modelling have developed in literature. The area of modelling is going to expand further.

Insights into Causes of Real World Phenomena

Models have provided insights into causes of change in the demographic variables. For example, using the simple multivariate regression analysis with total fertility rate as a dependent variable and GDP per capita, life expectancy, gross primary and secondary school enrolment rates, per cent urban, and contribution of agriculture as per cent of GDP as independent variables, Bryant drew the following conclusions:

a. Fertility declines in countries with low scores on development indicators cannot be explained by socio-economic theories
b. The relationship between development indicators and fertility is weaker than predicted by socio-economic theories

c. The relationship between development indicators and fertility has shifted over time

Some of the above conclusions would not be possible to make if the appropriate data did not exist or if the technique of multivariate regression analysis was not known. In an interesting article using data on homicide rates Cole and Gramajo (2009) showed that as female education increases the homicide rates also increase. It was an unexpected finding. Then they posited a number of factors that explain this unexpected relationship.

Maximum Longevity

It has been a matter of great interest to establish how much gain in life expectancy is ever possible. Can a person live for 500 years, or 200 years, or 100 years? Is it possible to improve life expectancy in the present day developed countries further? By how many years? How can it be done? In one such attempt Bongaarts (2006) built a model of life expectancy and showed that by reducing mortality due to causes related to smoking it should be possible to increase life expectancy in the high income countries further. His model is discussed below.

Bongaarts projected that in the future "longevity improvements will be larger and population aging will be more rapid than many governments of high income countries expect." To demonstrate this point he decomposed Life Expectancy (*LE*). As defined by him, the conventional life expectancy at any time equals senescent Life Expectancy (LE_s) minus the longevity-reducing effects of background and juvenile mortality.

$$LE = LE_s - B - J$$

where

$$B = LE_s - LE_j$$
$$J = LE_j - LE$$

Thus

$$\Delta LE = \Delta LE_s + \Delta B + \Delta J$$

LE_j is the life expectancy without juvenile mortality. It equals the average age of death for a newborn if there is no chance of dying before 25 years. In other words it is *LE* at age 25 plus 25. LE_s is the life expectancy if some causes of death, such as cardiovascular disease and cancer, risk of which increases with age, are removed. Background mortality, by causes such as accidents, violence, and some infectious diseases, is independent of age. Bongaarts studied changes in *LE*, LE_j, LE_s, *B* and *J* for 16 high income countries with records from 1850 to 2000, separately for males and females. The background mortality was estimated from the observed data on force of mortality using the model

$$\mu(a)=\frac{\alpha e^{\beta a}}{1+\alpha e^{\beta a}}+\gamma$$

In the above equation β measures the rate of increase in mortality with age (a) and γ measures the background mortality. Thus the estimate of senescent mortality by age

$$\mu_a(a,t)=\mu(a,t)-\gamma(a,t)$$

for ages above 25.

$$LE_s(t)=25+\int_{25}^{\infty} e^{-\int_{25}^{X}(\mu(a,t)-\gamma(t)^{da}} dx$$

To consider the effect of specific factors such as prevention of smoking

$$\mu_{NS}(a,t)=(1-s(a,t))\mu_s(a,t)$$

Decomposition of *LE*, therefore, provides an opportunity for making more informed projections of life expectancy for the future.

Popularity of Statistical Models over Mathematical Models

In the recent past, models based on advanced statistical techniques have become more popular than mathematical models (Jansen, 2007; Vandresse, 2008). Poisson regression (expressing log of rates as linear combination of independent variables), logit regression (expressing log odds as linear combination of independent variables) and multiple classification analysis are increasingly used by the social scientists. Guo and Harris (2000) used a structural equation model to examine effect of poverty and other factors on children's intellectual development.

STAGES AND LIMITATIONS

Modelling requires a through review of what is known and what is not known. Then the process to be modelled is analysed and represented in the form of mathematical equations, statistical relationships and/or probability distributions. The equations would contain some unknown characteristics of the population called parameters. They are estimated using an appropriate method of fitting. This is followed by testing whether the model reproduced the data accurately. If it did, then the model can be used for predictions or theorising. Thus modelling is done in four steps:

- specification of model;
- estimation of parameters;
- validation; and
- forecasting.

Specification

Specification refers to the process of expressing relationships between dependent and independent variables in the form of mathematical or statistical equations. These relationships contain variables and some constants. The constants of the equations are called parameters. Specification requires a sound understanding of the field of study and a thorough review of works done in the field, understanding of assumptions on which past models were based, how sound they are, and researcher's judgement. Suppose in a particular field such as study of waiting time in fertility past researchers have used mostly Poisson distribution and the researcher thinks that the population being heterogeneous a mixture of Poisson distributions will fit better, then the researcher has to specify waiting time as a linear combination of two Poisson distributions containing different parameters.

Estimation of Parameters

The next step in model building is to estimate parameters of the model. For this purpose demographers have to use a proper estimation technique. For example, if a dependent variable is expressed as a linear combination of a number of independent variables it contains certain parameters which may be estimated using the least square method or method of maximum likelihood. Thus the researcher has to use one method from a number of available methods of estimation given for a particular context. The researcher must know the merits and demerits of all the methods of estimation and choose one on the basis of knowledge and logic.

Validation

Validation refers to examination of whether the model predicts well. In other words validation is an examination of how close the estimated values of dependent variable are to the observed values of the variable when the model and available data on independent variables are used. In regression analysis R-square is used as a measure of goodness of fit of a model and a high value of R-square suggests that the model can be used for prediction and explanation.

Forecasting

Once the model is ready it can be used for forecasting. It must be noted that an advanced and complex model is not a guarantee of good forecasts. Simple models do sometimes result in better prediction than complex models. The accuracy of forecasts depends on a number of factors: (a) model specification; (b) accuracy of data; (c) estimation procedure: (d) stability of the system; and the (d) length of the projection period. Long term forecasts cannot be as good as short term forecasts because longer is the projection period greater is the likelihood of changes in the system dynamics (i.e., relationships between variables) and occurrence of unforeseen events.

Limitations of Modelling

Modelling has certain limitations. The first and foremost is the limitation caused by lack of perfect measurements. This problem is a general problem of mathematical social sciences and is not unique to population studies. Regression models for different measures of fertility, for example, may provide very different results. Therefore, demographers have to select their dependent and independent variables carefully.

Accuracy of models depends on whether the process has been correctly specified, whether observed data are accurate, whether appropriate method of fitting is used, and whether the fitness of the model to data is good. Error creeping in the modelling at any stage will introduce error in the results of modelling. Lack of literature, lack of reliable data or lack of data of certain kind, and inappropriate specification or curve fitting will cause serious problems.

When the validation of the model is made on the basis of past data, the used length of historical period may influence the results. One has to pay attention to periods and causes of abrupt and irregular changes, if irregular changes can be isolated, plausibility of outcomes, and whether the recent changes observed in the study variables justify the outcomes (Jansen and Kunst, 2007).

A serious limitation of modelling in population studies is that statistical data are not available on measures of socio-economic changes used by sophisticated socio-economic theories such as mobility strategies, opportunity cost of time spent with children, and non-familial mechanisms for obtaining labour and insuring against risk (Bryant, 2007). Correlation between fertility and growth of GDP per capita may not capture the process by which couples tend to limit family size in order to avoid further impoverishment.

CONCLUSION

Modelling in population studies has helped in answering questions which could not answered due to lack of data, or even lack of possibility of observations and experimentation. Yet, the models have certain limitations. The prediction based on models depends on various factors including state of art understanding in the field, nature of models employed, and accuracy of data. Modelling is a growing field of research and more and more advanced models have been developed in different branches of population to take care of advanced understanding of the subject, and to benefit from richer data available from diverse sources.

QUESTIONS AND EXERCISES

1. What is model? How does model building advance knowledge in a particular field?
2. What is the difference between mathematical and statistical models?
3. Describe the assumptions of stable population model? When does a stable population become stationary?

4. How did stable population model help in indirect estimation of fertility and mortality rates for countries for which reliable data were lacking?
5. What are current issues in modelling of demographic processes?
6. Discuss the major limitations of mathematical modelling.
7. What is logistic growth model? For what purposes was logistic model used?
8. Describe Zipf's model of migration. What improvements were made in this model to fit the empirical data?
9. What are Ravenstein laws of migration?
10. What is Brass's method of estimating total fertility rate?

REFERENCES

Alho, Juha M., and Spencer, Bruce D., 2005. *Statistical Demography and Forecasting*. New York: Springer.

Arthur, W. Brian, and McNicoll, Geoffrey, Large Scale Simulation Models in Population and Development: What Use To Planners? *Population and Development Review*, Vol.1, No. 2: 251-265.

Bongaarts, John, 2006, How Long will we Live? *Population and Development Review*, Vol. 32, No. 4: 605-628.

Bongaarts, John, Buettner, Thomas, Heilig, Gerhard, and Pelletier, Francois, 2008, Has the HIV Epidemic Peaked? *Population and Development Review*, Vol. 32, No. 4: 199-224.

Brass, W., 1979, Screening Procedures for Detecting Errors in Maternity History Data. In United Nations, Regional Workshop on Techniques of Analysis of World Fertility Survey Data, *Asian Population Studies Series No. 44*, Economic and Social Commission for Asia and the Pacific, United Nations.

Bryant, John, 2007, Theories of Fertility Decline and the Evidence from Development Indicators. *Population and Development Review*, Vol. 33, No. 1: 101-127.

Coale, Ansley, J., and Hoover, Edgar M., 1958, *Population Growth and Economic Development in Low-Income Countries.* Princeton: Princeton University Press.

Cole, Julio and Gramajo, 2009, Homicide Rates in a Cross-Section of Countries: Evidence and Interpretations. *Population and Development Review*, Vol. 35, No. 4: 721-748.

Crimmins, E.M., 2005, Socio-economic Differentials in Mortality and Health at the Older Ages. *Genus*, Vol. LXI, No. 1: 149-183.

Dorigo, Guido, and Tobler, 1983, Waldo, Push Pull Migration Laws. *Annals of the Association of American Geographers*, Vol. 73, No.1: 1-17.

Gabrielli, G. and Borgoni, R., 2007, Age at First Sexual Intercourse in Italy: A geographical approach. *Genus*, Vol. LXIII, No. 2: 149-183.

Guo, Guang, and Harris, Kathleen Mullan, 2000, The Mechanisms Mediating the Effects of Poverty on Children's Intellectual Development. *Demography*, Vol. 37, No. 4: 431-447.

Halli, Shiva S., and Rao, K. Vanandha, 1992, *Advanced Techniques of Population Analysis*. New York: Plenum Press.

Jansen, Fanny, and kunst, Anton, 2007, The Choice among Past Trends as a Basis for the Prediction of Future Trends in Old-Age Mortality. *Population Studies*, Vol. 61, No. 3: 315-326.

Judson, D.H., and Popoff, Carole L., 2004, Selected General Methods. In Siegel, Jacob S., and Swanson, David A. (eds.), *The Methods and Materials of Demography, Second Edition.* New York: Elsevier Academic Press.

Kendall, David G., 1949, Stochastic Processes and Population Growth. *Journal of Royal Statistical Society*, B, 11.

Keyfitz, Nathan, 1968, *Introduction to the Mathematics of Population*. London: Addison-Wesley Publishing Company.

________1975, How Do We Know the Facts of Demography? *Population and Development Review*, Vol. 1, 2: 267-288.

Keyfitz, Nathan, and Hal, Caswell, 2005, *Applied Mathematical Demography, 3rd edition*. New York: Springer.

Knud, Juel, 1983, Demographic Factors and Cancer Mortality. A Mathematical Model for Cancer Mortality in Denmark 1943-78. *International Journal of Epidemeology*, Vol. 12, 4: 419-425.

Krishnamoorty, S., 1989, Estimation of Fertility of Parents Generation from Data on Surviving Siblings. In Singh, S.N., Premi, M.K., Bhatia, P.S. and Bose, Ashish (eds.), *Population Transition in India*, Delhi: B.R. Publishing Corporation.

Leach, Donald, 1981, Re-Evaluation of the Logistics Curve for Human Populations. *The Journal of the Royal Statistical Society*, Series A (General), Vol. 144, No. 1: 94-103.

Lutz, W. Sanderson and Scherbov, S., 2003, The End of World Population Growth. *Vienna Yearbook of Population Research, 2003*, Vienna Institute of Demography, Austrian Academy of Sciences, Vienna: 1-18.

Lutz, Wolfgang, and Scherbov, Sergei, 2005, Will Population Ageing Necessarily Lead to an increase in the Number of Persons with Disabilities? *Vienna Yearbook of Population Research, 2005*, Vienna Institute of Demography, Austrian Academy of Sciences, Vienna: 243-259.

Mensch, Barbara S., Grant, Monica J., and Blanc, Ann K., 2006, The Changing Context of Sexual Inclination in Sub-Saharan Africa. *Population and Development Review*, Vol. 32, No. 4: 699-727.

Misra, B.D., 1980, *An Introduction to the Study of Population*. New Delhi: South Asian Publishers Pvt. Ltd.

Nath, D.C., 1989, A Two-Sex Quasi-Stable Population in the Presence of Immigration. In Singh, S.N., Premi, M.K., Bhatia, P.S. and Bose, Ashish (eds.), *Population Transition in India*, B.R. Publishing Corporation, Delhi.

Pathak, K.B. and Ram, F.1989, An Application of Life Approach in the Analysis of Fertility in India. In Singh, S.N., Premi, M.K., Bhatia, P.S. and Bose, Ashish (eds.), *Population Transition in India*, B.R. Publishing Corporation, Delhi.

Pathak, K.B., 1989, Some Approaches to Estimate Levels and Tempo of Fertility from Data on the Current Status of Women. In Singh, S.N., Premi, M.K., Bhatia, P.S. and Bose, Ashish (eds.), *Population Transition in India*, B.R. Publishing Corporation, Delhi.

Ravenstein, E.G., 1885, The Laws of Migration. *Journal of the Statistical Society of London*, Vol. 48, No. 2.

_______ The Laws of Migration, 1889. *Journal of the Royal Statistical Society*, Vol. 52, No. 2.

Roy, T.K., 1987, Measurement of Trends in Fertility: An Overview. In Saxena, P.C., and Talwar, P.P. (eds.), *Recent Advances in the Techniques for Demographic Analysis*, Bombay: Himalaya Publishing House.

Shryock, Henry S., Siegel, Jacob S., and associates, 1971, *The Methods and Materials of Demography.* New York: U.S. Bureau of Census.

Smith David, and Keyfitz, Nathan, 1977, *Mathematical Demography*. Berlin: Springer-Verlag.

Smith, David P., 1992, *Formal Demography*. New York: Plenum Press.

Stouffer, Samuel A., 1940, Intervening opportunities: Mobility and distance. *American Sociological Review*, Vol. 5.

Turra, Cassio M., Goldman, Noreen, Seplaki, Christopher L., Glei, Dana A., Lin, Yu-Hsuan, and Weinstein, Maxine, 2005, Determinants of Mortality at Older Ages: The Role of Biological Markers of Chronic Diseases. *Population and Development Review*, 31(4): 675-698.

United Nations, 1973, *The Determinants and Consequences of Population Trends, Vol. I.* New York: United Nations.

United Nations, 1974, *Methods of Projections of Urban and Rural Population.* New York: United Nations.

United Nations, 1983, *Indirect Techniques for Demographic Estimation*. New York: United Nations.

Vandresse, Marie, 2008, Estimation of a Structural Model of the Determinants of Neonatal Mortality in Hungary, 1984-88 and 1994-98. *Population Studies*, 62(1): 85-111.

Wadycki, Walter J., Stouffer's Model of Migration: a Comparison of Interstate and Metropolitan Flows. *Demography*, 12(1).

Weisstein, Eric W., 2009, Logistic Equation. From Math World-A Wolfram Web Resource. http://mathworld.wolfram.com/Logistic Equation. html [accessed on 14th December, 2009].

Weon, Byung Mook, 2004, Introduction to New Demographic Model for Humans, http://arxiv.org/ftp/q-bio/papers/0404/0404025.pdf [accessed on 8th October, 2008].

Zipf, George Kingsley, 1946, The P1 P2/D Hypothesis: in the Intercity Movement of Persons. *American Sociological Review*, 11 (6): 677-686.

5

History of World Population Growth and its Impact on Society

POPULATION IN ANCIENT TIMES AND MIDDLE AGES

The present population of the world is close to 6.8 billion and it is growing at the rate of 1.2 per cent per year with a doubling time of nearly 60 years. The rate of growth of population is, however, not a fixed quantity. For a long time world population remained stable. It was mostly in the second part of the eighteenth century that the world population started growing with an increasing rate, reaching a peak in the second part of the twentieth century. Since then although the population size is growing the rate of growth has been declining. The forecasts are that the rate of growth will decline further and the world population would reach a level of 9.1 billion in 2050. This section focuses on the historical rise and fall of population growth in the world and its major regions.

Population Growth in Ancient Society

Ancient societies were small in size and for them population was an asset. While the number of people in a tribal band or a community was small, the resources of nature were plenty. Rich forests, pure rivers, large species of various types of animals, mountains and oceans formed the outside environment of ancient human society. We do not know what the natural death rate in ancient society was. As far as natural environment is concerned it was pure and density of population was very low. Therefore many types of infectious diseases would not be prevailing. This implies that the longevity could have been higher. Moreover, those who survived the hardships of natural life during childhood may have lived longer. Yet, due to attack by wild animals, violence between different human groups, excessive or short rainfalls, floods, famines, and attack of epidemics the long term death rate was high. This means that even with natural fertility, i.e., absence of birth control, the long term rate of growth of population was extremely low.

Assuming that a man and a woman appeared on this planet earth about 5 lakh years ago (it is believed that man separated off from the animal kingdom a million years ago) and their progeny grew at an extremely low rate such as .1 per cent per year, today the world population would have been around $2.8e^{217}$. Is this size not just unimaginable and unsustainable? Even a much lower growth rate as .01 per cent on sustained basis would yield an unsustainable figure of $10.4e^{21}$, higher than the size of would population today. A rate of growth of .2 produces a population of $10.4e^{21}$ in just 50,000 years. Thus for a long time the rate of growth of would population must have been lower than .01 per cent per year.

Population growth rate depends on three factors: fertility, mortality and migration. When we are discussing the world population trends we may ignore the component of migration. This implies that in the past when population grew at extremely slow rate either the long term death rate was very high or the fertility could not keep pace with mortality. Reproduction rate was only as high as death rate. The two rates may have fluctuated: when mortality rate was high fertility was also high and when mortality was less fertility was also less or this may have happened with a small time lag. Alternatively, fertility was high and in short terms population would rise but periodically epidemics and wars would destroy a great proportion of population and the population size would come down to initial levels. In both cases, the result is that for a long time the world population was stationary or growing at a very slow rate.

Causes of Slow Growtn

We do not have exact demographic information on ancient society. There are only projections and conjectural estimates. These are mere speculations about the rate of growth and fertility and mortality.

Paleodemographers assume that ancient society had a long run tendency to remain stationary for various reasons. Hume (1977) suggested three reasons why ancient societies could not be more populated:

1. The ancient societies were almost in perpetual war and the war in a small state is more destructive than in a big state as most inhabitants of a small state must serve in the army; war could be caused by martial spirit, love of liberty, mutual emulation, and hatred for neighbour.
2. Not only in war time but even in peace time the condition of ancient society was unfavourable to growth: there was no law, no trial, no pardon and the nobles would butcher the opposite party at slightest provocation.
3. Ancient society had subsistence agriculture, without support of flourishing trade, manufactures and industry as in modern societies.

To quote (Valentey, 1977):

> There is good reason to assume that on the whole mortality levels in the primeval period were very high. Many of these people would perish from hunger or disease, or after being attacked by wild animals, or after encounters with hostile tribes or natural disasters. Life was particularly hard for people inhabiting lands in the temperate or cold belts, where food shortages in winter probably took a heavy toll of lives each year. Mortality was particularly high among young children and old people, the weakest members of the groups, who must have been the first to suffer from deteriorating conditions. When finding themselves exposed to unexpected dangers these clan or tribal groups often abandoned the old and the children to the mercy of fate. Traditional practices of infanticide as well as the killing of old people in times of hunger that have been discovered in some tribal societies (such as those of the Australians or the Eskimos) are more likely to have been widespread in this primitive period...
>
> The birth rate in this age of the primitive community must also have been high, on average a little in excess of the death rate, otherwise those primitive peoples would have died out.

No wonder it took a long period of time for the world population to reach the first billion mark in 1820 AD. Further, Bongaarts (1975) argued that in the high fertility societies birth rate too was not as high as could have been under sheer biological reproductive efficiency. To quote:

> ...a typical thirty-month birth interval in a natural fertility population may be divided as follows: twelve months postpartum amenorrhea, four months waiting time to conception before an intrauterine death, a one-month non-susceptible period associated with the intrauterine death, another four months' conception waiting time before a live birth, and finally a nine month full term pregnancy.
>
> In summary, the highest observed birth rates are much lower than is biologically possible because women in natural fertility societies are pregnant during only about one-sixth of their reproductive years. The rest of these potential childbearing years is spent in the unmarried, sterile, postpartum anovulatory, non-susceptible, or ovulatory states. As a result, birth rate rarely exceeded 50 in populations in which no deliberate actions are taken to affect the biological process of reproduction. Voluntary fertility control efforts by couples during the childbearing years are required to reduce birth control below the natural level.

Population in Middle Ages

It may be noted that in the beginning of our era the world population is estimated to be around 326.5 million. The region-wise break up shows that 35 million people lived in Europe, 220 million in Asia, 21 million in North and Central America, 19 million in South America, 30 million in Africa and 15 million in Oceania. Thus nearly 21.8 per cent of the world population lived in what may be called developed countries and 78.2 per cent in the developing countries (Urlanis, 1978).

Bennett estimated that the approximate population of the world in AD 1000 was 275,000,000 (Valentey, 1978). In five hundred years time, from AD 1000 to 1500, it grew by 171 millions only (Table 5.1). This gives an average annual growth rate of .00096 and a doubling time of 729 years.

Table 5.1: World Population, 1000-1500 AD

Year	Population (in millions)
1000	275
1100	306
1200	348
1300	384
1400	373
1500	446

Source: Valentey (1978).

Lack of Interest in Population Theory

The slow rate of population growth of ancient society explains why the early philosophers and planners gave little importance to population size and density. If for the philosophers and planners population is more or less a constant it cannot be part of their theory of change or progress. Economists of development would find little interest in a constant. Only sometimes it appears in planning for a city state in hypothesizing a relationship between size and density of population and quality of life in the city (in the context of fixed resources). Indian religious literature equates increasing burden of *asuras* on earth with *kaliyuga*, the age of sin, meaning thereby that uncontrolled population can produce normlessness and misery. Population became an issue at the end of 18th century and particularly after the Second World War because it started growing at an unprecedented rate.

DEMOGRAPHIC TRANSITION IN THE NINETEENTH AND TWENTIETH CENTURIES

Definition of Developed and Developing Countries

Due to differences in history as well as the present demographic regimes it is important to discuss demographic trends separately for developed and developing countries. Then the first question one would ask is: what are developed and less developed countries? United Nations has divided all countries of the world into two broad categories: more developed countries and less developed countries. Certain less developed countries are classified as least developed countries. The classification is as follows (United Nations Population Division, 2009):

- More developed regions: They comprise all regions of Europe plus Northern America, Australia/New Zealand and Japan.
- Less developed regions: They comprise all regions of Africa, Asia (excluding Japan), Latin America and the Caribbean plus Melanesia, Micronesia and Polynesia.

Least developed countries: The group of least developed countries, as defined by the United Nations General Assembly in its resolutions (59/209, 59/210 and 60/33) in 2007, comprises 49 countries, of which 33 are in Africa, 10 in Asia, 1 in Latin America and the Caribbean, and 5 in Oceania. The group includes 49 countries-Afghanistan, Angola, Bangladesh, Benin, Bhutan, Burkina Faso, Burundi, Cambodia, Central African Republic, Chad, Comoros, Democratic Republic of the Congo, Djibouti, Equatorial Guinea, Eritrea, Ethiopia, Gambia, Guinea, Guinea-Bissau, Haiti, Kiribati, Lao People's Democratic Republic, Lesotho, Liberia, Madagascar, Malawi, Maldives, Mali, Mauritania, Mozambique, Myanmar, Nepal, Niger, Rwanda, Samoa, São Tomé and Príncipe, Senegal, Sierra Leone, Solomon Islands, Somalia, Sudan, Timor-Leste, Togo, Tuvalu, Uganda, United Republic of Tanzania, Vanuatu, Yemen and Zambia. These countries are also included in the less developed countries.

Falling Death and Birth Rates

To follow Wilcox (1985), "there is nothing in the history of the last few centuries more notable than the increase in the population of the world" the prime cause of which is the decrease in the ratio of deaths to population.

In the second half of the eighteenth century the death rate in developed countries, particularly in Europe started declining (Valentey, 1977) under the impact of both economic and political factors, though the decline was slow and it took more than two centuries for death rates to come down to present levels. Since the birth rate remained high it led to increasing rate of population growth. The birth rate fluctuated. "It reached its highest level in the period of revival after the economic crisis at the beginning of the 1870, which was to prove the most severe of the whole century. The highpoint of that climb in the birth rate was 1876, which can be regarded as the turning point in the history of the European birth rate..."

Box 5.1: Walter Wilcox on the Expansion of Europe and its Influence of Population

Europe had more than three times as many inhabitants in 1900 as in 1750.

The persons of European stock living outside of in 1900 were three fourths as many as the entire number of inhabitants of that continent in 1750.

This vast increase of Europeans by blood in 150 years from 130,000,000 to 500,000,000 has not been secured at the cost of a decrease of other human beings.

On the contrary the native stocks reached by Europeans have usually increased in numbers.

This is true of nearly all numerous groups living mainly by agriculture in the tropical or sub-tropical regions of America, Africa, Asia, and Malaysia.

Where the influence of Europe has not gone and we have any clue to the facts, they indicate a stationary population, or at least a very low increase.

The enormous increase in the population of the earth from perhaps 1,000,000,000 in 1750 to 1,500,000,000 in 1900 must be ascribed mainly to the expansion of Europe.

Thus in the second half of the eighteenth century the world population started growing. This growth, however, was confined to developed countries. Population in the less developed countries remained almost stationary (Misra, 1995).

The world population reached the first billion mark in 1820. And after that it started growing at faster and faster pace, first due to greater decline in death rate in the developed countries and then due to decline in death rate in the developing countries.

Table 5.2 shows the various dates when the world population reached various billion marks. It exhibits that in the early nineteenth century population started growing. Yet, the growth rate was low. As explained above, the reason is that this growth was confined to the developed countries only which comprised one fifth of the world population. In the developing countries life expectancy at birth was around 20 and death rate was around 50. Thus despite a high fertility population was constant. World population started growing fast in the twentieth century, particularly in the second half of the twentieth century. This is the time when mortality rates declined with suddenness in the less developed countries and their fertility rates remained unchanged.

Table 5.2: Landmarks in World Population History

Billion mark	Year when the billion mark was reached (AD)	Time to add one billion
1st	1820	Cannot be estimated exactly but it is believed to have taken 5-10 lakh years
2nd	1930	110
3rd	1960	30
4th	1974	14
5th	1987	13
6th	1999	12

If we assume that it would take nearly 12 years again to reach the next billion, we can roughly say that sometime in year 2011 the world population will reach the 7 billion mark. Thus in the period 1820 to 2011 (less than two hundred years) the world population has grown nearly seven times. Nobody in eighteenth century could have imagined this explosion of population.

Kirk (1996) said that in Europe mortality decline, the chief cause of population growth occurred in four phases. In the first phase, up to the latter part of eighteenth century some improvement in mortality may have occurred due to improvement in income but nothing is known about this period. Beginning the latter part of eighteenth century mortality started falling mainly due to public order created by the modern state. Other factors such as improvement in agriculture, improved nutrition, improved hygiene, improvement in infrastructure and means of transportation and communication, and reduction in famines and epidemics, also helped in reducing mortality levels. Yet, the improvement in mortality occurred independently of medical intervention. In the third phase, from the last third of the nineteenth century to World War I, improvement in mortality occurred due to medical discoveries, particularly due to control of diseases like diarrhoea and tuberculosis. Finally, in the fourth phase, during World War II and afterwards, discovery of penicillin and other chemicals reduced mortality due to epidemic and contagious diseases. Thus it is perhaps not correct to say (though commonly believed) that advancement in medical sciences is the major factor in improvement in mortality in the nineteenth century.

The case of less developed countries is different. Here much of mortality decline occurred after World War II when a large number of them became independent and the national governments in the new countries took special interest in promoting health and nutrition with financial support from outside. This was the time when DDT, antibiotics and other drugs were already available in the developed countries and the less developed countries had to apply them to control infectious diseases as part of public health programme. In this period mortality improved in all less developed countries suddenly and this happened irrespective of culture, religion, level of economic development, ideology and social structure, though the positive correlation between development and life expectancy continued. This sudden decline in post-War mortality in the less developed countries caused population explosion and in several of them population was found growing at rate three per cent and above. This suddenness created disequilibrium in society. We do not yet understand the full implications of this.

On Wednesday, 13th October, 1999 BBC News announced the birth of the six billionth baby with the following photograph. UNFPA (2009) had estimated that around 12th October, 1999 the sixth billionth child would be born. According to UN symbolism it was a boy born in a clinic in Sarajevo, the Bosnian capital, a city scarred by years of war, where the six billionth baby was born in UN Secretary-General Mr. Kofi Annan's presence. The UN chose as "D6B", the day when humanity passed the symbolic threshold.

UN chief welcomes six billionth baby

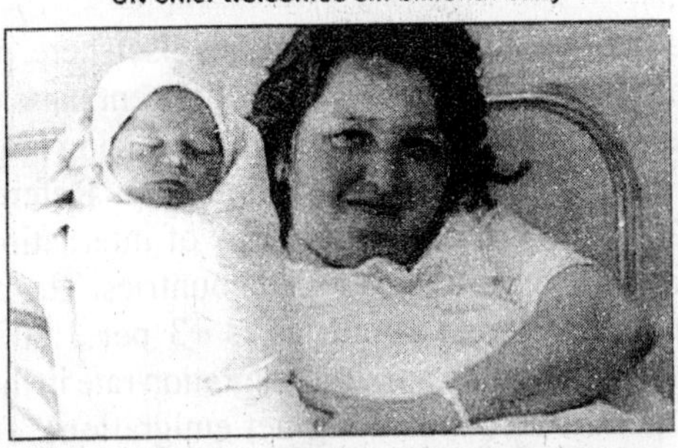

One in six billion: Fatima Nevic shows off her baby boy

Figure 5.1: Birth of the Six Billionth Baby

It cannot be said with certainty where exactly the six billionth baby was born but the event was significant. On the one hand there was something to be celebrated and on the other hand it was a moment for thinking and acting. We are reaching (or perhaps have already reached) the carrying capacity of earth and there is a need to plan for the future. Here it is important to make a distinction between physical carrying capacity and cultural carrying capacity. One may argue that it will be possible for earth to sustain more population. The question is: at what level of cultural standards? Are only numbers important and quality of life is not important?

The debate on possible population size cannot be separated from debate on desired quality of life. The earth can certainly support more population if the standards of the least developed countries are acceptable. But the earth cannot support that much population if the socio-economic and cultural standards of more developed countries are desired. There is a need to prevent the excessive growth of population in certain regions of the world and make reproductive decision a matter of choice for the individual couples and particularly for the women. As a matter of fact, it is in the interest of both developed and developing countries to achieve global improvement in mortality levels and reduce birth rate in the developing countries. In the increasingly globalized world the large socio-economic and demographic disparities cannot be sustained. They are going to produce political results which are not in the best interest of any country.

International Migration

Globalizaton and awareness of opportunities elsewhere, poverty, wars, political and ethnic conflicts going on in different parts of the world, natural disasters and climatic changes are producing large streams of international migration. As per the Population Reference Bureau estimates of 2008 there is a sizeable flow of international migrants from developing countries to developed countries. The net migration rate in the more developed countries is +3 per 1,000 population (+ indicating net immigration); the net migration rate in the developing countries is-1 per 1,000 (-indicating net emigration). The two rates suggest that the same amount of migration affects the developed countries more than it lessens the demographic burden in developing countries. Moreover, there are many developing countries with a large immigration rate (above 5 per 1,000). They are Western Sahara, Burundi, Seychelles, Botswana, Bahrain, Cyprus, and United Arab Emirates. According to Population Division of United Nations

Secretariat estimates made in 2005 in some countries like USA, Russian Federation and Germany, which come in the category of top 20 countries having largest numbers of international migrants, the migrants constitute more than 5 per cent of the total population of the country.

DEMOGRAPHIC SCHISM BETWEEN DEVELOPED AND DEVELOPING COUNTRIES AND FUTURE PROSPECTS

Growing Demographic Divide between Developed and Developing Countries

According to UNFPA's *State of World Population 2009* the world population has reached 6.83 million and it is growing at the rate of 1.2 per cent per year. There is a great demographic divide between developed and developing countries. The more developed countries have only 1,233.3 million and they exhibit a growth rate of only 0.3 per cent per year. The less developed countries have 5,596.1 million people and they exhibit a growth rate of 1.4 per cent per year. 835.5 million people in the less developed countries are living in what are designated as the least developed countries which exhibit a growth rate of 2.3 per cent. Table 5.3 shows the size of population, rate of growth and doubling time for developed and developing countries of the world.

Table 5.3: Size and Growth of World Population and Major Regions, 2009

World/region	*Size of Population (millions)*	*Growth rate, 2005-2010*	*Doubling Time (years)*	*Projected Population in 2050*
World	6,829.4	1.2	58.3	9,150.0
More developed countries	1,233.3	0.3	233.3	1,275.2
Less developed countries	5,596.1	1.4	50.0	7,875.0
Least developed countries	835.5	2.3	30.4	1,672.4

The divide in population dynamics of developed and developing countries has implication for economic, political and social divides. There are also such divides within the less developed countries, caused by their colonial past and unequal and capitalist development.

Differences in Vital Rates

Table 5.4 shows the life expectancy and a few other measures of mortality in selected high life expectancy and low life expectancy countries.

Table 5.4: Expectancy and Other Measures of Mortality for Selected Countries, 2009

Life expectancy	*Country*	*IMR per 1000 live births*	*Life Expectancy (M/F)*	*Maternal Mortality ratio*
High				
	Japan	3	79.4/86.5	6
	Hong Kong SAR, China	4	79.6/85.3	–
	France	4	78.0/84.9	8
	Italy	4	78.3/84.3	3
	Switzerland	4	79.6/84.3	5
	Iceland	3	80.4/83.5	4
Low				
	Mali	104	48.1/49.2	970
	Mozambique	86	47.4/48.8	520
	Nigeria	108	47.6/48.7	1,100
	Lesotho	67	45.0/45.7	960
	Swaziland	62	47.1/45.5	390
	Afghanistan	154	44.3/44.3	1,800

The above table shows that in a number of countries, such as Japan, Hongkong, France, Italy and Switzerland life expectancy for females has gone beyond 84. Life expectancy for males is 5-6 years less than for females but that is also above 79. On the other hand there are still countries such as Afghanistan, Swaziland, and Lesotho where life expectancy for females is below 46. These countries are decades behind the developed countries. Interestingly, there is very little difference in these countries in life expectancy between males and females.

Table 5.4 also shows that in high mortality countries Maternal Mortality Ratio (MMR) is particularly high. In Afghanistan it stands at 1,800 and in Nigeria at 1,100. Infant mortality is also high but it varies from a moderate level of 67 to a very high level of 154. This suggests that it is easier to improve infant mortality as compared to maternal mortality. For improvement in MMR mere public health measures are not enough. There is also a need for improved transportation, empowerment of women, and change of culture and traditions.

Table 5.5 shows the differences in total fertility rates.

Table 5.5: Total Fertility Rate for Selected Countries, 2009

Total fertility rate	*Country*	*Total fertility rate*
High		
	Hong Kong SAR, China	1.01
	Korea, Republic of	1.22
	Japan	1.26
	Singapore	1.26
	Poland	1.27
	Germany	1.32
Low		
	Chad	6.08
	Uganda	6.25
	Somalia	6.35
	Togo	6.38
	Afghanistan	6.51
	Niger	7.07

The above table shows that the total fertility rate varies from 1.01 (in Hongkong) to 7.07 (in Niger). In most developed countries fertility is below 2.1 and there are several countries in which average rate of population growth is negative.

Differences in International Migration

Table 5.6 shows data on international migration flow in the world as well as separately for the developed and developing countries. The table shows the changing nature of pattern of international migration. It shows that between 1990 and 2005 developed countries absorbed most of the increase in the number of international migrants. In the developing countries during this period the migrant stock virtually stagnated: the number of migrants in developing countries increased only by barely 3 million. It is possible that actual amount of new outflows to the developed countries (emigration) was more but the return flows cancelled it out.

Table 5.6: Estimated Number of International Migrants and their Percentage Distribution by Development Group and Major Area, 1990-2005

Development group and major area	*Number of international migrants (millions)*		*Increment (millions)*	*Percentage distribution of international migrants*	
	1990	*2005*	*1990-2005*	*1990*	*2005*
World	154.8	190.6	35.8	100.0	100.0
More developed regions	82.4	115.4	33.0	53.2	60.5
Less developed regions	72.5	75.2	2.8	46.8	39.5
Least developed countries	11.0	10.5	-0.5	7.1	5.5
Africa	16.4	17.1	0.7	10.6	9.0
Asia	49.8	53.3	3.5	32.2	28.0
Latin America and Caribbean	7.0	6.6	-0.3	4.5	3.5
Europe	27.6	44.5	16.9	17.8	23.3
Oceania	49.4	64.1	14.7	31.9	33.6
	4.8	5.0	0.3	3.1	2.6

Source: Population Division of United Nations Secretariat, *Trends in Total Migrant Stock: The 2005 Revision* (POP/DB/MIG/Rev.2005). Quoted in United Nations (2009).

Table 5.7 summarizes the broad characteristics of population in developed and developing countries.

Demographic Window in Developing Countries

Population growth has both positive and negative consequences. Negative consequences are commonly mentioned in literature. Among the positive consequences, several of the developing countries are having the advantage of opening of demographic window. This concept implies the bulging of population in working ages. Demographic window occurs because of the following three reasons:

- Constant decrease in fertility level leading to reduction in proportion of population at younger ages
- Lack of significant improvement in life expectancy at older ages leading to slower rise in proportion of population at older ages
- Entry of baby boom generation into labour farce.

It is estimated that this advantage of demographic window will remain for about 20 years. After that the low fertility cohort will start entering the working ages and there may also be an improvement in life expectancy at older ages. Then the proportion of population in working ages may decline. The Planning Commission says that opening of demographic window in India can be a matter of great advantages (Box 5.2).

Table 5.7: Broad Characteristics of Population in the Developed and Developing Countries

Characteristic	*Developed countries*	*Developing countries*
Density of population	Varies greatly	Varies greatly
Growth rate	Near zero or negative	Varies from a low growth rate to continuing high growth rate (1-2.5)
Fertility	Below replacement level (1.2 –1.6)	Declining from moderate to low level (3-4)
Mortality	High life expectancy with a difference of 4-7 years between males and females (above 80 for females)	Low to moderate level of life expectancy with less differences between males and females (58-68 for females)
Migration	Emigration often leading to internal reaction against liberal migration policies	Varies. While most countries are sending migrants to other countries, several countries are having significant inmigration of professionals and workers
Average age of population	Going up. Not only proportion of aged is high, among the aged (60+) proportion of more aged (80+) is increasing.	The process of aging is on. Several countries like India have the advantage of opening of demographic window
Income levels	Very high	Low to moderate, with some countries having high income (one ninth of the world income level)
Human development (HDI)	High	Low to medium
Share in the world population	Decreasing	Increasing
Future predictions	Negative natural growth rate	Low to moderate, yet positive growth rate. Population to stabilize at much higher levels
Population policy	Pronatal-aiming at raising the fertility rate	Antinatal-aiming at reducing the fertility rate
Are policies effective	Not effective or less effective	Difficult to assess as both population policy and improvement in social development are leading to reduction in fertility

Yet, then is a caveat here. If the youths can be provided suitable skills then they will fill the labour force shortage facing the industrially advanced, aging economies of the world and this will help both the labour force and the national economy. If the youths are not provided employment the demographic window may turn into demographic nightwave.

Box 5.2: Demographic Window

Demographic window may be an advantage or a disadvantage. If the increasing population in working ages may be provided skills, suitable employment and resources, they can contribute to society and economy considerably. If they cannot be provided work and resources, the society may face alienation, resistance and anomy.

Future Prospects

Table 5.8 shows the UN projections of world population and major regions. As per *The State of World Population 2009* the world population is likely to reach the figure of 9.1 billion in 2050. There is a caveat here. It is not easy to make predictions of population. Their accuracy is based on several factors: accuracy of data on size and composition of population, fertility and mortality rates, and assumptions regarding future trends in fertility and mortality. The most difficult among them is to predict fertility.

Table 5.8: Projections of World Population and Major Regions

World/region	*Size of population (millions), 2009*	*Share in the world population, 2009*	*Projected population in 2050*	*Share in the world population, 2050*
World	6,829.4		9,150.0	
More developed countries	1,233.3	18.06	1,275.2	13.94
Less developed countries	5,596.1	81.94	7,875.0	86.06
Least developed countries	835.5	12.23	1,672.4	18.28

The above table shows that the share of developed countries in the world population is declining. Almost all the growth in the world population in the period 2009-2050 will take place in the developing countries only. Thus the share of developed countries which was more than 20 per cent in the beginning of the Christian era is going to decline to 14 per cent and the share of developing countries will increase from less than 80 per cent to 86 per cent.

Future is unpredictable. Different countries will have different demographic paths in the future. We can have various scenarios:

- Universally low fertility, characteristic of second demographic transition and national governments worried about it, but not doing anything to raise fertility, leaving it to market forces, civil society and individuals
- Universally low fertility, and national governments using ideology and political resources at their disposal, to encourage women to withdraw from work temporarily and produce right number of children
- While most parts of the world have low fertility, some countries, for cultural, religious, political or socio-economic reasons, continue to maintain moderate fertility levels and they fulfil the demographic need of the world community, partly or fully
- There is another demographic transition and after reaching a below replacement fertility levels more and more countries move towards a replacement level fertility or higher fertility.

At the moment it appears to be more likely that in the future more and more countries will face the problem of fertility going below the replacement level and its impact on aging.

QUESTIONS AND EXERCISES

1. What is the present size of the world population and at what rate is it growing? What is its doubling time?
2. Why did population of the world grow at extremely slow rate till the beginning of the nineteenth century?
3. What are the regional differences in world population growth and what are the reasons behind them?
4. What are difficulties in predicting the future of world population?
5. Who is described as six billionth baby? What is the significance of celebrating the birth of six billionth baby?
6. Classify the countries on the basis of birth and death rates. Do you find any relationship between the two?

7. What are developed and less developed countries?
8. Write an essay on patterns of international migration and its causes.
9. Should the developed countries show interest in improving mortality rates in the developing countries? Why do you think so?
10. Define:
    a. cultural carrying capacity
    b. demographic window.

REFERENCES

Bongaarts, John, 1975, Why High Birth Rates are So Low. *Population and Development Review*, Vol. 1, No. 2: 289-296.

Hume, David, 1977, On the Populousness of Ancient Nations. *Population and Development Review*, Vol. 3, No. 3: 323-329.

Kirk, Dudley, 1996, Demographic Transition Theory. *Population Studies*, Vol. 50, No. 3: 361-387.

Misra, B.D., 1995, *An Introduction to the Study of Population*. New Delhi: South Asian Publishers Pvt Ltd, p.5.

The National Intelligence Council, 2001, The US National Intelligence Council on Growing Global Migration. *Population and Development Review*, Vol. 27, No. 4: 817-819.

UNFPA, 2009, Fast Facts, *http://www.unfpa.org/6billion/facts.htm* [accessed on 13th December, 2009].

United Nations Population Division, 2009, The World Population Prospects: The 2008 Revision, *http://esa.un.org/unpp/*[accessed on 6th January, 2010].

United Nations Population Fund, 2009, *The State of World Population 2009*. New York: UNFPA, p. 8, *http://www.unfpa.org/swp/2009/en/pdf/EN_SOWP09.pdf* [accessed on 13th December, 2009].

United Nations, 2009, International Migration Report 2006: A Global Assessment. Department of Economic and Social Affairs, Population Division, *http://www.un.org/esa/population/publications/2006_MigrationRep/exec_sum.pdf* [accessed on 19th January, 2009].

Urlanis, B.T., 1978, World Population Growth. In Valentey, D.I. (eds.), 1978, *The Theory of Population*. Moscow: Progress Publications: 232.

Valentey, D.I. (eds.), 1977, *An Outline Theory of Population*. Moscow: Progress Publications: 33-34, 103.

________ (eds.), 1978, *The Theory of Population*. Moscow: Progress Publications: 232.

Wilcox, Walter, 1985, Walter Wilcox on the Expansion of Europe and Its Influence on Population. *Population and Development Review*, Vol. 11, No. 3: 515-527.

6

Population of India

POPULATION GROWTH IN INDIA

Introduction

The first question in population sociology of a country is: what is the size of population in that country and at what rate is it changing? As suggested by demographic transition theory the population was more or less constant for a long time due to high fertility and high mortality. Then as mortality starts improving population begins to rise. Eventually when fertility rates fall (in response to economic development and improvement in mortality) growth rate of population starts declining and population moves towards the stationary state. Indian population history is no exception to this. This chapter looks at the growth of India's population.

Population in Ancient India

The first population census was conducted in 1872 and that too was not synchronous. The first synchronous and nearly complete census was conducted in 1881. We do not have very precise estimates for India's past. Yet, there are some scholarly estimates which are consistent with the theoretical framework of demographic transition theory. Table 6.1 presents the estimates of population of ancient India.

Phases of Population Growth in India, 1901-2001

Table 6.2 presents census data on population of India from 1901 to

Table 6.1: Estimates of India's Population, 300 BC-1871 AD

Date	Population (in millions)	Source
300 BC	100-140	Pran Nath
1600 AD	100	Moreland
1800	120	Playfair (adjusted)
1834	130	M'Culloch
1845	130	M'Culloch
1855	175	Statistical Abstract of UK Possessions (adjusted)
1867	194	Parliamentary Papers (adjusted)
1871	255	Census

Source: Devis (1951)

Table 6.2: Growth of Population in India, 1901-2011

Year	Population	Average annual rate of growth	Progressive growth rate over 1901 (per cent)
1901	238,396,327	—	—
1911	252,093,390	0.56	5.75
1921	251,321,213	-0.03	5.42
1931	278,977,238	1.04	17.02
1941	318,660,580	1.33	33.67
1951	361,088,090	1.25	51.47
1961	439,234,771	1.96	84.25
1971	548,159,652	2.20	129.94
1981	683,329,097	2.22	186.64
1991	846,421,039	2.16	255.05
2001*	1,028,737,436	1.97	331.52
2011	1,210,193,422	1.64	407.64

2011 (Census of India, 2011). The table shows that in 2011 the total population of the country is 1,210,193,422 or 1,210 million. It is growing at the average annual rate of growth of 1.64 per cent. Thus the doubling time of population of India is nearly 42.7 years. This means that in absence of any change in the growth rate the population of India may grow to 2,430 million by year 2054. But the rate of growth would not remain same during 2011-2054. It has not remained same during last one hundred years. The table also shows that in the last century population of India grow by 33.52 per cent. The major part of the growth occurred in the last four decades. After independence in 1947 the population of India grew more than three times by the year 2011.

Table 6.3 shows the stages of growth in India's population. On the basis of data one may divide the population history of India into four distinct stages: before 1921; 1921-1951; and 1951-1981; and after 1981. Before 1921 the population of India had erratic growth rate, sometimes increasing and sometimes decreasing, though growing slowly on long term basis. After 1921 it started growing at a rate more than 1 per cent per year. The cause of this increased growth rate was not a rise in fertility but a decline in mortality that set in due to better health facilities, education and overall development. During 1951-1981 the process of improvement in the mortality rate was accelerated and the population started growing at rate above 2 per cent. After 1981, though the population initially grew at rate above 2 per cent, the rate of growth started falling. Increasing success in family planning programme was a major cause of this. The last decade has seen a significant fall, from 1.97 per cent during 1991-2001 to 1.64 per cent during 2001-2011.

Table 6.3: Stages of Growth in the Population History of India

Stage	*Period*	*Chief characteristics*
Stage I	Before 1921	Population changing at erratic rates: sometimes rising and sometimes falling
Stage II	1921-1951	Population continuously rising at rate more than 1 per cent per year
Stage III	1951-1981	Population rising at rate above 2 per cent
Stage IV	After 1981	Population still rising at rate above 2 per cent but the decadal rate of growth declining

The October 2009 Bulletin of Sample Registration Scheme shows that for the year 2008 the natural growth rate of India is 15.4 per thousand. This means that if we exclude the effect of international migration (which is estimated to be-.0 per 1,000) the growth rate of India's population is 1.54 per cent per year. This is much less than the decadal growth rate for 2001-2011 (2.16%) indicating a further reduction in fertility after 2001.

Sex Ratio

Next to size and growth rate of population, demographers are interested in sex ratio of population. According to Census of India

2011, the sex ratio of India's population is 940 females per 1,000 males, showing a relative deficit of females. Table 6.4 shows the changes in sex ratio in India. It shows that in the last century the overall sex ratio of population has declined. This could partly be due to the fact that males were the earlier beneficiary of improvement in mortality. The last census, however, showed an improvement of 7 points.

Table 6.4: Sex Ratio in India, 1901-2011

Year	*Sex ratio*
1901	972
1911	964
1921	955
1931	950
1941	945
1951	946
1961	941
1971	930
1981	934
1991	927
2001	933
2011	940

There are urban-rural differences in sex ratio, mostly indicating male selectivity in rural-urban migration. In 2001 the urban sex ratio was 900 and the rural sex ratio was 946. There are also state-wise differences. Today Kerala with a sex ratio of 1,084 has the highest sex ratio. At the bottom is Daman & Diu which has a sex ratio of 618. Sex ratio in age group 0-6, called child sex ratio, is of special interest.

To quote JSK (2009):

> Sex Ratio is a sensitive indicator that displays the status of women. Concerted efforts are needed to create equal regard and affection for the girl child. The sex ratio among children (0 to 6 years) is showing a continuous decline in Punjab, Haryana, Himachal Pradesh, Delhi and Gujarat. Many families willfully decide to remove the female foetus in a quest for sons. Unfortunately this happens in the more educated and affluent localities. The motivation is primarily to protect property, family business and to avoid giving dowry. If there has to be a change

in mindset, leaders in society have to show the way. Otherwise the population will become skewed leading to a host of societal problems like increased crime against women.

It is estimated that during 2001-2011 child sex has declined from 927 to 914. This large decline in child sex ratio has been attributed to the practice of female feticide. Table 6.5 shows ten districts with extreme child sex ratios (JSK, 2009).

Table 6.5: Districts with Extreme Child Sex Ratios

District with highest sex ratios	*Sex ratio*	*District with lowest sex ratios*	*Sex ratio*
East Kamang (Arunachal Pradesh)	1035	Fatehgarh Sahib (Punjab)	766
Pulwama (Jammu and Kashmir)	1033	Kurukshetra (Haryana)	771
Kupwara (Jammu and Kashmir)	1021	Patiala (Punjab)	777
Dantewada (Chhattisgarh)	1014	Ambala (Haryana)	782
Upper Siang (Arunachal Pradesh)	1010	Mansa (Punjab)	782

Age Composition of Population

Table 6.6 shows the age composition of population of India as shown by Census of India, 2001. It shows that India has a young age structure with 35 per cent population of India in the age group 0-14 years. The percentage of old (60+) is only 7.8. Earlier it was higher. A thumb rule states that in the pre-transitional society, marked by high birth rate and high death rate nearly 40 per cent population is found in the age group 0-14. Thus the data show that as a result of fall in birth rate the percentage population in age group 0-14 has somewhat declined.

Marital Status

In India marriage is early and universal. So around the age of 15 girls start getting married. NFHS-3 (2005-06) data show that by the time they reach age group 25-29 the percentage of never married women drops to 5.8; and by the next age group 30-34 it drops to 1.8 per cent. NFHS reported that for women in the age group 20-49 average age of marriage is 17.2 years. Median age is 17.7. This means that more than half of the women are still marrying below the age of 18, the legal minimum age of marriage. Among men the percentage never married is found to be 29.4 in the age group 25-29, and 8.7 in 30-34. Then it drops to 3.0 in age group 35-39, and further to 1.9 in 40-44.

Table 6.6: Age Distribution of India

Age group	*Total*	*Males*	*Females*
6 years and below	163,819,614	84,999,203	78,820,411
Proportion to total population (%)	15.9	16	15.9
7 to 14 years	199,791,198	104,488,119	95,303,079
Proportion to total population (%)	19.4	19.6	19.2
15 to 59 years	585,638,723	303,400,561	282,238,162
Proportion to total population (%)	56.9	57	56.9
60 years and above	76,622,321	37,768,327	38,853,994
Proportion to total population (%)	7.5	7.1	7.8
Age Not Stated	2,738,472	1,500,562	1,237,910
Proportion to total population (%)	0.3	0.3	0.3

Caste/Tribe

There are no authentic data on OBC population. The censuses give data on SC and ST only. However, NFHS-3 provides useful information on this subject. NFHS-3 data shows that nearly 19 per cent population of India belongs to SC, 8 per cent to ST, 39 per cent to OBC, and the rest to others.

Wealth Index

NFHS 3 data divides population in five categories according to wealth index. It shows that 27.7 per cent rural population belongs to lowest quintile, 26.1 to second, 22.8 to middle, 16.0 to fourth and only 7.4 to highest quintile. This indicates the widespread urban-rural disparity in the country with only 7.4 per cent of the rural population being in the highest weaith quintile according to national (i.e., combined urban-rural) standards of wealth. NFHS-3 produces data on housing characteristics, specifically, type of house (kachcha, semi-pucca and pucca), persons per room and cooking fuel. It also gives data on household possessions, ownership of agricultural land, house and farm animals, and reach of media. For those pursuing work in structural characteristics of India's population these data can be of immense use.

TRENDS IN DEATH AND BIRTH RATES

Rise and fall in the growth rate of India is the result of systematic changes in death and birth rates from high levels to moderate levels. In the beginning of the last century death and birth rate of India were in the vicinity of 50 per thousand (Sharma, 1996). Death rate declined to 31 during 1931-41 and to 15 in 1971-81. After that due to socio-economic development and efforts made by Government of India to provide health facilities to its population, mortality rate started declining further. By 2008 the death rate of India has come down to 7.4. Life expectancy which was around 20 in the beginning of the century rose to 31 in 1971-81 and 50 in 1971-81. At present the life expectancy is above 64 for males and above 66 for females. However, birth rate remained above 40 till 1971. Birth rate started declining only during 1971-81. It has come down to 22.8 and there is evidence that it will decline further. In the future, since life expectancy has already reached 65 it will be more and more difficult to improve it further, though there is lot of scope for this (Box 6.1). India's life expectancy is 10-15 years lower than that of the industrially advanced countries. The fertility will decline and, therefore, the growth rate of population is expected to decline further.

There is one more reason why the growth rate will decline further. That is the effect of age distribution, called population momentum. It can be shown that the decline in average fertility does not immediately affect the growth rate of population. If a high fertility country achieves a total fertility rate of 2.1 its growth rate will not become zero immediately. It will take a few decades for the population to stabilize because in the meantime more and more people will enter reproductive ages and produce their first and second child. When fertility was high nearly 40 per cent population of India was below the age of 14 years. With decline of fertility this percentage has come down but the number of children is still very large. As time passes they will grow, enter the reproductive period, marry and produce children. Therefore, the country will continue to have positive growth rate for several decades. In the Tenth Five Year Plan it was estimated that the contribution of age distribution to growth of India's population is about 60 per cent.

Box 6.1: Excerpt from Eleventh Five Year Plan, Vol. 2: 57

Considerable achievements have been made over the last six decades in our efforts to improve health standards, such as life expectancy, child mortality, infant mortality, and maternal mortality. Small pox and guinea worm have been eradicated and there is hope that poliomyelitis will be contained in the near future. Nevertheless, problems abound. Malnutrition affects a large proportion of children. An unacceptably high proportion of the population continues to suffer and die from new diseases that are emerging; apart from continuing and new threats posed by the existing ones. Pregnancy and child birth related complications also contribute to the suffering and mortality.

Regional Diversity

Table 6.7 presents the SRS estimates of death rates, birth rates and natural growth rates for different states of India, separately for rural and urban areas, for the year 2008. It also presents the estimates of infant mortality rates for different states. Natural growth rate is simply the difference between birth and death rates. The table clearly demonstrates that there is a large variation in birth rate in different States of India. Variations in death rates are comparatively small. The table also shows that there are significant variations in birth and death rates by urban-rural residence. As a rule urban areas have lower birth rates as well as death rates. Yet, since the urban-rural difference in birth rates is larger than in death rates, urban areas show a lower rate of natural growth than rural areas. Uttar Pradesh, Madhya Pradesh, Chhattisgarh and Orissa have a high death rate. Normally the states which have high death rate also have high birth rate but there are exceptions: Orissa has low birth rate but high death rate; Bihar has high birth rate but relatively low death rate. Orissa has the highest value of infant mortality rate. One may say that differences in Indian states are analogous to the differences in the world regions. Demographically, Kerala constitutes the Europe of India; Orissa, Uttar Pradesh and Bihar constitute the Africa of India. There is a need to fight the spatial differences in demographics. The political unity of India will depend heavily on the extent to which we can curtail the demographic diversity between different states and Union Territories.

Table 6.7: Birth and Death Rate, India 2008

India/States/Union Territories	*Birth Rate*			*Death Rate*			*Natural Growth Rate*			*Infant Mortality Rate*		
	Total	*Rural*	*Urban*	*Total*	*Rural*	*Urban*	*Total*	*Rural*	*Urban*	*Total*	*Rural*	*Urban*
1	2	3	4	5	6	7	8	9	10	11	12	13
India	**22.8**	**24.4**	**15.5**	**7.4**	**8.0**	**5.9**	**15.4**	**16.5**	**12.6**	**53**	**58**	**36**
Bigger States												
1. Andhra Pradesh	18.4	19.1	16.8	7.5	8.3	5.7	10.9	10.8	11.1	52	58	36
2. Assam	23.9	25.3	15.7	8.6	9.0	5.6	15.4	16.2	10.1	64	66	39
3. Bihar	28.9	29.7	22.5	7.3	7.4	6.0	21.6	22.3	16.5	56	57	42
4. Chhattisgarh	26.1	27.6	19.3	8.1	8.5	6.4	18.0	19.2	12.9	57	59	48
5. Delhi	18.4	20.2	18.1	4.8	5.1	4.7	13.6	15.1	13.4	35	40	34
6. Gujarat	22.6	24.1	20.3	6.9	8.0	5.4	15.7	16.1	14.9	50	58	35
7. Haryana	23.0	24.2	20.4	6.9	7.3	5.9	16.1	16.8	14.5	54	58	43
8. Jammu and Kashmir	18.8	20.2	14.0	5.8	6.0	4.9	13.1	14.2	9.1	49	51	37
9. Jharkhand	25.8	27.5	18.9	7.1	7.5	5.2	18.7	19.9	13.7	46	49	32
10. Karnataka	19.8	20.9	17.9	7.4	8.5	5.5	12.4	12.4	12.4	45	50	33
11. Kerala	14.6	14.6	14.6	6.6	6.7	6.4	8.0	7.9	8.2	12	12	10
12. Madhya Pradesh	28.0	30.0	21.1	8.6	9.4	6.0	19.4	20.7	15.1	70	75	48
13. Maharashtra	17.9	18.4	17.2	6.6	7.4	5.6	11.3	11.0	11.6	33	40	23
14. Orrisa	21.4	22.2	16.0	9.0	9.4	6.9	12.3	12.9	9.1	69	71	49
15. Punjab	17.3	18.0	16.1	7.2	8.0	6.0	10.1	10.1	10.1	41	45	33
16. Rajasthan	27.5	28.8	23.5	6.8	7.0	6.1	20.7	21.8	17.4	63	69	38
17. Tamil Nadu	16.0	16.2	15.8	7.4	8.2	6.3	8.6	8.0	9.4	31	34	28
18. Uttar Pradesh	29.1	30.0	25.1	8.4	8.8	6.6	20.7	21.2	18.4	67	70	49
19. West Bengal	17.5	19.4	12.4	6.2	6.1	6.6	11.2	13.3	5.8	35	37	29

(Contd.)

(Contd.)

1	2	3	4	5	6	7	8	9	10	11	12	13
Smaller States												
1. Arunachal Pradesh	21.8	23.1	15.2	5.2	5.6	3.0	16.6	17.5	12.1	32	34	19
2. Goa	13.6	13.4	13.8	6.6	8.1	5.7	7.1	5.3	8.2	10	10	11
3. Himachal Pradesh	17.7	18.2	12.1	7.4	7.4	4.7	10.3	10.6	7.4	44	45	27
4. Manipur	15.8	15.9	15.7	5.0	4.8	5.4	10.9	11.1	10.3	14	16	8
5. Meghalaya	25.2	27.3	15.6	7.9	8.4	5.4	17.3	18.9	10.2	58	60	43
6. Mizoram	17.8	22.0	13.4	5.1	5.9	4.2	12.8	16.1	9.2	37	45	24
7. Nagaland	17.5	17.8	16.4	4.6	5.0	3.3	12.9	12.9	13.0	26	25	28
8. Sikkim	18.4	18.7	16.6	5.2	5.4	3.7	13.2	13 3	12.8	33	33	19
9. Tripura	15.4	16.1	12.0	5.9	6.0	5.2	9.5	10.1	6.8	34	36	26
10. Uttarakhand	20.1	21.0	16.5	6.4	6.7	5.6	13.6	14.4	10.9	44	48	24
Union Territories												
1. Andaman and Nicobar Islands	16.9	16.9	17.1	4.8	5.5	3.6	12.1	11.4	13.4	31	35	23
2. Chandigarh	16.4	22.6	15.8	4.4	3.1	4.6	11.9	19.6	11.2	28	22	29
3. Dadra and Nagar Haveli	27.0	26.4	29.2	5.4	6.1	3.0	21.6	20.4	26.2	34	38	20
4. Daman and Diu	17.5	17.3	17.9	5.3	5.4	5.2	12.2	12.0	12.6	31	29	36
5. Lakshadweep	14.3	15.7	12.9	7.1	6.4	7.8	7.1	9.3	5.0	31	28	35
6. Pondicherry	16.4	16.4	16.4	7.5	8.8	6.9	8.9	7.6	9.5	25	31	22

Note: Infant mortality rate for smaller Sątes and Union Territories are based on three year period 2006-08.

Source: SRS Bulletin, October 2009, Office of the Registrar General of India, Ministryof Home Affairs, Government of India.

Implications of High Growth Rate

We have seen that after independence population of India grew at a rate of more than 2 per cent a year. This had serious implications for Indian society. The issue to what extent high population growth rate hampered development is controversial and can never be settled. Development is influenced by ethical and ideological factors, resources, and state policies. Those who claim that population growth is bad for development they may argue as follows: if the national income (total value of goods and services produced in a country) grows at 2.5 per cent a year and the population also grows at the same rate, in terms of income per capita the country will remain where it is. In crude terms just to maintain the same level of standard, education, jobs, housing and health facilities the country must grow at 2.5 per cent level. Assuming a capital-output ratio of 4 it means that a country must invest 10 per cent of national income to achieve this. It is not easy for a poor and backward country to save 10 per cent for investment but this has to be done, and without any promise in the near future. Even a good growth of say 5 per cent a year, requiring 20 per cent investment, would result in a very slow improvement in the economic standards. This is one of the reasons why in the post-independence period India experienced a *Hindu growth rate* (i.e., a nearly stable and low growth rate).

Others may argue that population is a resource. In the long run a higher population is better than the lower population. Children born today will start contributing to production nearly 21 years from now. If they are provided education and other productive resources, more number will mean more development. It is only in the short run, up to next 20 years, that population growth may adversely affect development. Even here one may say that higher family size may force people to work more and, therefore, contribute to economic development.

India has had ambitious economic plans and declarations on the part of political leaders that India is fast catching up with the West. This created fast rising aspirations among the masses. The country has also made progress on many fronts. It has made progress by large investments (not always fair for a poor country) partly by internal mobilization and partly by borrowings and, yet, the reality is that it's not possible for India to catch up with the Western countries. Over the years development has produced more inequalities: between regions, males and females, social classes, urban and rural areas and the rich and the poor. The gap between those working in organized sector, mostly in big cities, and those working in unorganized sector in small towns and villages is widening. The result is the widespread discontent and anarchy.

FUTURE PROSPECTS

Present Assessment of the State of Demographic Transition in India

According to NFHS-3 the following seven states have reached below replacement level fertility (TFR less than 2.1): Andhra Pradesh, Goa, Tamil Nadu, Kerala, Himachal Pradesh, Punjab, and Sikkim. Three other states have replacement level fertility (TFR of 2.1). There is a need to examine in-depth what factors have led to below replacement level fertility in these diverse states and whether it is possible to design programmes for the high fertility states (such as Nagaland, Meghalaya, Uttar Pradesh and Bihar where TFR is 3.7 or above) based on lessons learnt from these states. Another issue is: whether in these states fertility will stabilize at the present low levels or it will continue to decline? Will they ever experience a third demographic transition and move towards replacement level fertility after attaining the below replacement fertility?

In this context, the case of low fertility in Himachal Pradesh is particularly interesting. Himachal Pradesh has some unique characteristics:

1. Himachal Pradesh has the lowest incidence of spousal physical or sexual violence (6%).
2. It also has the highest contraceptive prevalence rate (73%). What has made all this possible in Himachal Pradesh? In Himachal Pradesh, knowledge and availability of family planning methods are universal and, therefore, the unmet needs are minimum (7.3%).
3. Ironically, Himachal Pradesh is not at the top in terms of improvement in infant and child mortality, antenatal care or institutional delivery.
4. It has the lowest level of urbanization.
5. In the state only 45.3 per cent deliveries are institutional and only half of the deliveries (50.2%) take place in presence of doctor/nurse/LHV/ANM/other health personnel (NFHS 3,

2009). Does the state have high rate of abortion? Collecting data on abortions is difficult. It is very personal, intimate and often a painful event.

6. There is a need to know: what is the level of spontaneous and induced abortion in Himachal Pradesh and what are the factors behind it?

There is vast literature on demographic transition. It is believed that in the West demographic transition occurred in two phases: first, in response to socio-economic development and modernization; and second time in response to developing separation between sex and reproduction due to development of contraception. The second transition has produced the below replacement fertility. In a recent article Chesnais (2000) identified the following factors behind demographic transition to below replacement level fertility: (1) social atomization and related feminism; (2) implementation of collectivized pension benefits; (3) globalized nomadism; (4) youth loss of majority; and (5) the "end of work" syndrome". In simple terms it means that individualization, increasing freedom of women, pension benefits, migration and economic deprivation (because many youths are earning less than their parents and there is rise in unemployment) have changed the calculus of fertility in favour of low fertility.

Fertility levels are outcome of a number of factors:

- Age of marriage and length of reproductive period
- Sexuality within marriage
- Use of modern family planning methods
- Abortion practices

In literature, the above factors are divided into two categories: family planning; and beyond family planning factors. While family planning factors include knowledge, attitude and practice (KAP) of contraceptive methods, the beyond family planning factors include the whole matrix of socio-economic factors which impinge upon value of children, reproductive decision making, and motivation to limit family size.

India is making progress on all fronts: knowledge of family planning is almost universal, about 60 per cent couples are using family planning methods, there is improvement in socio-economic condition and women are more empowered today. Due to

Westernization, modernization and state efforts significant changes are taking place in age of marriage. Parents have started recognizing the importance of girls' education and empowerment of women has increased desire to provide as much education to girls as to boys. All this is going to help India in proceeding further on the path of demographic transition. Yet there are several impediments also. Traditionally, Indian society is patriarchal, and patrifocal. Marriage has been early and universal. In most parts of the country great value is placed on having a son. After marriage women join their husband's family and live almost permanently there or with husband if he is working elsewhere. They are subjected to physical, emotional and sexual violence. In certain parts of the country there is avoidance of girl child and illegally cases of female feticide are also taking place.

Projections of Future Population

It is almost impossible to predict the future population with great accuracy. Population projections require an exact understanding of the present day processes and intelligent understanding of future possibilities (Box 6.2). United Nations estimates show that by the year 2050 India will be the most populous country of the world and its population will be larger than that of China (Box 6.3). This will affect international relations as well as India's place in globalization.

Box 6.2: Uncertain Future

Many people who mark dire predictions about the ecological future do so out of genuine concern; others seem to be doing no more than cashing in on the public's seemingly inexhaustible appetite for nightmares. There are opposing 'no-problem' or 'the market will adjust' schools whose optimism cannot be shared either. It is more honest to admit that we do not know what the future holds; that it will be good or bad depending on some things that are within human control and others that are not. The business of the academic observer is to point to the areas where action is most needed and also—and this is one of our self-confessed aims—to create a climate of opinion for balanced judgement about future development.

From: Cassen (1978).

Migration as a Burning Issue

Indian population has become mobile. As per the Registrar General of India out of the 1.02 billion people in the country, 307 million (or 30%) were reported as migrants by place of birth data in 2001 census.

Box 6.3: Future Population Prospects

...it seems extremely unlikely that the country's population will not exceed 1.5 billion at sometime in the coming decades. Indeed, a figure of about 1.6 billion seems fairly likely. And, while it is unlikely, even a figure approaching 1.7 billion cannot be ruled out. Personally I feel that a figure just short of 1.6 billion is most probable. And in this context it is worth noting that Natarajan and Jayachandran's projections (2001a, 2001b)-which also extend to the year 2051—yield a figure of 1.646 billion. Moreover, the latest UN medium-variant (i.e. 'best-guess') projection puts the total population of India at 1.572 billion in 2050. The corresponding population figure for China then is only 1.462 billion (United Nations 2002).

Source: Dyson (2003)

This proportion in case of India (excluding J&K) is slightly more than what was reported in 1991 (27.4%). Thus there has been a steady increase in the number of migrants in the country. Whereas in 1961 there were about 144 million migrants by place of birth, in 2001 Census, it was 307 million. With time migration is going to become a burning issue with ethnic conflicts between migrants and natives being reported from several parts of the country.

Table 6.8 presents the data on migration based on place of birth data. State-wise details, showing 1991 population, number of net in-migrants 1991-2001, migration rate and a comparison with 1991-2001 growth in population, and contribution of migration in the growth of each state are given in Table 6.9. It clearly shows that Bihar and Manipur are two most outmigrating states while Chandigarh, Dadra and Nagar Haveli, Daman and Diu, and Delhi are most inmigrating Union Territories/States.

Table 6.10 shows the reasons behind migration. The table shows that women are more mobile than men but the reason for that is essentially marriage migration among women. Among men work and employment is the major reason. 37.6 per cent of them have migrated for work and employment. Interestingly, though only one-sixth of men, women too are migrating for work and employment.

CONCLUSION

It appears that demographically, in the future India will experience hyperdifferentiation, a term used in postmodern literature for extreme differentiation leading to dedifferentiation or new forms of integration, uzncertain and unpredictable at the moment. While some states will be moving towards lower death and birth rates as

Table 6.8: In-Migration by Place of Birth and Sex: 2001

Category	Persons	Males	Females
(a) Total Population	1,028,610,328	532,156,772	496,453,556
(b) Born in India	1.022,442,977	528,981,861	493,461,116
(c) Born in the place of enumeration	721,460,171	441,746,082	279,714,089
(d) Total migrants (a-c)	307.149,736	90,410,496	216,739,240
(e) Born within the state of enumeration	980,101,274	509,306,087	470,795,187
(i) Born elsewhere in the district of enumeration	181,799,637	42,781.678	139,017.959
(ii) Born in other districts of the state	76,841,466	24,778,327	52,063,139
(f) Born in other States in India beyond the state of enumeration	42,341,703	19,675,774	22,665,929
(g) Born abroad	6,166,930	3,174,717	2,992,213
(h) Unclassified	421	194	227

Note: India excludes 2001 Census data on population and other characteristics for Mao Maram, Paomata and Purul sub-divisions of Senapati district of Manipur.

Source: Table D1, Census of India 2001.

predicted by classical demographic transition theory, others will be experiencing a second demographic transition, and in some there will be a demand for the third transition leading to higher fertility levels. There will be more of poor and rich divide. Then within each state there will be high and low fertility districts, within each district high and low fertility blocks, and within blocks high and low fertility social classes. Within classes again there will be fragmentation due to Westernization, individualization and women's education. Urban and rural differences are likely to continue.

Migration will, however, become a more important issue than fertility and family planning. There are two types of migration: international and internal. In terms of statistics international migration will remain small as compared to population of India. But its impact on economy, culture and state policy may be quite substantial. Internal migration will increase further. There will be rapid migration from population surplus areas to resource surplus areas, often leading to violent conflicts at the place of destination.

Table 6.9: 1991 Population, 2001 Census Data on Inter-State Migration Based on Last Residence (0-9), Migration Rate and Growth Rate of Population—States/UTs

States/UTs	*Population (1991)*	*In-migrants From other states (2001)*	*Out-migrants (2001)*	*From other countries (2001)*	*Net-in migrants (2001)*	*Migration Rate (per 100) 1991-2001*	*Growth Rate of Population (1991-2001)*
India	846,387,888	16,826,879	16,826,879	740,867	740,867	0.09	21.54
1. A&N Islands	280,661	29,538	8.011	728	22,255	7.9	26.90
2. Andhra Pradesh	66,508,008	421,989	637,360	6,292	209.079	(0.3)	14.59
3. Arunachal Pradesh	864,558	71,789	12,507	2931	62213	7.2	27.00
4. Assam	22,414,322	121,803	281,510	5,053	154,654	(0.7)	18.92
5. Bihar	64,530,554	460,782	2,241,413	57.724	1,722,907	(2.7)	28.62
6. Chandigarh	642,015	239,263	106,734	5,108	137,637	21.4	40.28
7. Chhattisgarh@	17,614,928	338,793	444,679	2,615	103,271	(0.6)	18.27
8. Dadra and Nagar Haveli	138,477	47,649	3,440	964	45,173	32.6	59.22
9. Daman and Diu	101,586	48,362	5,401	1,835	4,796	44.1	55.73
1.0. Delhi	9,420,644	2,172,760	457,919	49,281	1,764,122	18.7	47.02
11. Goa	1.169,793	120,824	32,578	4,775	93,021	8.0	15.21
12. Gujarat	41,309,582	1,125,818	451,458	14,800	689,160	1.7	22.66
13. Haryana	16,463,648	1,231,480	588,001	26,639	670,118	4.1	28.43
14. Himachal: Pradesh	5,170,877	188,223	165,776	28,276	50,723	1.0	17.54
15. J & K @	7,718,700	86,768	122,175	2,938	32,469	(0.4)	29.98
16. Jharkhand	21,843,911	502,764	616,160	2,309	111,087	(0.5)	23.36
17. Karnataka	44,977,201	879,106	769,111	20,533	130,528	0.3	17.51
18. Kerala	29,098,518	235,087	431,821	32,077	164,657	(0.6)	9.43
19. Lakshadweep	51,707	4,444	1,149	17	3,312	6.4	17.23
20. Madhya Pradesh	48,566,242	814,670	842,937	6,939	21,328	(0.0)	24.26
21. Maharashtra	78,937,187	3,231,612	896,988	48,394	2,383,018	3.0	22.73

(Contd)

(Contd)

States/UTs	*Population (1991)*	*In-migrants From other states (2001)*	*Out-migrants (2001)*	*From other countries (2001)*	*Net-in migrants (2001)*	*Migration Rate (per 100) 1991-2001*	*Growth Rate of Population (1991-2001)*
22. Manipur	1.837,149	4,529	30.867	182	26,156	(1.4)	24.56
23. Meghalaya	1,774,778	33,710	20,434	1,154	14,430	0.8	30.65
24. Mizoram	689,756	22,599	31,739	8,436	704	(0.1)	28.82
25. Nagaland	1.209,546	33,594	51,857	1,752	16,511	(1.4)	64.53
26. Orissa	31,659,736	229,687	440,893	3,931	207,275	(0.7)	16.25
27. Pondicherry	807,785	105,208	35,755	1,426	70,879	8.8	20.62
28. Punjab	20.281,969	811,060	501,285	26,861	336,636	1.7	20.10
29. Rajasthan	44,005,990	723,639	997,196	11,873	261,684	(0.6)	28.41
30. Sikkim	406,457	22,519	6,238	7,655	23,936	5.9	33.06
31. Tamil Nadu	55,858,946	270,473	674,304	25,671	378,160	(0.7)	11.72
32. Tripura	2,757,205	40,262	23,538	11,246	27,970	1.0	16.03
33. Utter Pradesh	132,061,653	1.079,055	3,810,701	32,110	2,699,536	(2.0)	25.85
34. Uttaranchal@	7.050,634	352,496	354,718	29,138	26,916	0.4	20.41
35. West Bengal	68,077,965	724,524	730,226	259,204	253,502	0.4	17.77

Source: Table D2, Census of India 2001.

Note: @ Population of new states for 1991 Census is recast from the states from which they are formed. For Jammu and Kashmir estimated population is shown.

Table 6.10: Reasons for Migration of Migrants by Last Residence with Duration (0-9 Years), India, 2001

Reason for migration	*Number of migrants*			*Percentage to total migrants*		
	Persons	*Males*	*Females*	*Persons*	*Males*	*Females*
Total migrants	98,301,342	32,896,986	65,404,356	100.0	100.0	100.0
Reason for Migration						
Work/Employment	14,446,224	12.373,333	2,072,891	14.7	37.6	3.2
Business	1,136,372	950,245	186,127	1.2	2.9	0.3
Education	2,915,189	2,038,675	876,514	3.0	6.2	1.3
Marriage	43.100,911	679,852	42,421,059	43.8	2.1	64.9
Moved after birth	6,577,380	3,428,6734	3,148,707	6.7	10.4	4.8
Moved with Households	20,608,105	8,262,143	12,345,962	21.0	25.1	18.9
Other	9,517,161	5,164,065	4,353,096	9.7	15.7	6.7

There will also be more migration caused by new development projects, climate change, environmental risks, political and ethnic reasons and new economic policies. There are forces of globalization and glocalization. All this would make the future more uncertain and less amenable to understanding in old sociological terms.

QUESTIONS AND EXERCISES

1. Discuss the 20th century population trends in India.
2. What is the difference between decadal growth rate and natural growth rate?
3. Which are the most outmigrating and inmigrating states of India? What is the result of the rapid movement of people from one part of the country to another?
4. What is the possibility of third demographic transition in the low fertility states of India?
5. What are the future prospects of India's population?
6. Collect data on fertility, mortality, education and income for different states of India and explore if it is possible to classify the states of India in some way.
7. What is demographic momentum?
8. How is sex ratio of India changing? What does a low sex ratio in age group 0-6 imply?
9. Will a large population be a resource in India? Discuss the advantages and disadvantages of large population in the globalized world.
10. Write a note on migration patterns in India.

REFERENCES

Cassen, R.H., 1978: *India: Population, Economy, Society*. London: The Macmillan Press Ltd.: 330.

Census of India, 2001, *http://www.censusindia.gov.in/Census_Data_2001/India_at_glance/variation.aspx* [accessed on 17th November, 2009].

Census of India, 2011, *http://www.censusindia.gov.in/2011-prov_results_paper1_india.html* [accesses on 27th April, 2011].

Chesnais, Jean-Claude, 2000, Determinants of below-replacement fertility. In United Nations, *Below Replacement Fertility*. New York: Population Division, Department of Economic and Social Affairs, 127-136.

JSK, 2009, *http://www.jsk.gov.in/child_sex_ratio.asp* [accessed on 20th January, 2009].

Davis, Kingsley, 1951, *The Population of India and Pakistan*. Princeton: Princeton University Press.

Dyson, Tim, 2003, India's Population: Past, Present and Future, The Pravin Visaria Public Lecture, delivered at Gujarat Institute of Development Research, Conference Hall of the Ahmedabad Management Association on March 4.

Sharma, A.K., 1996, *Gandhian Perspectives on Population and Development*. New Delhi: Concept Publishing Company.

7

Urbanization and Development

URBANIZATION IN INDIA

Introduction

This chapter focuses on the growth of urbanization in India. It deals with the concept of urbanization, difference between urbanization and urbanism, level and trend of urbanization, causes of urbanization, relationship between urbanization and development, and future of urbanization in India

Definition of Urban Areas

There is no universal definition of urban areas. Different countries define urban localities in terms of different factors such as size and density of population, amenities considered to be commonly available in urban areas, major economic activities of population, etc. Also not all those countries which define urban areas in terms of the same factors use the same threshold values for distinguishing urban localities from rural localities. For example, among those countries which define urban areas in terms of minimum size of population, some countries define an area with a minimum population of 5,000 as urban while many countries define smaller places also as urban areas (say areas with a population of 2,000). This makes comparison between levels of urbanization between different countries as somewhat problematic.

Box 7.1 presents the census definition of urban areas that was used in Census of India, 2001. The same definition was used in 2011 census. The box also defines urban agglomerations and cities. The definition shows that size is one major factor in defining urban areas but this is not the only factor. Density of population, being a seat of local administration and composition of male labour force are others. Thus not all urban areas are large. Some urban areas have a population of less than 5,000. Badrinath, the famous pilgrimage place of Hindus has zero population at the time of census enumeration but it is defined as urban. The urban areas which have a population above 100,000 are called cities or Class I cities.

Urbanization and Urbanism

Urbanization does not imply urbanism. Urbanization refers to growth of urban population, in relation to rural population, but urbanism refers to presence of a distinct culture in urban areas. The term urbanism was coined by Louis Wirth (2009) to refer to ways of life in cities. Wirth published a classic essay on this theme "Urbanism as a Way of Life", in the *American Journal of Sociology* in 1938. In this essay he focused on city life, minority group behaviour and mass media. His research was concerned with how Jewish immigrants adjusted to life in urban America, as well as the distinct social processes of city life. He applied the concepts and theories of sociology to study the city life. For those who followed Wirth's ideas, the way of life of urban areas has been a more important subject of study than urbanization. Looked at from this perspective, a country may have high degree of urbanization but in terms of culture its urban areas may not be very different from the rural areas. Alternatively, urbanism need to be defined varyingly in the context of different countries. Since the history and processes of growth of cities in the developing countries are markedly different from those of the developed countries it is natural that the urban areas in the two world regions acquire different characters, or different styles of urbanism.

In general, however, in studies of population processes a distinction is made between urban and rural areas. All social and demographic characteristics of population vary according to urban-rural residence. Urban areas are normally marked by:

- Higher literacy, higher educational achievements and higher vocational education
- Higher standard of living, higher aspirations and more amenities and services

- Higher age of marriage
- Lower ideal family size, greater use of family planning methods and lower fertility
- Better health infrastructure leading to lower mortality and fertility rates
- Higher autonomy and empowerment of women
- Lower impact of religiosity and supernatural beliefs
- Greater impact of globalization, individualization and secularization.

Applying the Wirth's framework of urbanism, some demographers call the urban areas of India as rurban, i.e., showing the characteristics of both urban and rural areas. Thus urban population of India lives in urban areas but shows the characteristics of rural areas. It may be noted that while some sociologists use rurban as a distorted form of urbanization many sociologists use it as a descriptive category suggesting a new form of urban pattern. For some it is positive concept implying an emerging integration of rural and urban communities with respect to principles and practices governing land use, energy, transportation, governance, and all aspects of economic, ecological, and social development. Indiresan (2008) argues that rurbanisation is a solution to India's development problems.

Measurement of Urbanization

Urbanization is measured in terms of level (or sometimes called degree) of urbanization and speed of urbanization. Level of urbanization is defined as the percentage of total population of an area that is living in urban localities. All countries classify localities into urban and rural and collect data on their population. Thus

$$\text{Level of urbanization} = (\text{Urban population/Total population}) \times 100$$

Thus if the level of urbanization of a country is 32 per cent it implies that out of 100 persons in that country 32 are living in localities classified as urban (i.e., towns and cities). It may be stressed that the level of urbanization is dependent on the definition of urban and rural areas; change in the definition of urban localities may produce change in the level of urbanization.

Speed of urbanization during a given period is defined as

percentage change (per year) in the level of urbanization. Thus the speed of urbanization during 1991-2001 may be calculated as follows:

> Speed of urbanization, 1991-2001 = [(Difference in the level of urbanization between 1991 and 2001)/Level of urbanization in 1991]*100/10

Box 7.1: Urban and Rural Areas in Indian Census

In the Census of India 2001, the following definition of urban areas was used:

(a) All statutory places with a municipality, corporation, cantonment board or notified town area committee, etc.

(b) A place satisfying the following three criteria simultaneously:

i) a minimum population of 5,000;

ii) at least 75 per cent of male working population engaged in non-agricultural pursuits; and

iii) a density of population of at least 400 per sq. km. (1,000 per sq. mile).

For identification of places which would qualify to be classified as 'urban' all villages, which, as per the 1991 Census had a population of 4,000 and above, a population density of 400 persons per sq. km. and having at least 75 per cent of male working population engaged in non-agricultural activity were considered. To work out the proportion of male working population referred to above against b)(ii), the data relating to main workers were taken into account.

An Urban Agglomeration is a continuous urban spread constituting a town and its adjoining urban outgrowths (OGs) or two or more physically contiguous towns together and any adjoining urban outgrowths of such towns. Examples of OGs are railway colonies, university campuses, port areas, etc., that may come up near a city or statutory town outside its statutory limits but within the revenue limits of a village or villages contiguous to the town or city. Each such individual area by itself may not satisfy the minimum population limit to qualify it to be treated as an independent urban unit but may deserve to be clubbed with the town as a continuous urban spread.

For the purpose of delineation of Urban Agglomerations during Census of India 2001, following criteria are taken as pre-requisites: (a) The core town or at least one of the constituent towns of an urban agglomeration should necessarily be a statutory town; and (b) The total population of all the constituents (i.e. towns and outgrowths) of an Urban Agglomeration should not be less than 20,000 (as per the 1991 Census). With these two basic criteria having been met, the following are the possible different situations in which Urban Agglomerations would be constituted: (i) a city or town with one or more contiguous outgrowths; (ii) two or more adjoining towns with their outgrowths; and (iii) a city and one or more adjoining towns with their outgrowths all of which form a continuous spread.

City—Towns with population of 1,00,000 and above are called cities.

Since the level of urbanization can vary from zero to 100 only as the level of urbanization increases the potential to urbanize faster decreases.

According to one United Nations study, urbanization follows a logistic growth model. This means that in the beginning when the total population lives in rural areas, urbanization level increases at a slower pace but as the level of urbanization rises the rate of urbanization also rises. A point comes when the population observes highest speed of urbanization. Beyond this point, although the level of urbanization may continue to rise further but the speed of urbanization starts decreasing.

At some level below 100 per cent urbanization stops increasing further. As the level of urbanization increases a similar amount of rural-to-urban migration would result in smaller speed of urbanization. One cannot expect a highly urbanized country with a level of urbanization above 80 per cent to be urbanizing at the same speed as a lowly urbanized country with a level of urbanization at 5-10 per cent. In such cases ratio of urban to rural population multiplied by 100 may be seen as a better mesure of urbanization than the per cent urban.

Urbanization in India

Table 7.1 shows the levels and trends of urbanization in India in the twentieth century. It shows that in the beginning of the last century only 10.84 per cent population of India was living in urban areas. There is no doubt that there were some world famous religious, political and educational cities in all parts of the country but an overwhelming majority of population was living in rural areas. Thus India lived in its villages. Till 1931 the speed of urbanization was rather small. As a matter of fact during 1901 to 1911 the level of urbanization decreased. The major improvement in urbanization took place during 1931-1951 and 1971 to 1981. The period 1931-1951 was politically turbulent and millions of people moved cross-border after the partition of the country into India and Pakistan. After that the speed of urbanization has been slower and erratic (partly due to definitional changes). The 2001 census showed that 27.81 per cent of India's population was living in urban areas and the speed of urbanization is 0.82 per cent per year.

Census data have also shown that Goa state has the highest proportion of urban population (49.76%), Himachal Pradesh has the lowest (9.30%). Among the Union territories Delhi has the highest proportion of urban population (93.18%), and Dadra and Nagar Haveli the lowest (22.89%).

The towns and cities are usually divided into five classes: Class I Cities with population above 100,000; Class II Towns with population

50,000-100,000; Class III Towns with population 20,000-50,000; Class IV Towns with population 10,000-20,000; and Class V Towns with population 5,000-10,000. More than half of India's urban population lives in Class I cities, and nearly one-third in Class II or Class III towns. The share of towns with population less than 20,000 is rather small (Registrar General India, 2009).

Table 7.1: Level and Trend of Urbanization in India, 1901-2001

Year	*Total*	*Rural*	*Urban*	*Level of urbanization*	*Speed (trend) of urbanization*
1901	238,396,327	212,544,454	25,851,873	10.84	–
1911	252,093,390	226,151,757	25,941,633	10.29	-0.51
1921	251,321,213	223,235,043	28,086,170	11.18	0.86
1931	278,977,238	245,521,249	33,455,989	11.99	0.72
1941	318,660,580	274,507,283	44,153,297	13.86	1.56
1951	361,088,090	298,644,381	62,443,709	17.29	2.47
1961	439,234,771	360,298,168	78,936,603	17.97	0.39
1971	548,159,652	439,045,675	109,113,977	19.91	1.08
1981	683,329,097	523,866,550	159,462,547	23.34	1.72
1991	846,302,688	628,691,676	217,611,012	25.71	1.02
2001	1,028,737,436	742,490,639	286,119,689	27.81	0.82

Three Million Plus Cities

There are about 4,000 cities and towns in India. About 300 cities have population over 1,00,000. Among them seven cities have population more than 3 million (Indiamart.com, 2009). According to U.S. Census Bureau Mumbai ranks third in the world after Tokyo and Mexico. Kolkata is at the 9th place and Delhi at 14th. The names and populations of 3 million plus cities are given in Table 7.2.

Table 7.2: Cities in India with three Million Plus Population

City	*Population in 1991*	*Population in 2001*
Greater Mumbai (Bombay)	9,925,891	11,914,398
Delhi	7,206,704	9,817,439
Kolkata (Calcutta)	4,399,819	4,580,544
Bangalore	2,660,088	4,292,223
Chennai (Madras)	3,841,396	4,216,268
Ahmedabad	2,876,710	3,515,361
Hyderabad	2,964,638	3,449,878

CAUSES OF URBANIZATION

Causes of Growth of Urban Population

Urbanization, being a process of population concentration, is caused by all those factors which change the distribution of population by size of locality. Thus all those factors which make people move from places of lower population concentration to places of higher concentration lead to urbanization. In practice, it refers to growth of urban population in relation to rural population (Box 7.1) and is dependent on the definition of urban and rural localities. One may say that urbanization is caused primarily by migration of people from rural to urban areas (or smaller town to large cities). This assumes that the natural growth rate of urban and rural areas is similar. If urban areas have better health facilities and lower mortality, they also have lower fertility. However, sometimes this is not the case and urbanization may also be caused by differences in natural growth rate between urban and rural areas. In India, in the past natural growth in urban areas has been a major factor in the country's urban growth (Box 7.3). Yet, as a rule natural growth and the rural to urban migration are two main sources of growth of urban population and increase in level of urbanization. In addition, urban areas and city limits expand and as time passes they tend to incorporate a few villages at the outskirt leading to increase in urban population. Sometimes urban population also grows due to graduation, i.e., growth of population of localities which are classified as rural in one census and as urban in the subsequent censuses. Lastly, change of definition of urban areas may also increase or decrease urban population. Therefore, whenever we analyse trend in urbanization it is important to ask whether the definition of urban population has remained unchanged.

Box 7.2: Causes of Growth of Urban Population

There are five major causes of growth of urban population:

1. Natural growth in urban areas (i.e., the difference between births and deaths)
2. International and internal migration (mostly rural to urban migration within the country)
3. Absorption of peripheral rural localities in city limits
4. Graduation of small villages to small towns
5. Reclassification of urban and rural localities

According to the Sample Registration Scheme (SRS) data, in year 2008 the natural growth rate of urban areas is 12.6 per thousand (or 1.26%) while the natural growth rate of rural areas is 16.5 per thousand (or 1.65%). This implies that now it is rural-urban migration that will primarily decide the fate of urbanization. In absence of rural-urban migration the level of urbanization in India is likely to decline. But in the future the natural growth rate of rural areas will also change producing a further change in components of urban population growth.

Box 7.3: Causes of Urban Population Growth

The most important contributory factor behind the growth of India's urban population during the past five decades has been *urban natural increase*, i.e. the excess of urban births over urban deaths. My preliminary estimates suggest that between 1991 and 2001 at least 56 per cent of the growth of India's urban population was due to urban natural increase. During recent decades migration from rural to urban areas has been an important, but nevertheless secondary factor behind urban population growth.

-Quoted from Dyson (2003).

Causes of Rural-Urban Migration

Now the issue is: why do people move from rural to urban areas? Migration is a complex issue and the answer to this question is not simple. One major problem in studying the causes of migration empirically is that it is difficult to measure migration. The volume of migration depends heavily on the definition of migration. Overall, the pattern of migration depends on a number of factors:

- Whether the definition is based on place of birth criterion, last residence criterion, duration of residence, residence at a fixed prior date or any other criteria
- Whether the level of analysis is national, state, district, locality or urban-rural residence
- Whether the interest is in long distance or short distance migration
- Whether the interest is in total migration or male migration
- Whether the interest is in development induced migration or migration in general.

Yet, researches on the theme of migration show that several factors are important:

- Factors operating at the place of origin because of which people have to think of migrating to other places
- Factors operating at the places of possible destination because of which people at other places feel attracted to migrate
- Awareness and evaluation of the factors of migration
- Economic and psychological costs of migration
- Possibility of assimilation at the place of migration determining whether the migrants continue to stay there or must consider to return back or move to some other places
- Individual level factors—some people at some stage of life are by nature (personality) more mobile than others. Among the individual level factors the three most important factors are: psychological factors; demographic factors; and family background.

Sociologists and demographers divide causes of migration in terms of push and pull factors. Certain negative factors may push people to move away from place of origin and certain positive factors may attract them to place of destination. In case of rural-urban migration there are several possible push factors operating in the rural areas: lack of work and employment; domination, exploitation and oppression; inequality; lack of education and health facilities; caste hierarchy; disliking for traditions; and lack of opportunities to do something meaningful. Figure 7.1, produced in UNFPA's *State of World Population 2009,* shows how push factors induce people to migrate. The pull factors operating in urban areas are: better work and employment situation including possibility oi getting a more decent work; higher wages; greater social equality; better education and health facilities; closeness to seat of development and power; charm of city life; modernization; better connectivity with the outside world; and better living condition. In India we also talk of certain push-back factors operating in urban areas because of which rural-urban migrants feel pushed back to native, rural places. They are: lack of expected employment opportunities, ethnic segregation and discrimination; greater vulnerability to various risks; poor quality of life; and work place exploitation.

However, migration is not a simple function of push and pull factors. Various geographical and legal barriers prevent people from migrating even when they are aware of potential advantages of migration. Other factors remaining same, people will have the tendency to move to such places which are socially, culturally and politically closer to the place of origin. Also there are individual differences which are better explained in socio-psychological terms. Certain types of personalities could be more prone to migration than others. While this is true that certain sociological factors are closely associated with migration this is also true that in the same conditions some people migrate while others do not. This indicates the existence of relationship between personality and migratory tendency.

Figure 7.1: A Woman on the Move

One may argue that as the natural increase decreases the growth rate of urban population may also decrease. Further, if rural development policies aiming at greater investment in agriculture (such as Mahatma Gandhi National Rural Employment Guarantee Scheme) and expansion of provision for employment generation succeed in mitigating the effect of push factors in rural areas, the growth rate of urban population may decline substantially. In this situation India may achieve a higher level of development without having a high level of urbanization.

THEORIES OF URBANIZATION AND DEVELOPMENT

Urbanization and Development

In demographic and economic literature urbanization is frequently used as an indicator of development. There is a very intricate relationship between urbanization and development. *State of World Population 2009* shows that the more developed countries are all highly urbanized countries; the least developed countries are all low on urbanization. However, while the level of urbanization in the more developed countries has almost stabilized, in the less developed countries urbanization is occurring at a fast rate. A high rate of growth of urban population in the least developed countries shows that their urban populations are growing due to both natural increase (births-deaths) and rural to urban migration. Several of them are urbanizing at a rate which is higher than the rate at which the developed countries had urbanized when they had similar level of urbanization. The report exhibits the following:

- In year 2009 the world is around 50 per cent urban.
- The level of urbanization in the more developed countries is 75 per cent.
- The level of urbanization in the less developed countries is 45 per cent.
- The level of urbanization in the least developed countries is 29 per cent.
- The urban population in the world is growing at 2.0 per cent per year.
- The urban population in the more developed countries is growing at 0.6 per cent per year.
- The urban population in the less developed countries is growing at 2.6 per cent.
- The urban population in the least developed countries is growing at 4.1 per cent per year.

In the history of urbanization the year 2009 is specially marked. In 2009 the world is half urban and as the trends show in the coming years more than half of the world population will be living in urban areas.

Urbanization, industrialization and development are concomitant processes. It is difficult to say what exactly is the cause of what. The changes are symmetrical. Agricultural society was a village society. Industrialization caused urbanization by providing better opportunities to work in the urban areas. Better employment situation, better wages and charm of city life attracted people to move towards cities and urbanization started. This is the reason why the more developed countries which started urbanizing in 19th century are the most urbanized countries today. Less developed countries most of which were colonies of the developed countries did not experience industrialization and remained less urbanized. It was only in the second half of the twentieth century when they became independent that they started building infrastructure, providing various services to their population and developing industry. Then they started urbanizing. Several of their cities have now developed as business, service and administrative cities. On the other hand cities too promote development and industrialization. The reasons are associated with high density of population, economy of scale, culture that promotes creativity and innovation and frees individual from traditional institutions, greater participation in global processes, better transportation and communication facilities, better infrastructure and conditions that promote need for achievement.

Yet, there is a huge difference between urbanization and development. Urbanization is quintessentially a demographic phenomenon while development is an economic phenomenon. Urbanization is a process of population concentration. When people move from rural areas, where density of population is lower, to urban areas, where density of population is higher, urbanization takes place. Looked at from this perspective when wanderers and food gatherers developed settled agriculture and started living in villages urbanization started. Gradual increase in the size of village/habitation led to more urbanization. In the developing countries where urbanization is occurring quite fast this is because people are moving from rural areas to urban areas, and also from smaller urban areas to big cities. On the other hand, development requires huge investments and improvement in productivity.

Some political analysts see the relationship between urban and rural areas as exploitative. They focus on urban-rural conflict and ways in which urban areas grow at the expense of rural areas. According to this thesis, growth of urbanization may not lead to development of all and growth and expansion of urbanization may simultaneously lead to marginalization and exploitation of rural masses.

Demographic Transition and Urbanization

It is also possible to argue that in developing countries demographic transition, and not the development, contributed to growth of cities, weakening the correlation between urbanization and development. When the population of developing countries started growing at a fast rate (above 2%) due to fall in the death rate it could not be absorbed in agriculture which was almost stagnant. Therefore, the surplus population started moving towards cities, whether there was any need for them there or not. This led to rapid growth of urbanization, though without development. Undoubtedly, India, a developing country has one of the oldest civilizations and has had a long history of cities. Old cities of India were, however, fort cities or places of pilgrimage and were small in number and size. Their functions were political and religious. The large cities of today are so large that their population is larger than the population of many countries. Administration, trade and commerce, industry, and transport and communication have emerged as the new functions of cities.

Studies of urbanization in the less developed countries, therefore, contradict that there is a positive correlation between urbanization and development and produce the overurbanization thesis. According to this thesis the present day less developed countries are more urbanized than the developed countries were at the same level of development and the quality of urban population in the developing countries is very poor.

In the less developed countries three things were especially marked:

- Rapid growth of large cities
- Division of city into two different parts, one modern and developed, and the other as traditional and poor
- Overpopulation in the urban areas, particularly large cities, leading to creation of large squatter settlements and slums.

Data show that the large cities are growing faster than the smaller cities. As a matter of fact many tiny towns have experienced a declining trend (Registrar General, 2009). This phenomenon produces city primacy. i.e., a situation in which large cities have disproportionately more population than smaller cities and towns, making them unmanageable by city planners and requiring large investments to keep them liveable. For development planning, a good option would be to develop smaller cities and towns and restrict movement of people towards the largest cities.

Consequently, though cities are still the places and sources of modernization, and, yet, they have a traditional part, slum areas or squatter settlements, where the rural social institutions and arrangements are maintained. Most of the Indian cities including Delhi have a new city (e.g., New Delhi), or a civil lines area, and an old city (e.g., old Delhi, old Hyderabad, old Lucknow). Thus they may be called dual cities. In the old city one finds continuity of traditional kinship, caste and regional networks. The new, poor migrants depend upon them for decisions regarding the choice of destination and also for their adjustment to the harsh conditions of urban living (De Souza, 1983).

In this context, there are a few new concerns:

- Growing size of slums, informal sector and its role in modernizing economy
- Influence of kinship, caste, religion and region of origin on the migrants' adaptation to the new situation
- The condition of urban poor and structural and cultural marginalization: income, savings and loan pattern, organization, health, education, welfare and self-reliance among the poor
- Slum improvement programmes
- Consequences of urban poverty for women and family
- Identity and social stereotypes

Based on an ethnographic study in steel town of Bhilai, Parry (2004) writes:

> It is true that even forty years on, regional identities continue to be marked in terms, for example, of diet, dress, the worship of deities and the language of home. It is in the 'home' rather than the 'world' that the distinctions are most manifest, and the maintenance of them is significantly gendered. Even after years in Bhilai, the Hindi spoken by many south Indian women remains rudimentary. In the masculine space of the plant, regional ethnicity is the focus of legitimised joking;

but outside the topic is more touchy and ethnic stereotyping has a harder edge. Malayalis are clever, cunning and clannish, and always get on; Telugus are feckless and often inebriated, and generally do not. Where there are Bengalis there is *netagiri* (political bos-ism), and where 'Biharis', *dadagiri* (gangsterism). This last identity (which includes people from eastern Uttar Pradesh) is particularly strongly freighted and Bhilai's social problems are routinely laid at their door.

Future of Urbanization in India

There are diversities between cities and towns. Large cities have grown faster. Diversity in employment is one important factor. Table 7.3 shows the differences in proportion of employed persons in urban areas of different sizes (Government of India, 2009). In the future more people may move to larger cities and towns which have better employment potential.

There are several other factors and policies such as Jawaharlal Nehru Urban Renewal Mission (JNNURM) which would provide further impetus to growth of some selected cities. JNNURM can promote rural-urban migration by making cities more attractive by developing infrastructure and scaling-up delivery of civic amenities. Sharma (2008) shows that there are significant differences in amenities between cities and towns of different sizes and the Class I cities are more attractive than other towns (Table 7.4). Cities participate in global network of exchange of capital, technology, labour and information. There is a synergistic relationship between international markets and cities. Globalization and modernization will promote migration further and lead to more urbanization.

For people migrating from population surplus areas to cities there was a hope of better life though for some it turned out to be a nightmare and they were pushed back. Increasing regionalism and son-of-soil politics may prevent the growth of urban areas in the future. This is clear that India will urbanize further. There is no doubt about this. Yet, it is difficult to say what model of growth it will follow. Future is uncertain and unpredictable. There will remain diversities in levels and patterns of urbanization between various regions of the country. At the same time, decentralization, and transfer of fiscal authority and responsibility for services from national to local units of the government implies that smaller towns play increasingly more

Table 7.3: Proportion (Per 1000) of Usually Employed Persons (of Age 15 years and above) According to Usual Status (PS+SS) for Each Size Class of Town During 2004-05

Class 1 City/ Size Class of Town	*Male*	*Female*	*Person*
(1)	(2)	(3)	(4)
Class 1 cities			
Agra	833	147	494
Ahmedabad	795	214	516
Bangalore	841	202	549
Bhopal	782	151	490
Chennai	749	168	471
Delhi	714	112	442
Faridabad	726	118	464
Howrah	779	158	469
Hyderabad	770	190	472
Indore	835	283	557
Jaipur	766	377	573
Kalyan-Dombivili	730	203	486
Kanpur	776	77	435
Kolkata	751	190	496
Lucknow	695	93	399
Ludhiana	834	128	528
Meerut	790	51	434
Mumbai	786	267	545
Nagpur	720	289	515
Nashik	610	187	411
Patna	528	18	313
Pimprichinchwad	774	212	525
Pune	712	291	512
Surat	876	182	591
Thane	736	223	499
Vadodara	717	197	447
Varanasi	860	411	667
All Class I Cities	762	198	498
Size Class II Towns Combined	756	218	498
Size Class III Towns Combined	777	276	530
Urban India	763	227	506

important role. Central and State Governments are increasingly concerned about rapid growth of large cities and would like to decelerate migration towards them. This can be done by adopting policies aimed at development of rural areas. Schemes such as National Rural Employment Guarantee programme may reduce need to migrate to cities by providing wage employment at the village level.

In addition, there are other factors which may retard the process

Table 7.4: Percentage of Households with Basic Amenities by Size Class of Urban Centres in India, 2001

India	*Toilet*	*Drinking water*	*Kerosene*	*LPG*	*Drainage*
Class-I	80.38	89.07	21.63	56.56	56.85
Class-II	66.75	81.48	13.76	43.78	73.09
Class-III	63.06	78.08	12.17	35.88	67.06
Class-IV	57.58	78.83	12.61	29.82	63.78
Class-V	53.05	78.77	9.24	26.04	57.63

of urbanization. Identity politics, hostility towards 'outsiders' coupled with contractualization of labour and mass unemployment, lack of open space in large cities where the migrants built illegal settlements in the past, expansion of IT industry, improved city planning, and increasing vulnerability of migrants to various risks in the cities would also discourage people from migrating towards cities. This will mean that the migration flows may change direction. Potential migrants would find Delhi, Bangaluru, Mumbai, Chennai and Kolkata less attractive than in the past and move towards other cities where they have a greater chance of finding employment and facing less hostility.

To quote the Committee on Population (2003):

> A paradox of globalization is that, while creating more linkages and interdependencies, it also underscores the importance of comparative advantage of the sub-national and local levels. Transnational corporations become increasingly aware of the niches where cheap and reliable labour can be found, and learn in detail of the constraints of local transport and infrastructure. Hence when seen from a global corporate perspective, the cities of low-income countries are likely to appear increasingly diverse.

QUESTIONS AND EXERCISES

1. Define urbanization. What are the causes of urbanization in less developed countries?
2. What is the relationship between urbanization and demographic transition, i.e., changes in birth and death rates?
3. Write an essay on urbanization in India.
4. How does census define urban and rural localities in India?

5. Distinguish between:
   a. push and pull factors of migration
   b. urbanization and overurbanization
6. What is urbanism? How is it different from urbanization?
7. Write an essay on the character of cities in the less developed countries.
8. On what factors depends the future of urbanization in India?
9. Can you identify how urban areas can exploit rural areas?
10. Why have the larger cities grown faster than smaller cities and towns?

REFERENCES

Committee on Population, 2003, *Cities Transformed: Demographic Change and its Implications in the Developing Countries*. Washington, D.C.: The National Academic Press: 76-77.

De Souza, Alfred, 1983, The Challenge of Urban Poverty. In De Souza, Alfred (ed.), The *Indian City: Poverty, Ecology and Urban Development*. New Delhi: Manohar Publications.

Dyson, Tim, 2003, India's Population: Past, Present and Future, The Pravin Visaria Public Lecture, delivered at Gujarat Institute of Development Research, Conference Hall of the Ahmedabad Management Association on March 4.

Government of India, 2009, Press Note on Employment and Unemployment Situation in Cities and Towns in India, 2004-05, *http://www.mospi.gov.in/press_note_520_2april07.htm* [accessed on 28th December, 2009].

Indiamart.com, 2009, India Finance and Investment Guide, *http://finance.indiamart.com/india_business_information/indian_cities_population.html* [accessed on 28th December, 2009].

Indiresan, P.V., 2008, Rurbanisation is Solution, *Business Line*, *http://www.thehindubusinessline.com/bline/2008/05/12/stories/2008051250240800.htm* [accessed on 25th December, 2009].

Parry, Jonathan P., 2004, Nehru's Dream and the Village 'Waiting Room': Long-distance Labour Migrants to a Central Indian Steel Town. In Osella, Filippo and Gardner, Katy (eds.), *Migration, Modernity and Social Transformation in South Asia*. New Delhi: Sage Publications.

Registrar General India, 2009, *http://www.google.co.in/search?hl=en&q=Class+V+towns+India&meta=cr%3DcountryIN&aq=f&oq=* [accessed on 28th December, 2009].

Sandhu, Ranvinder Singh, 1989, *The City and its Slums: A Sociological Study*. Amritsar: Guru Nanak Dev University Press.

Sharma, S.P., 2008, Keynote Address. *Population and Environment Bulletin*,

Vol. 5, Nos. 2-3. *http://www.iipsenvis.nic.in/Newsletters/vol5no2_3/Volume5_no2_3.htm* [accessed on 28th December, 2009].

United Nations Population Fund, 2009, *The State of World Population 2009*. New York: UNFPA, p. 8, *http://www.unfpa.org/swp/2009/en/pdf/EN_SOWP09.pdf* [accessed on 13th December, 2009].

Wirth, Louis, 2009, *http://en.wikipedia.org/wiki/Louis_Wirth* [accessed on 25th December, 2009].

8

Population Theories

THEORIES IN HISTORICAL PERSPECTIVE

This chapter deals with canons of population theory. We will first discuss the theories of Malthus, Marx and a few others which have had the greatest impact on theorizing about population and development. Then we will discuss if there is any possibility of synthesizing some of these theories or whether different theories co-exist without competing with each other. This is followed by demographic transition theory which summarizes the empirical data on 19th and 20th century demographic processes in the North-West Europe. Finally, we will discuss Gandhian theory of population which would be of some interest to Indian students of population sociology.

MALTHUSIAN LAW OF POPULATION

The first major study of population was taken up by Thomas Robert Malthus. He produced his essay entitled *The Principle of Population as it Affects the Future Improvement of Society*, anonymously, in 1978. It created lot of controversy. Subsequently, to defend him Malthus produced six editions of the essay between 1798 and 1826. With his writings, an era of fear of over-population started (Paul, 1948). Malthus was Britain's first professor in political economy at the East India Company College. In 1797 he had taken orders and become an Anglican country parson. Being a clergyman Malthus seems to be guided by the idea that sex is at the root of all problems of man. He thought that passion for sex not only degrades and eventually kills a man but also degrades and kills human society. He was a pessimist and is called a doomsday philosopher.

Malthus started with two postulates. First, that food is necessary to the existence of man. Secondly, that the passion between the sexes is necessary, and will remain in its present state. Assuming these postulates to be true, he said that the power of population is indefinitely greater than the power of the earth to produce subsistence for man (Malthus, 1965). Unchecked population increases in a geometric ratio, but subsistence can increase only in an arithmetical ratio.

> In the United States of America, where the means of subsistence have been more ample, the manners of the people more pure, and consequently the checks to early marriages fewer than in any of the modern states of Europe, the population has been found to double itself in twenty five years.

Malthus said that the human species would increase in ratio of—1, 2, 4, 8, 16 ... and subsistence only as 1, 2, 3, 4 ..., creating a continuously rising imbalance between the size of population and availability of means of subsistence. For Malthus, animals and plants are all impelled by a powerful instinct to reproduce. Man is no exception to this. Afterwards their growth is checked by want of room and nourishment.

Malthus thought that due to the basic conflict between sexuality and subsistence humans can never be happy and population is brought down to lower levels periodically. He divided all the factors leading to decline in the size of population into two categories: positive checks and preventive checks. If the population growth is not checked by human reason, it produces misery and vice, i.e., pestilences, famines, deaths, infant deaths, starvation, exposure, and customs such as homosexuality, prostitution, abortion and improper acts. The checks to population growth that has already begun are the positive checks. They manifest in the form of high death rates. Preventive checks appear in the form of vice (sexual practices not leading to childbirth) or moral restraints on sexual activities.

Ironically, Malthus was against use of birth control methods. He believed that there are several forms of voluntary restraints to human population which are oscillatory in nature. They change depending on the cycles of material conditions. Restraints increase when the population is more and food is less and decrease when population is less and food is plenty.

Malthus accepts that population growth is not the only factor that influences development. There are many other factors. Yet he maintains that in all animated life there is a constant tendency to increase beyond the nourishment, and this is the most important cause of human misery. The institutional changes alone—without preventing the growth of population—cannot solve the problem of poverty and destitution on a permanent basis.

To Malthus the natural inequality of the two powers—one of population, and another of production in the earth—and the great law of nature which must constantly keep their effects equal form the great difficulty that appears to be insurmountable in the way to the perfectibility of society. He says that all other arguments are of slight and subordinate consideration in comparison with this. He sees no way by which man can escape from the weight of this law which pervades all animated nature. "No fancied equality, no agrarian regulations in their utmost extent, could remove the pressure of it even for a single century."

Malthus accepts that temporarily a number of other factors such as introduction or failure of certain manufacturers, greater or less prevalent spirit of agricultural enterprise, invention of processes for shortening labour without proportional extension of market, difference between nominal and real wages, and conspiracy of the rich class do affect the conditions of labourers, but their influence is temporary. The action of misery is constant.

To quote:

> Human institutions appear to be the obvious and obtrusive causes of much mischief to mankind; yet, in reality, they are light and superficial, they are mere feathers that float on the surface, in comparison with those deeper seated causes of impurity that corrupt the springs, and render turbid the whole stream of human life.

Malthus was aware of the relationship between population growth and the social inequalities too and showed a clear understanding of the class basis of pressures to exercise restraints on population and consequences of population growth. He said that even though all classes defer marriages to check the reproduction, the motives are different for different classes. Among the lower classes, it is the fear of not providing well for the family, and among the higher classes, it is the fear of lowering their life condition. If a society is equal the misery due to population growth is for all, but in an unequal society, the misery is more for the poor people. The labourers have to work harder, the wages decrease, marriages are discouraged, freedom is lost, many of the poor persons are reduced to severe distress and the population becomes constant. The positive checks are confined mainly to the lowest stratum of the society. Poor people are malnourished and infant deaths among the poor are more than among middle and rich classes. In the meantime, cultivators can use the cheap and efficient labour and increase the production of food. When the food-population balance is re-established the labourers can again live comfortably and the restraints to population are weakened.

Thus population and development maintain a cycle of growth and decline. Many people use the term Malthusian state to refer to a situation in which birth and death rates are high, population is more or less stationary, and there is a lack of development.

The most controversial aspect of Malthus's ideas was that he was opposed to the Poor Law which classified and supported various categories of the poor and destitute people in his time. According to him, Poor Law had eradicated the spirit of independence, caused population increase, drove more labourers to ask for support as their quantities of provisions declined, diminished the shores of more industrious and worthy members of society and encouraged dependent poverty. The poor people would not save in the presence of the Poor Law even when they could, and would spend in drunkenness and dissipation. Poor Law cannot, therefore, improve the living conditions of the poor people even when the money that is collected for them is well managed.

He suggested that to remove the poverty of the lower classes all parish-laws should be abolished, the wages of the agricultural labourers should be increased to the level of wages of labourers in trade and manufacturing, and country work-houses must be established for the cases of extreme distress where a person can do a day's work at market price.

Malthus is against the socialist and equalitarian ideas. In the views of Malthus societies by their very nature are divided into unequal classes: upper classes and the labourers. Between them the misery and vice caused by rapid population growth are observed mainly by the labourers.

> ...that a society constituted according to the most beautiful form that imagination can conceive, with benevolence for its moving, principle, instead of self-love, and with every evil disposition in all its members corrected by reason and not force, would, from the inevitable laws of nature, and not from any original depravity of man, in a very short period, degenerate into a society, constructed upon a plan not essentially different from that which prevails in every known state at present; I mean, a society divided into a class of proprietors and a class of labourers, and with self-love for the main-spring of the great machine.

Evaluation of Malthusian Theory

Malthus was heavily criticised for his pessimistic ideas. He revised his essay six times and by the time of last revision he had become more flexible and optimistic: he had accepted that growth of education and awareness among the masses may lead to population control. The main charges against Malthus are as follows:

- There is no empirical basis of his laws of population and subsistence.
- His theory became popular simply because after French revolution it attempted to divert people's attention towards population growth while the social institutions and unequal access to resources were the major reasons behind poverty and unemployment. Thus it helped to legitimize the capitalist system.
- History showed that population growth need not be negatively associated with development. Moderate population growth may even lead to more development through its effect on infrastructure and work force. The ultimate resource is the human spirit (Simon, 1998).
- There can be no natural law of population. All laws pertaining to human society depend on the socio-economic and cultural contexts.

Spengler attempted to make a modification in Malthus's theory by suggesting that a growing population can continue to escape deterioration in its average choices if it can orient its tastes away from relatively non-augmentable goods toward highly augmentable goods (Spengler, 1962). He argued that this can solve the problem to some extent at least in the short run. Yet the changing tastes will constitute an increasingly less effective means to improve a population's situation since substitutability is limited.

Peacock (1952) showed that the Malthusian theory of population as a theory of economic development is general and different patterns of assumptions about the relation between population growth and development can be considered within the Malthusian framework. It is not necessary to accept the Malthusian remedies along with the Malthusian analysis.

Undoubtedly, Malthus has had a very strong influence on thinking about relationship between population and society for a long time. All family planning programmes in the developing countries are based on a Malthusian understanding of population.

MARXIST THEORY OF POPULATION

Marx was very critical of Malthus. He said that an abstract law of population did not exist for men (Marx, 1974). All historical modes of production have their own special laws of population which are valid only within their limits.

Marx discussed the law of population, applicable to capitalist mode of production in chapter XXV of *Capital*, entitled, "The General Law of Capitalist Accumulation". Two books *An Outline Theory of Population* and *The Theory of Population*, both edited by Valentey and published by Progress Publishers, provide a lucid discussion of Marxist theory of population. To understand Marxist theory of population it is important to understand his concept of surplus labour. According to Marx, capitalist society consists of two basic classes:

- Capitalists, who own means of production; and
- Workers, who own nothing except their labour power

To Marx, in a capitalist society, production is controlled by the capitalist class. They earn from profit only. They hire workers and supply them the wherewithal of work-instruments of production and raw material. According to the labour theory of value, it is only workers who create value addition through their labour, i.e., work done by the labourers only creates value and the means of production on their own cannot produce anything. The workers are, however, given wages which are always less than their contribution. The difference (surplus) is expropriated by the capitalists and added to fixed capital under their possession.

To put it in other words, capital consists of two parts: constant capital and variable capital. The part of the capital which is represented by the means of production, raw and auxiliary material, and instruments of labour is the constant capital. The part of capital represented by labour power is the variable capital. While the constant capital does not undergo any change of the quantitative value, the variable capital produces its own value and a surplus.

Accumulation of capital, though originally appearing as its quantitative extension only, results eventually in the change in its composition, under a constant increase of its constant constituent, and a constant decline in variable constituent.

On several occasions when the total capital increases, its variable part may also increase, but it will increase in a constantly diminishing proportion. Technological development, rise in productivity of labour and centralization of economic activities tend to decrease the ratio of variable capital further. Since in a capitalist society the demand for labour depends on the variable constituent only, it falls progressively, and the labouring, population, therefore, produces, along with the accumulation of capital, the means by which it is rendered superfluous and surplus to an increasing extent. Accordingly, the advancement of modern industry leads to unemployment and underemployment.

For Marx, therefore, the correlation between accumulation of capital and rate of wages is nothing else than the correlation between the unpaid labour transformed into capital and the additional paid labour necessary for the setting in motion of this additional capital. It is not to be seen as a relation between two independent factors—population and capital. It must be seen as the relation between the unpaid labour and the paid labour of the same labouring population. Thus Marx shows that the existence of what has been considered as surplus population is a necessary product of accumulation of wealth on a capitalist basis. It is also a lever of capitalistic development (Ananyeva, *et al.*, 1974).

If the quantity of unpaid labour supplied by the working-class, and accumulated by the capitalist class, increases so rapidly, that its conversion into capital requires an extraordinary addition of paid labour, then wages rise, and, all other circumstances remaining equal the unpaid labour diminishes in proportion. But as soon as this diminution touches the point at which the surplus labour that nourishes capital is no longer supplied in normal quantity, a reaction sets in: a smaller part of revenue is capitalized, accumulation lags, and the movement of rise in wages receives a check. To explain this Marx would use a simile: as in religion man is governed by the products of his own brain, so in capitalistic production, he is governed by the products of his own hand.

With progressive advancement of capital, labourers are set free more rapidly than the reduction in the variable part of capital as compared with the constant because it enables the capitalists to exploit the labour power. It also leads to progressive replacement of superior labour power by inferior labour power. Ultimately, the overwork of labour, reduction in the variable constituent of capital, and greater exploitation expand the ranks of industrial reserve army and force the workers to subjugate under the dictates of capital, independently of the natural increase of population. The development in this way increases both the demand and supply of labour by setting them free.

There are four different forms of the relative surplus population or industrial reserve army: floating surplus; latent surplus; stagnant surplus; and paupers. Any member of the working class who is unemployed or partially employed belongs to this pool. In modern industries where modern division of labour exists, only a small number of workers continue to find employment in them, while the majority of them are regularly discharged. This majority constitutes the floating surplus and this sector is marked by contradiction: in this sector complaint of the want of hands and unemployment exist side by side. Latent surplus is associated with agricultural sector. Capitalist development of agriculture causes a latent surplus in the countryside and constant movement of pauperized agricultural workers towards centres of industries. The stagnant surplus forms a part of the labour with extremely irregular employment.

As some branches of the industries decay, handicraft leads to manufacturing and manufacturing to mechanization, it provides a large reservoir of stagnant surplus to capital, consisting of labourers with extremely irregular employment, low wages, and longer working hours. One example of this type of surplus is in domestic industry. Lastly, pauperism, consisting of the lowest sediment of the surplus population, consists of the so-called "dangerous classes" of vagabonds, criminals, prostitutes. They consist of: (a) those who are able to work but have become pauper due to economic crisis; (b) orphans and pauper children; (c) the demoralised and ragged; and (d) those unable to work. The last category of people includes those who lack power to adapt due to prevailing division of labour, who have crossed the normal age of work, and the victims of industry (the mutilated, the sickly, and the widows). To Marx, pauperism is "the hospital of the active labour-army and the dead weight of the industrial reserve army."

On the relationship between development and employment Marx says:

> The law by which a constantly increasing quantity of means of production, thanks to the advancement in the productiveness of social labour, may be set in movement by a progressively diminishing expenditure of human power, this law in a capitalist society—where the labourer does not employ the means of production, but the means of production employ the labourer—undergoes a complete inversion and expressed thus: the higher the productiveness of labour, the greater is the pressure of the labourers on the means of employment, the more precarious, therefore, becomes their condition of existence, viz., the sale of their own labour-power for increasing another's wealth, for the self-expansion of capital. The fact that the means of production and the productiveness of labour, increase more rapidly than the productive population, expresses itself, therefore, capitalistically in the inverse form that the labouring population always increases more rapidly than the conditions under which capital can employ this increase for its own self-expansion.

While for Malthus the fundamental cause of poverty, unemployment, high mortality, malnutrition, and destitution is the tendency of population to grow beyond the means of subsistence available to it, for Marx the cause of these factors is the capitalist mode of production. From the Marxist perspective the changes in population dynamics are governed by the social systems that are created on the basis of relations of productions. The solution to the problems of underdevelopment from this perspective lies basically in the socialistic reconstruction of present day capitalist societies. When population is analysed from historical perspective, it is taken as a socio-economic category. Marx was of the view that population is an abstract notion if the classes of which it consists are disregarded. These classes are also empty sound if relations of production in general and wage, labour, and capital—three elements in production—are not explicitly considered.

Evaluation of Marxist Theory of Population

The Marxist theory is based on the idea of history of class struggle. Those who do not believe in Marxist theory of change would also not accept his theory of population. Moreover, the population reality of today is complex and in many important aspects different from what it was during the times of Malthus and Marx. The two lived in an age in which both birth and death rates were high (death rates had only begun to fall in the industrially advanced countries) and the rate of population growth was very low. National policies of today are pragmatic and responsive to new realities.

OTHER MAJOR THEORIES

In the second part of the twentieth century, especially in the context of developing countries, Malthus's ideas influenced the planners and social scientists a great deal. They explored the negative linkages between population and human welfare. Two important theorists of this period adopting Malthusian line are Hardin and Ehrlich. Hardin, a professor of Human Ecology at the University of California, having very strong views on the matter, even raised doubt about the ethics of saving lives in poverty stricken developing countries. Paul R. Ehrlich was an entomologist, associated with Stanford University, who specialized in studies of butterflies.

To Hardin, poverty and epidemics are nature's way of maintaining demographic equilibrium. By preventing deaths without putting a condition that the developing countries should control their population size, the developed countries are creating a situation in which a much larger number of people would die in the developing countries in the future. And those acting altruistically today will be responsible for a larger number of deaths and misery in the future.

Some of his major ideas are: in place of shortages of supply in the developing world attention should be shifted to longage of population; if the world is to be treated like a spaceship then it has to have a powerful captain and in absence of this the different countries should be seen as life boats some of which are overcrowded; commons cannot be managed because it is in the individual interest of all that they are exploited to the detriment of collective welfare; and, therefore, developed countries should not supply food to less developed countries facing starvation unless they decide to reduce their population size. To him the combination of welfare and freedom is the root cause of what he calls the run away growth. To prevent this either social welfare considerations have to go or *laissez-faire* birth control (freedom to breed) will have to be restrained. It is not possible to maximize two things simultaneously: population size and welfare. There is a need for mutual coercion, mutually agreed upon by the majority of people affected.

Paul R. Ehrlich declared that the battle to feed humanıty is over and in the coming years the world will face scarcities, famines, drop in life expectancy, extinction of life in several regions, and smog disasters. He drew the attention of people to connection between hunger, deforestation, droughts, traffic congestion, drug abuse, global warming, widening hole in ozone layer, acid rains, increasing use of pesticide, inadequate sewage treatment plant, and aid and population growth. *The Population Bomb*, published in 1968, summarises his major ideas. The argument was further carried out in *The Population Explosion* written by Paul R. Ehrlich jointly with Anne E. Ehrlich. Ehrlich looked at the future state of mankind as an alarmist and attributed the emerging crisis not only to population growth (P) but also to rising affluence (I) and technology (T). Affluence is defined as per capita level of resource consumption, and technology as the environmental impact per unit of consumption.

Using the equation I = PAT, he showed that the environmental impact is the product of population size, affluence and technology. It may be noted that unlike neo-Malthusians of England, Hardin and Ehrilch give more importance to population control (i.e., reduction in population size) rather than birth control which focuses on reduction in fertility levels only and aims to reduce population growth rate.

More on Malthusian and Marxist Theories of Population

Even though demography, the science of population has gained tremendously in last few decades both from methodological sophistication and more data, the essential dividing line in the theories of population is still the controversy between Malthusian and Marxian paradigms. The controversy has strengthened mainly due to their roots in two dominant, political philosophies of modern times: rational capitalism *versus* socialism. All social science thinkers from the West, including those critical of Malthus, are attacked by socialists for defending the interests of the capitalist class and providing a misleading theory. To quote:

> Bourgeois sociological theories of population are extremely contradictory. On the one hand they criticize the positions of Malthus, Spencer, and the Social Darwanists; but on the other hand, bourgeois sociologists, while recognizing the decisive importance of social factors in demographic processes, do not accept the concept of a socio-economic formation. They replace the concept of classes by a vague concept of social stratum. They depict the antagonistic contradictions of capitalism as those of industrial society as well; ... (Smulevich, 1978)

Yet, as argued by Caldwell (1998), Malthus's essay played a powerful role in the establishment of family planning programmes in India, Pakistan, Bangladesh and many other countries. Lee and Feng (1999) examine the influence of Malthus on Chinese population policy and say that Malthusian focus on the potentially precarious balance between population and resources is one of the central present day preoccupations. Therefore, it should not cause surprise if the Malthusian pronouncement can be located in the population policy of a communist country or a concern with the institutional changes can be found in the capitalist thinking about population control programmes. The goals of the national policies are chiefly determined by the economic and demographic profile of the population. The countries where population is stationary or is declining and the level of development of productive forces is high, there is a pro-natalist policy; and the countries where population growth is rapid and the level of development is low there is an anti-natalist policy, directly or indirectly, strong or weak. There is a need to maintain a balance between population and resources. It is not a controversial issue. Thus a document of Chinese Population Policy says:

> Confronting us today are two possibilities either we control population growth strictly and effectively or we exercise no strict control, carry cut no effective measures, and let the population continue to grow, thus leading to a state in which neither the people's living standard can be improved nor our economic, cultural and defense construction can be successfully carried out. Our option will certainly be one of these two possibilities. We believe that the comrades of the whole party and the people of the whole country can soberly realize the seriousness of this issue, and will voluntarily implement the policy and stipulations regarding the control of the population. (Chinese Population Policy Draft, 1982).

It was made a constitutional duty for Chinese citizens to practice family planning under Article 49 of the country's Constitution approved by the Fifth National People's Congress on 4th December, 1982. Commenting on the results of the Chinese Census conduct on 27th October, 1982. Le Chengrui (1982), the Director, State Statistical Bureau, said:

> Thus, of the more than 300 million increases in the 18 years, close to two-thirds occurred during the first nine years. This was mainly caused by the 'leftist' tendency in the guiding ideology during the first nine years. Because effective measures were not adopted in family planning, there was a drastic increase in the size of the population. This was a major mistake in population policy. The new Constitutional amendments in China enunciate the reciprocal duties of parents and children.

In USSR, another socialist country, differences in population growth rates of Slavic, Baltic and Muslim groups have ultimately led to endorsement of a regionally differentiated demographic policy at the 26th Party Congress in February 1981 (Wever and Goodman, 1981).

Although the role of administrative pressure on individual Chinese families by family planning cadre and other officials is well documented (Aird, 1982), Greenhalgh (2003) argues that the core ideas underlying the one-child policy in China came from Western discourse. They were shaped by the Club of Rome's work on the future crisis of the world.

A synthetic approach to population is found in the explicit aim of the World Population Plan of Action-Bucharest 1974: "to help coordinate population trends and trends in economic and social development", prepared after an intense conflict between countries divided in two major camps: incrementalists, and redistributionists. The incrementalists group consisted of the Western European Nations, United States and Canada, which favoured increase in "Commitment of governments to family planning." The redistributionists consisted of the majority of developing countries and the countries of Soviet Bloc, which emphasized the need for developing better redistributive policies.

India stood for the middle path (Berelson, 1975). The Indian slogan was: "development is the best contraceptive", by which the Indian representative Dr. Karan Singh actually meant that we should simultaneously focus on the development of the underdeveloped sections, and propagate contraceptive through both development and family planning (Singh, 1975). Since then India has adopted a synthetic model that has gradually become the most popular policy model in the world.

In sum, Malthus warned that the world is suffering from large population and Marx warned that the problems of unemployment etc. cannot be solved within the capitalist framework. Subsequent writers on the subject emphasized population control not only for improvement in employment and income but also for the sustainability of development and the very planet itself. The question is not of either or type. If the global zero population growth has to be achieved through low and not high birth and death rates (Espenshade, 1991) efforts are needed at all the levels:

- Limit the growth of population
- Move from economic prosperity to economic sustainability
- Promote the value of simplicity, equality, brotherhood and peace
- Replace machine by man wherever possible and progressively everywhere.

DALY's SYNTHESIS AND OPTIMUM POPULATION THEORY

Daly's Synthesis

Recognizing the importance of both demographic and institutional factors in the developmental planning in general, and inadequacy of either or type of question, some social scientists have attempted to develop a combination of Malthusian and Marxian views of poverty and development. Among them, Daly (1971) suggests that the theories of Malthus and Marx are complementary. Populations are marked by both differences in ownership of property and fertility. A simple definition of poverty is the per capita income, or the ratio between income and population (Y/P). The cause of poverty or low per capita income, according to Malthus is high population (P), and according to Marx low income (Y). The two theories will be complementary if the growth of population and income are independent. But they are not.

Daly argues that the two are independent only within limits, Given Y, there is maximum value of P that is possible and a minimum value of P that is technically necessary. Also the growth of P affects Y directly through age distribution and its influence on saving, education, and size of surplus. However, the effect of Y on P is less clear than of P on Y. Malthus says that development or increase in Y leads to growth of population (P) but the empirical correlation between income and population growth of the global level is negative. Daly maintains that the empirical does not necessarily contradict theoretical because the relation between Y and P is medicated by a number of factors as traditions and customs, norms, ethics, material standards and law. Daly divided the population into four groups by nature of income (those earning from wages or property) and birth control (those using or not using birth control methods). He expresses that the Marxian theory of stratification is based on the experience of nineteenth century when population was growing rapidly. If the rate of population growth is less than the rate at which workers are displaced by machines, there cannot be any surplus population or reserve army. Daly analyses what happens to four groups as time passes and society moves from primitive to classless society of the future.

Optimum Population Theory

For some the theory of optimum population initially developed by Marshall, Sidgwick, Cannan and Gini provides a more realistic alternative to Malthusian and Marxist theories. According to this theory due to law of diminishing returns and limited substitutability of factors of production, as population grows the long run tendency of per capita income is to decline. For the reason of economy of scale initially for sometime per capita income may also rise as population grows but beyond reaching a certain size further growth of population would lead to reduction in per capita income (Figure 8.1). This size is the optimum size of population. Beyond this there is surplus population. Below this there is shortage of population (UN, 1973). Some scholars use welfare measures other than per capita income but the logic of optimum population is the same. Box 8.1 presents the economic logic behind optimum population theory.

Optimum population theory is part of economic theory of production. It assumes: (a) there are five factors of production, namely, land, labour, capital, organization and enterprise; (b) one single factor produces nothing; (c) cost of production falls with increasing use of one factor and increases thereafter; (d) perfect substitution is impossible; (e) optimum point arises when the ratio of marginal productivity of factor A to that of B is same as the ratio of the price of factor A to that of B; and (f) population is a non-specific factor which can be put to alternative uses. The optimum population theory draws attention to situational factors and gives an objective ideal according to which changes in population should be controlled.

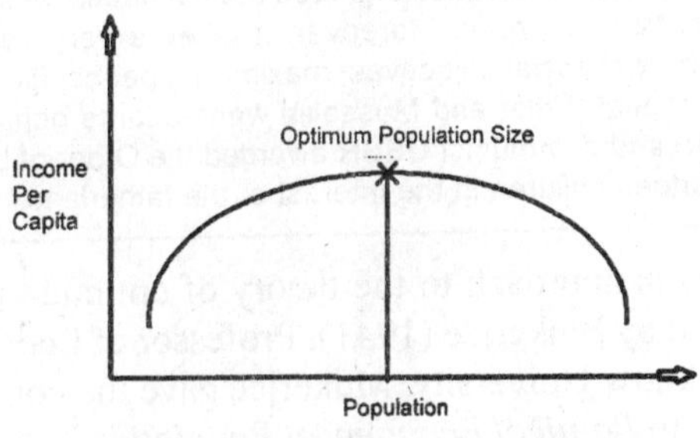

Figure 8.1: Optimum Population

Evaluation of Optimum Population Theory

Myrdal and Gottlieb criticize this theory on various grounds. Myrdal has expressed that the optimum theory is associated with neo-Malthusianism and demand for a smaller population on policy grounds. Gottlieb (1945) stressed that it is impossible to compute an optimum number that maximizes social welfare. The optimum population size depends on a variety of factors such as resources, level of technology, structure of economy, model of ownership, and international situation and, therefore, as time passes the value of optimum will also change. Moreover, the optimum population size would depend on the criterion used for maximization of welfare.

Box 8.1: Optimum Population Theory (OPT)

- OPT is part of the economics theory of population.
- According to economics, there are five factors of production: land, labour, capital, organization and enterprise.
- One single factor produces nothing.
- Initially the cost of production falls with increasing use of a factor but it starts increasing thereafter.
- Up to the optimum size there are conditions of increasing returns as economics of large scale production is enjoyed by any increase in output. However, beyond the optimum size the diseconomies of large scale production or decreasing returns begin to set in.
- Perfect substitution is impossible.
- At the optimum level the ratio of marginal productivity of a factor to price of that factor is same for all the factors.
- Optimum point is not fixed. It depends on other factors.
- OPT gives an objective ideal according to which changes in population should be controlled.
- The limitation of the OPT is that it ignores the distributional aspects of increase in national income. Moreover, it takes a very narrow and materialistic view of social objectives; maximizing per capita income is not always the goal (Hitler and Mussolini wanted large population for military power) and communist USSR awarded the Order of Lenin to a mother of fourteen children in the interest of the fatherland.

A more realistic approach to the theory of optimum population has been presented by Mukerjee (1941), Professor of Economics and Sociology in Lucknow University, Mukerjee gave the concept of the integral optimum. In *Political Economy of Population* he writes: "The true optimum of population is the integral optimum which is based on a harmonious co-ordination of the optima in the successive levels of ecology, economy and state in respect of (a) the expectation of life, (b) real income, and (c) personal happiness and self-expression, all these from the individual standpoint, and of (a) the stability of the economic base and occupational balance, (b) the regularity and continuity of employment, and (c) national security and power, all of the latter from the collective standpoint." Mukerjee said that this optima was, however, only a hypothesis (though of a great analytical value) and cannot be quantitatively measured or expressed.

GANDHIAN THEORY

There are certain practical difficulties in discussing Gandhian theory of population. First of all, Gandhi was not a social scientist. He was a practical idealist who had no time or the aptitude for constructing systematic theories (Iyer, 1986). Therefore, his ideas are open to several interpretations. One way of looking at his social theory is to assume that: (a) his theory of society is rooted in his own understanding of mystical tradition of India that provides a common framework of moral action in the midst of a number of religious and moral philosophies existing in the country for a long time; (b) it needs to be constructed partly from his own writings, speeches, notes, etc. and partly from his social experiments; and (c) it evolved with time, sometimes contradicting the earlier position in some respects, without ever negating its mystical and moral substratum.

Gandhi had expressed a deep concern for population control on several occasions. The main source of his ideas on population are his autobiography and the report of the summit meeting on birth control in 1935, in which he had held lengthy discussion with Margaret Sanger of the International Planned Parenthood Federation (IPPF). It may be noted that at that time there were not many people to support birth control: the world had not seen the phenomenon of population explosion. The writings of Paul R. Ehrilch or Garrett James Hardin did not exist. Margaret Sanger had undergone a jail term for 30 days (in her country) for holding views favourable to birth control.

Gandhi courageously spoke in favour of population control. Yet his argument in favour of population control was not the usual Malthusian fear of over-population. As early as 1925, he had written in *Young India* that if suitable improvements could be made in the laws relating to land and the state of agriculture, and an allied occupation could be provided, India could support twice its population. Gandhi said:

> This little globe of ours is not a toy of yesterday. It has not suffered from the weight of over-population through its age of countless millions. How can it be that the truth has suddenly dawned upon some people that it is in danger of perishing of shortage of food unless birth rate is checked through the use of contraception?

This and other ideas of Gandhi on birth control are well presented in Chapter LVI: Birth Control in *India of My Dreams*. The population of India at that time was about 262 million. Today, as per the 2011 Census, it stands at 1,210 million. Therefore, today, there is all the more reason to control the population, particularly since the perception of the ecological crisis is more vivid than it was in Gandhi's time. His support for birth control was related to the "political" situation prevailing in the country. He said that there could be no two opinions on the necessity for limiting births (Suman, 1969). But, like Marx, he rejected the idea of a universal theory of population. To him, in some circumstances it may be considered quite rational to encourage reproduction but in many others it may be considered irrational. According to Gandhi, in his days, religion favoured a small family and birth control had become a political duty. Some of his committed supporters found his involvement with birth control a little embarrassing, but for Gandhi, the political situation at that time demanded that people avoid any kind of wastage of the vital force (Desai, 1973) and take up the task of ending colonization and poverty more seriously. Thus, politics had become a religious activity.

Gandhi made two observations (Margaret, 1969):

(a) The burden of large families falls on the middle class; as far as fertility is concerned, it is greater among the middle than the lower classes. If that were not true one would not have the low average of five children per family in India.
(b) Women do not want many children but they cannot resist their husbands. If they could do so without causing bitterness, birth control would be possible in 99 per cent of the cases.

Gandhi was the first person in India to make an observation on the correlation between family size and class. Later, empirical data collected through research studies confirmed the theoretical validity of his observations. In the pre-transitional stage too fertility in India was certainly nowhere near the biological maxima (Bongaarts, 1975). Culture must have been a major fertility depressing factor in India. Research has also shown than in India development and modernization caused a rise in fertility in the early years of the post-Independence period (Srinivasan, 1986).

In observation (a) above, the term middle class requires some clarification. In the Gandhian framework, middle class is not an income category. It is a class of people who have begun to Westernize their lifestyle and serve as go-betweens. They are most influenced by Westernization and they controlled the consciousness of masses. Behavioural changes among the members of this class have ensued as a result of both modernization and Westernization. Modernization may lead to a short term increase in fertility through its effects on coitus frequency, separation between spouses caused by cultural and familial reasons and intrauterine deaths. In the West, this rise was arrested by a simultaneous change in social mobility aspirations which motivated couples to control family size. This fertility-depressing effect of modernization did not operate among the middle classes during the early phases of development.

It is true that empowerment of women, or a lack of it, is associated with fertility. Demographic surveys have shown that women have lower fertility desires than men but due to force of patriarchy they were not in a position to act as per their desires. Education among women has now paved the way for fertility decline and fertility among the educated women has already declined to the below replacement fertility.

Gandhi rejected artificial birth control methods and this is the most controversial aspect of his theory of population. In this respect, he is closer to Malthus than to Marx. Interestingly Malthus was a clergyman and Gandhi too strongly believed in religion. Except for a brief period during his stay in England as a student, Gandhi was always against using *external* family planning methods. His commitment to *brahmacharya* (celibacy) was basic. Initially, he used it for the limited purpose of restricting family size but as his thoughts matured, he advocated it essentially for Truth realization. To follow *brahmacharya* completely is to realize Truth, said Gandhi. He claimed to have found it experientially and continuously, step-by-step (Gandhi, 1957) and subsequently confirmed it with statements enshrined in religious literature. It may be said that for Gandhi *brahmacharya* in itself, was not a means but a value. According to him, the sole purpose of the reproductive organs was to produce offspring (of high quality); it was wrong to use them for gratification.

Gandhi was not addressing the *sanyasins*: he was proposing *brahmacharya* to ordinary householders. He said that a householder can also lead a life of *brahmacharya* if he controls his semen, except on the occasion of cohabitation for the purpose of childbirth. If he does so he is as good as an avowed *brahmachari*. He said that in the life of a healthy and virile man or woman, there may be only one such occasion. One may argue that a man or a woman may want more than one child. In that case, among ordinary householders, sex for the purpose of childbirth (once or more) may not lead to violation of the vow of celibacy, but sex for pleasure does.

Socio-economic consequences of celibacy are obvious. It may look difficult or even impossible to practice celibacy but if practiced, it would lead to replacement level or even lower levels of fertility quite fast. Many Western countries have limited family size using natural methods at a time when state and religion were not supportive of birth control at all. But Gandhi was not looking for solution to population problem only. For Gandhi the root meaning of celibacy or *brahmacharya* was different: it is a conduct which puts one in touch with God. "The conduct consists in the fullest control over all the senses. This is the true and relevant meaning of the word" (Gandhi, 1954).

Control over the organ of generation is impossible without proper control over all the senses. "My experience says that one who has not won palate cannot win sexual desire", said Gandhi (1999). A householder lives for his household creating a boundary wall around their love. In order to rise to the height of universal love one would have to remain unmarried or live with his wife as brother and sister.

Evaluation of Gandhian Theory of Population

For those who believe in Gandhian values of good life, Gandhian theory of population presents a fresh approach to population control that goes beyond the birth control and raises the issue of constructing a good society. The question is: a population can achieve a low growth rate using birth control but can it achieve the moral values required to establish an egalitarian and non-violent order? Such questions cannot be answered on empirical basis. Gandhi provided a critique of modernity, and presented a practical alternative to it, which is neither traditional nor from within the modernity. Can Gandhi be called postmodern? One thing is clear that he was one of those early thinkers who could connect population growth with gender, political power, voluntarism, religion and social values.

DEMOGRAPHIC TRANSITION THEORY

Demographic Transition Theory (DTT) is an attempt to capture the process of change from a situation of high mortality and high mortality to a situation of low mortality and low fertility. The demographic transition theory states that ancient society was marked by high and fluctuating death rate. At that time survival of human society required that it reproduces at the highest level to counter the high force of mortality (caused by small pox, plague, malaria and other deadly infectious diseases, wars, natural disasters, shortage of food, violent conflicts and wars). If a year was free from natural catastrophes mortality was relatively lower and if there were outbreaks of diseases, wars, fire, famine or abnormal rainfall, then mortality was high. Demographers suggest that such a society may be placed in Stage I of demographic transition. In this stage the rate of growth of population fluctuates with a long run tendency to remain around zero. Chapter 5 has already thrown enough light on the nature of demographic transition in the world.

The theory says that as a society develops its death rate starts falling. The reasons are not adequately understood. Yet they include formation of nation state, improvement in working conditions, improvement in means of transport and communication, developments in the field of medical sciences and medicine, and improvement in income. Development of antibiotics and better surgical techniques has certainly played an important role in reduction of death rate though the role of socio-economic and political factors cannot be ignored. This reduction in death rate leads to population explosion. Thus all Stage II societies experience rapid population growth. Finally, equilibrium between birth and death rates is restored when couples start limiting number of children. Thus in Stage III when death rates are low and birth rates are also low Zero Population Growth (ZPG) is restored.

Figure 8.2 shows the nature of demographic transition (Montgomery, 2009).

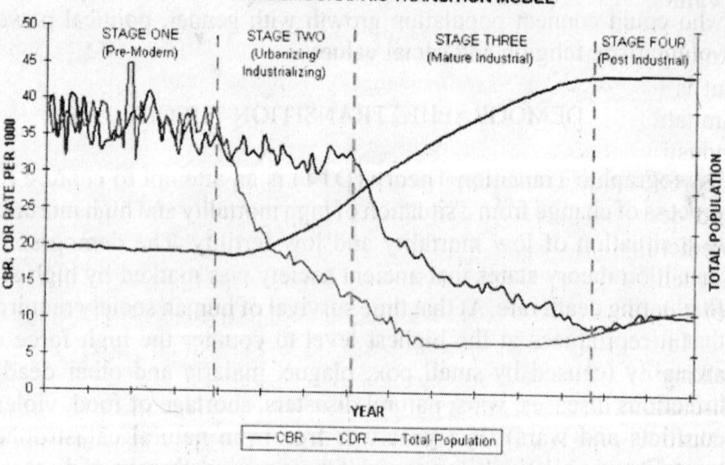

Figure 8.2: Demographic Transition

It may be noted that demographic transition has not followed the same course in all parts of the world (Figures 8.3-8.5). In the developed countries it took a very long time for mortality and fertility to decline and since the changes in both of them was slow they did not experience population explosion (i.e., a very high rate of growth of population). In less developed countries mortality remained high till the middle of the twentieth century and declined suddenly in the third quarter of the century. In absence of corresponding decline in fertility, which is taking much longer time, they experienced very rapid growth of population, often exceeding three per cent, implying a doubling time of 23 years. It is easy for any state to work effectively towards reducing death rates and improving health facilities that everyone welcomes but it is difficult to change reproductive behaviour which requires sustained motivation on the part of individual couples. For fertility to decline the couples must perceive:

- ⌘ A smaller family is better than a larger family
- ⌘ It is possible to decide how many children one should have
- ⌘ There are several methods of birth control that people are practicing
- ⌘ There is at least one birth control method which is easily available, affordable, safe, legitimate, and acceptable.

Evaluation of Demographic Transition Theory

Among all the theories DTT is most known to population sociologists but is also the most criticized theory. It suffers from a number of limitations: (a) it only summarizes the empirical experience of some, industrially advanced, countries but does not present a coherent theoretical framework to establish relationship between development and demographic transition; (b) it cannot be used for making predictions; (c) it completely ignores the role of migration; (d) it does not tell how much time the demographic transition will take; and (e) it does not explain the causes of changes in death and birth rates.

In the recent literature on demographic trends social scientists are talking of second and third demographic transitions. The transition discussed above is called the first transition. Second demographic transition refers to rapid fall in fertility to the below replacement level in the industrially advanced countries, mostly after a brief period of baby boom after World War II. The third transition refers to the possibility of increase in fertility in the lowest low fertility countries whose mechanism is not yet understood. It is difficult to say whether societies will experience increased fertility after the second transition, and in what circumstances. This is a new issue. Today it confronts the developed countries. As and when the developing countries will achieve the replacement or below replacement level fertility this issue will become important for them also.

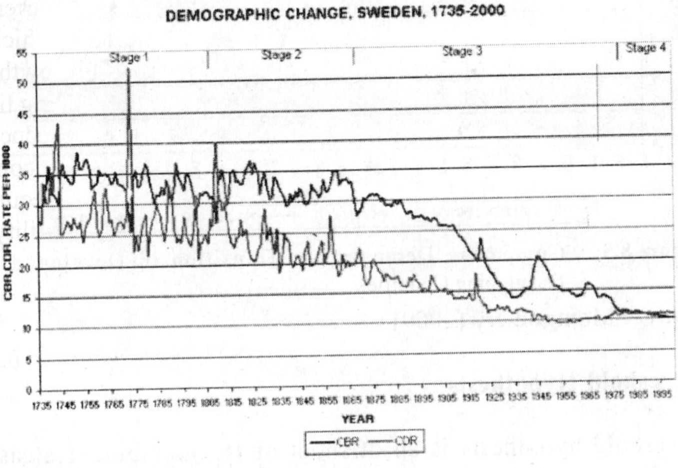

Figure 8.3: Demographic Transition in a Developed Country

Source: Montgomery (2009).

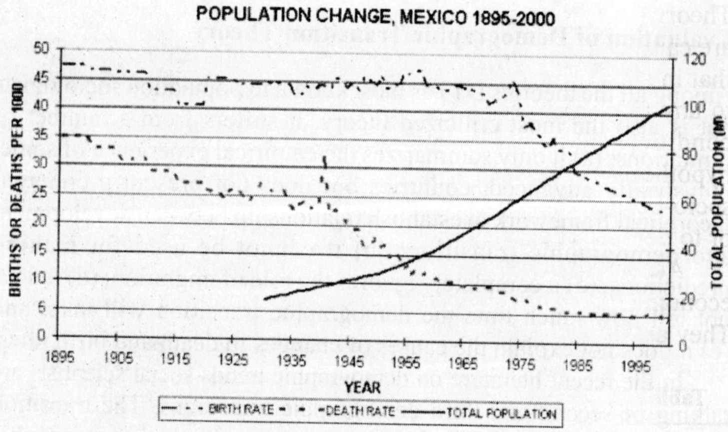

Figure 8.4: Demographic Transition in a Developing Country

Source: Montgomery (2009).

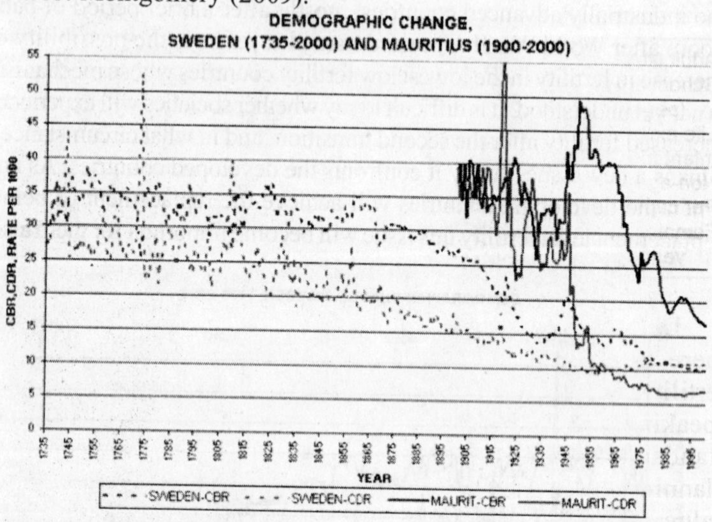

Figure 8.5: Comparing Demographic Transition in Developed and Developing Countries

Source: Montgomery (2009).

Threshold Hypothesis

Threshold hypothesis is an offshoot of Demographic Transition

Theory (DTT). According to DTT changes in mortality and fertility are caused by development and modernization. Yet, one may argue that in a less developed country minor improvements may not lead to any change in mortality and fertility. Improvement in people's condition must be substantial and perceptible. Thus threshold hypothesis attempts to operationalise how much improvement in socio-economic indicators is required for fertility to start declining or to decline to a given level.

According to Berelson there are certain threshold values of socio-economic indicators which should be achieved to lower birth rates. They are given Table 8.1:

Table 8.1: Threshold Values for Reduction in the Birth Rate

Indicator	*Threshold value for Crude Birth Rate*	
	30 per thousand population	*20 per thousand population*
Adult literacy (per cent)	70	93
School enrolment, age 5-10 years (per cent)	55	69
Life expectancy (years)	60	69
Infant mortality rate (per thousand)	65	32
Non-agricultural labour force (per cent)	55	80
Per capita GNP (US $)	450	1080
Females, never married, age 15-19 years (per cent)	80	100

Demographic studies in different settings have shown that there are no fixed thresholds for the decline of mortality and fertility. Vital rates have fallen in different circumstances. Broadly speaking, one may say that some minimum level of change in standard of living is required before people start thinking of planning family size, but it is not possible to fix any particular value of the indicators which sufficiently predict the onset of fertility decline. Moreover, there is also no agreement regarding which variables must be given top priority in applying threshold hypothesis. The question is not easy to answer: Is it education, income, urbanization, age of marriage, women's empowerment or what that determines beginning of demographic transition or a combination of all of them?

CONCLUSION

Like Marx, it can be said more confidently today that there is no law of population that applies to all societies. Trends in vital rates and their causes are all shaped greatly by the socio-economic, political and cultural milieus as well as human intervention. Thus the search for a universal law is in vain. At the same time we cannot forget the warning given by Malthus that unrestrained population could lead to underdevelopment, especially in the context of developing countries which require a more balanced and an optimum approach to fertility and mortality. We must pay particular attention to migration, the process which was ignored by demographic transition theory as well as many other theories.

QUESTIONS AND EXERCISES

1. Can Malthusian or Marxist theories be applied to deal with population and development issues in any country today?
2. What is your assessment of Hardin's argument that the poor countries are suffering from longage of population and not from shortage of resources?
3. Write a short note on four types of surplus labour.
4. What are the major differences in Malthusian and Marxist theories of population?
5. State the demographic transition theory.
6. Describe threshold hypothesis.
7. What are the major differences in demographic transition between developed and developing countries?
8. What are the economic assumptions behind optimum population theory?
9. Does the environment depend on population size only? What are all the factors determining environment impact?
10. Discuss Gandhian theory of population and its relevance in the present times.

REFERENCES

Aird, John, 1982, Population Studies and Population Policy in China. *Population and Development Review*, 8(2): 267-297.

Ananyeva, *et al.*, 1977, Underlying Patterns of Population Development. In Valentey, D.I. (ed.), *An Outine Theory of Population*. Moscow: Progress Publishers.

Berelson, Bernard, 1975, The World Population Plan of Action: where Now? *Population and Development Review*, 1(1).

_______, 1978, Prospects and Programmes for Fertility Reduction. *Population and Development Review*, 1(1).

Bongaarts, John, 1975, Why High Birth rates are so Low. *Population and Development Review*, 7(2): 289-306.

Caldwell, J.C., 1998. Malthus and the Less Developed World: The Pivotal Role of India. *Population and Development Review*, 24(4): 675-696.

Chengrui, Li, 1982, On the Results of the Chinese Census. *Population and Development Review*, 9(2): 327. Also Chinese Population Policy, 1982. *In*: *Population and Development Review*, 8(3): 633-35.

Coale, Ansley, J. and Hoover, Edgar M., 1958, *Population Growth and Economic Development in Low-Income Countries.* Princeton: Princeton University Press.

Daly, H.E., 1971, A Marxian-Malthusian View of Poverty and Development. *Population Studies*, 25(1): 25-38.

Desai, M., 1973, *Day-to-Day with Gandhi*, Varanasi: Sarva Seva Sangh.

Espenshade, T.J., The Population Explosion. *Population and Development Review*, 17(2): 331-339.

Gandhi, M.K., 1954, *Sarvodaya*, Ahmedabad: Navajivan Publishing House.

_______, 1957, *Satya Ke Prayoga*, Ahmedabad: Navajivan Mandir (Hindi).

_______, 1999, *Ramnam*, Ahmedabad: Navajivan Prakashan Mandir.

Gottlieb, Manuel, 1945, The Theory of Optimum Population for a Closed Economy. *The Journal of Political Economy*, 53(4): 289-316.

Greenhalgh, Susan, 2003, Science, Modernity, and the Making of China's One-Child Policy. *Population and Development Review*, 29(2): 163-196.

Iyer, Raghavan (ed.), 1986, *The Moral and Political Writings of Mahatma Gandhi*, Vol. 1-3, Oxford: Clarendon Press.

Lee, James, and Feng, Wang, 1999. Malthusian models and Chinese Realities: China's Demographic system 1700-2000. *Population and Development Review*, 25(1): 33-65.

Malthus, T.R., 1965, *First Essay on Population, 1798*. New York: Augustas, M.Kelley.

Margaret, Sanger, 1969, A Summit Meeting on Birth Control, in Cousins, Norman (ed.), *Profiles of Gandhi: America Remembers a World Leader*, New Delhi: Indian Book Company.

Marx, Karl, 1974, *Capital: A Critical Analysis of Capitalist Production*, Vol. 1. Moscow: Progress Publishers.

Montgomery, Keith, 2009, The Demographic Transition. *http://www.marathon.uwc.edu/geography/Demotrans/demtran.htm* [accessed on 14th December, 2009).

Mukerjee, Radhakamal, 1941, Population Theory and Politics. *American Sociological Review*. [*http://www.jstor.org/sici?sici=0003-1224(194112)6%3A6%3C784%3APTAP%3E2.0.CO%3B2-T* accessed on 4th October, 2008].

Paul, Mantoux, 1948, *The Industrial Revolution in the Eighteenth Century*. London: Jonathan Cape.

Poston Jr., Dudley L., Micklin, Michael and Baumle, Amanda K., 2007, Demography. In Bryant, Clifton D. and Peck, Dennis L. (eds.), *21st Century Sociology: A Reference Handbook*. Thousand Oaks: Sage Publications, 508-517.

Simon, Julian L., 1998, *The Ultimate Resource* 2, PrincetonUniversity Press.

Singh, Karan, 1975, *Jansankhya, Garibi aur Bharat ka Bhavishya,* New Delhi: NIFP (Hindi).

Smulevich, B.Y., 1978, Sociological Theories of Population. *In*: Valentey, D.I. (ed.), *The Theory of Population*. Moscow: Progress Publishers.

Spengler, J.J., 1962, Population and Freedom. *Population Review*: 74-82.

Srinivasan, K., 1986, Has Modernisation Increased Fertility in Karnataka India?" *Demography India*, 15 (2): 281.

Suman, Ramnath, 1969, *Samaj Sudhar: Samasyayen aur Samadhan*. Allahabad: Gandhi Sahitya Prakashan (Hindi).

United Nations, 1973, *The Determinants and Consequences of Population Trends, Vol. 1*. New York: United Nations.

Wever, Cynthia, and Goodman, Ann, 1981. Demographic Policy Debate in the USSR. *Population and Development Review*, 7(2).

9

Population Policy and Family Planning Programmes

POPULATION POLICY

Introduction

This chapter focuses on the subject of population policy. It shows the various kinds of policies which governments in different countries have and problems they encounter in implementing them.

Population Policy

As mentioned earlier, population is intricately linked with development. Therefore, the National Governments may want to examine population dynamics with reference to development goals, identify problems, and take a corrective action. This results in population policy. Here the term population policy refers to statements of state's understanding of population trends, their causes and consequences and measures adopted to influence some aspects of the population trends. Most governments have a clearly stated policy on population, but some have only a broad understanding and a broad vision of population processes. The world over, population policy addresses one or more of the following issues (UN Population Division, 2007).

- Population size

- Growth
- Age composition
- Size of population in working ages
- Regional differences in size or growth rate of population
- Fertility
- Adolescent fertility
- Mortality
- International migration
- Internal migration—from one region to another and rural to urban areas
- Age of marriage
- Social differentials in fertility or mortality or other aspects of population
- Social class mobility or shift from agriculture to urban, industrial employment
- HIV/AIDS

Governments have often taken action on the front of population, even without having a clearly stated and officially accepted population policy. For example, in India it was only in year 2000 that the Parliament approved the National Population Policy 2000 but the government has had a long history of adopting measures to reduce fertility rate at the national and regional levels. Chapter 10 discusses that the Central Government issued population policy statements at least two times: one in 1976 during Congress rule; and another in 1977 during Janata Party rule. In addition the policy statements of different departments and the various Five Year and Annual Plans have shown government's commitment to check the growth rate of population.

Pronatal and Antinatal Policies

As the second half of the twentieth century witnessed development of various theories linking population growth rate to development and environment and both developed and developing countries are undergoing significant changes in their demographic profile, population policies have largely focused on whether they encourage or discourage the prevailing reproduction rates. As far as mortality rate—the other vital component of growth—is concerned everybody favours reduction in death rate and improvement in life expectancy. On migration there has not been a consensus but most countries welcome those migrants who fill certain vacuum in their labour force structure and discourage large streams of migrants for the fear of declining cultural standards and overpopulation.

Overall, the countries may be divided into three categories on the basis of population policy:

- Countries having no explicit policy, i.e., no deliberate intervention in population processes;
- Countries having pronatal policy; and
- Countries having antinatal policy.

Not all countries have an officially declared population policy. There are countries which have high growth rate of population but did not deem it necessary to change the situation. Some of them want the growth rate to remain high for religious, political or other reasons. Those who have no policy may be satisfied with the present trends or believe that socio-economic development will change the family size in desired direction. Pronatal policy implies a policy that favours raising fertility rate. Antinatal policy implies a policy that attempts to bring down fertility rates.

Candidly, the developed countries which have a declining fertility and fear aging of population and declining growth rate favour pronatal policy, the developing countries favour the opposite. The developing countries have faced the population explosion in much of 1960s and 1970s and fear adverse effects of population on savings and capital, and culture and society. They have antinatal population policy.

The policy statements are expected to include: discussion of the present demographic scenario; their implications for development; statement of a preferred demographic scenario commensurate with the short term and long term development goals of the country; and strategies to materialize the preferred demographic scenario, often combined with time bound targets and calculations of requirements of resources. The policy statement is issued with the approval of the head of the state and is not simply a statement of goals of its intellectuals, academicians, political parties, or one particular department of government.

Participants in Population Policy

Jain (1998) identifies the following *nine* participants in population policy.

1. Political leaders
2. Religious groups
3. Ethnic groups
4. Feminist factions and women's groups
5. Non-governmental organizations
6. Census and survey organizations
7. International agencies which influence the national population policies
8. International conferences on population and development.

Political leaders play a critical role in making of population policy. They are responsible for developing the statements of vision and mission. Yet, they would not be able to ignore popular sentiments on contraception and abortion, views of major religious groups and their doctrines, politics of ethnic communities/identities, and role and views of national and international non-governmental organizations. In plural countries, religious leaders can influence the policy debate in a significant manner. They wield powerful influence on the community and they may think that by declaring population policy government is intruding in their religious matters. In some countries like Bangladesh and Malaysia Governments has been able to obtain support of the religious leaders in population control. Here the religious leaders support the idea of family planning, including use of sterilization. But involving religious leaders in plural societies is fraught with risks. If government manages support from one specific cleric this may boomerang and isolate that cleric in the community. In that case whatever was achieved through secular appeals may be lost to communal frenzy. Secular appeals through media and neutral and respected persons may be more effective than involvement of religious leaders. Yet, if it is possible to have a broad consensus among the different religious schools on a few aspects of the policy that can go a long way to make the population policy more effective.

In the late 20th century women' groups (often called feminists) became a major civil society actor exerting influence on population policy. They have raised issues about women's autonomy, contraception and abortion. Feminist groups have supported the idea of birth control as it empowers them to decide how many children they should have and whether they should produce children or work. Yet, they have raised objections to a few family planning methods included in the programmes of certain countries such as female sterilization, abortion, emergency pills and Depo-Provera (injections) on health grounds as well as social grounds. According to them several family planning methods such as Depo-Provera have been introduced in the programme without examining their adverse health impacts and informing women about the risks. Some of them who reject abortion on moral grounds say that abortion works to the advantage of the exploitative male and not for the female. It makes the male free from all financial, legal or social obligations associated with childbirth by eliminating the possibility of birth. Feminist maintain that the males have made the females a perpetual and re-usable sex object.

Feminists have also viewed seriously that due to patriarchy if families decide to go for sterilization they go for female sterilization rather than male sterilization though the latter is simpler and safer than the former method. DLHS-3 shows that among the current users of family planning for every male sterilization there are 34 female sterilizations (IIPS, 2010).

Apart from feminists groups, government needs support from other Non-Governmental Organizations (NGOs) for:

- Generating public opinion
- Implementation of programme (under public-private-partnership)
- Independent feedback on programme implementation through operations research
- Innovative ideas
- Resources
- Support of local communities
- Linkages with development initiatives

Nevertheless, to support their claims all the participants in population debate depend on data, which are provided by national and international agencies. Population censuses provide useful data on size and growth of population which are supplemented by estimates of demographic rates by international, national and sub-national surveys. Further, the World Population Conference, held in Bucharest in 1974, and subsequent international conferences on population too have influenced the perceptions and ideas of politicians, bureaucrats, academicians and NGOs, by raising new questions, sharing experiences, providing a platform to discuss and debate various issues, and presenting scientific analysis on population processes. Such conferences have led to paradigmatic shifts in the theory of population and approaches to family planning programmes. Lastly, the consultants, academicians and media persons too play a role in population policy by providing data, perspectives and creating a public opinion favourable to population policy.

EFFECTIVENESS OF POPULATION POLICIES

Defining Effectiveness

Since to implement population policy a nation state has to spend resources it is legitimate to ask whether the policy is effective. In discussing effectiveness of population policies the starting point is: how does one define the effectiveness of a policy? A simple definition of effectiveness may be that it is the degree to which a policy is able to achieve its desired objectives (regarding development, regional equality, long term needs of society etc.).

Prerequisites of Effective Population Policy

Now you may ask : what are the prerequisites of effective population policy? Experience shows that population policy will be effective if:

- Policy is stated in unambiguous and unequivocal terms
- There is good governance
- Strategies are based on good understanding of the socio-economic and cultural milieus
- There is good political support for the policy
- Adequate resources are mobilized to implement the policy
- Socio-economic development and the population policy are influencing the targets in the same direction
- Civil society is in agreement with the goals of the policy.

Difficulties in Assessing Effectiveness of Population Policy

Evaluation of population policy is problematic. The reason is that one cannot have an experimental method to evaluate the implementation of policy. Population trends depend on policy as well as on multitude of other factors, such as the institutional context, economic conditions, culture, value of children, religious doctrines, autonomy, etc. For example, how can one separate the effect of family planning programme from the effect of modernization and development? Some other difficulties are:

- Lack of consensus regarding the major goals of the population policy
- Lack of adequate measurement of parameters of population system
- Lack of reliable data
- Conversion of statistics of family planning users into reduction in total fertility rate
- Lack of a clear theoretical understanding of population-development nexus and how the effect of policy be separated from the effect of development and modernization
- Lack of appreciation for monitoring and evaluation of population programmes.

Lack of consensus regarding the major goals of the population policy is a serious problem. Therefore, even those governments that now have an officially stated policy have taken decades to arrive at the policy statement and get it approved by appropriate state bodies. Lack of data raises another level of problem. Economically less developed countries are also statistically less developed countries. They lack detailed data on family planning and population parameters. The available data may be incomplete or unreliable. Then there are technical problems too. How does one convert the data on number of users of family planning methods into measures of number of births averted and the percentage impact on the birth rate? For this one needs:

- Reliable data on family planning users by method, age, sex and duration of use;
- Rate of continuation and discontinuation by age; and

- Effectiveness of the different methods included in the programme.

To evaluate the effectiveness of population policy the evaluators need a clear definition of whether the goal of the stated policy is to reduce population growth rate (which depends on three things—fertility, mortality and migration), or fertility rate or mortality rate or all. This goal has to be clear, measurable and meaningful. Suppose the goal is to reduce fertility. Then the question is: should the government aim at reducing birth rate or total fertility rate or other measures of fertility (such as net reproduction rate)? Indian Government has aimed at reduction of total fertility rate but Chinese government has directly, influenced birth rate through the concept of birth quotas. A clear analysis is required to identify all factors on which the target indicators depend. For example, it is easier to reduce total fertility rate than birth rate because birth rate depends on both age specific fertility rates and age distribution of population. It is not in the hands of planners to change the age distribution of population. Obviously, reducing the population growth rate is a rather more difficult task. As discussed previously, reduction in age specific fertility rates does not immediately reduce the growth rate of population and for several decades population would continue to grow despite reduction in total fertility rate.

Difficulty in analytical and empirical separation of the effects of population policy from those of development and modernization poses another serious problem before the planners and programme managers. The two processes may work in the same or different directions. Finally, a lack of appreciation for monitoring and evaluation of population programmes is another issue. The programme managers may not see the direct utility of evaluation studies. Population programmes require expenditure of huge resources. In absence of these studies, however, one cannot judge how effective the population policies are, and whether it is worth spending money on population programmes.

Are Developed Countries more Effective in Implementing Population Policy?

There is no doubt that developed countries are worried about low fertility, particularly because it causes aging. It not only raises proportion of the old in the total population of the country it also causes aging among the aged, i.e., increasing proportion of very old (80+) among the old (say 60+). This requires analysis of the causes of fertility decline.

The comparison between developed and developing countries in performance in implementing population policies is not sound because they are dealing with different types of problems. McDonald (2006) avers that there are several causes of low fertility in the developed countries. Two main causes are: social liberalism or reflexive modernization; and economic deregulation or the new capitalism. The former refers to the conditions of postmodernism. Modernization (coupled with organized capitalism) with emphasis on reason, certitude of science and industrialization caused the first demographic transition and fertility declined to 2-3 children. Reflexive modernization or postmodernization led to fulfilment of women's claims for gender equity, individualization of the individual, and lifted the lid on divorce. Simultaneously, economic deregulation made a revolutionary impact on the labour market: the end of "jobs for life"; increased demand for higher level of human capital; flexible employment; contractualization of jobs; unemployment; and uncertainties. Consequently, the reflexive modernization produced the second demographic transition in which fertility has gone below the replacement level. Will the industrially advanced, postmodern societies be able to have third demographic transition and improve fertility levels through state intervention or community action? There is no simple answer.

One can compare India and Bangladesh because they have similar policies and similar socio-economic characteristics. Both are developing countries with low income, large rural base and strong influence of religion and tradition. Both have antenatal policies. One cannot compare effectiveness of population policy between Mexico and France. In the two cases institutional mechanisms and conditions are very different.

It appears that with the end of value of children it is impossible to raise fertility unless new institutional mechanisms are developed which virtually coerce women to produce children. Merely giving them more facilities for producing children will not help. For Keyfitz (1986), the low fertility problem is a very difficult problem. Population policy based on more money, more privileges or professionalization of motherhood have uncertain contribution. Any attempt to predict post-transitional fertility in the developed countries is in vain. It is more difficult to implement population policy effectively in the developed countries than in the developing countries. Yet, there are some who see that it is possible. For this society has to support family, particularly women.

McDonald argues:

> The solution to low fertility lies neither in the moral Right's call for a rolling back of social liberalism nor in the old Left's agenda of rolling back economic deregulation. Both waves of change have achieved many of the desirable outcomes for which they were intended. Most people prefer to live in a society that offers social freedoms and personal choices. Most prefer to work in an environment that rewards enterprise and endeavour. But most people prefer to have long-lasting intimate relationships and to have children. The solution, therefore, lies in a third wave of social change, new and substantial priority to the support of family life—especially the bearing and rearing of children. New perspectives on the family are required that recognize the vital social and personal significance of family life and that understand that family life will be played out amid the social liberalism and the new capitalism that are integral to twenty-first-century economies and societies.

To follow McDonald, the population policy in the developed, postmodern, societies, would not be effective unless family life is supported. The question is how to do this. Another issue is what will be its repercussions for the very institutions and values that have produced the weakening of family—the freedom and individual choices.

The developing countries have their own problems (Box 9.1). Lack of conceptual clarity and disagreement among the opinion makers, academics and planners is the biggest problem. But there are other problems too: fear of misuse of funds; lack of governance; religious or ethnic resistance; and lack of clarity regarding transfer of responsibilities to private sector, individuals or non-governmental organizations.

Box 9.1: Prospects for Success

...ICPD makes some very unrealistic demands on national governments. The implementation of a broader population policy as embedded in ICPD recommendations would require a cross-sectional approach to policy-making. Experience in policy-making with such an approach, however, has not been promising so far, either in the population field or in other fields. At least six factors would hamper implementation of such an approach in any setting. The extent to which these issues are resolved would determine the degree to which a broader population policy is implemented in a country and succeeds in reducing growth and improving individual well-being. These factors are:

1. Lack of conceptual clarity,
2. Disagreement among academics and intellectuals,
3. Concern about losing funds for family planning,
4. Absence of effective bureaucratic structures,
5. Lack of effective accountability mechanisms, and
6. Waning role of government

Quoted from Jain (1998b).

FAMILY PLANNING PROGRAMME AND BEYOND FAMILY PLANNING MEASURES TO CONTROL FERTILITY

Policy Options in the Developing Countries

Developing countries are still struggling with the problem of having fertility levels perceived to be higher than what they should be. Also several social groups in these countries still have high mortality levels particularly among infants, children and women in the reproductive ages. A practical issue is: what needs to be done in this context? Here a distinction has to be made between family planning programme and beyond family planning measures. The former focuses on promotion of birth control methods, the latter on all other factors which can be regulated to reduce fertility. Success of family planning programme is not the necessary and sufficient condition for fertility decline, and fertility decline is not a necessary and sufficient condition of decline of growth rate of population. Thus a distinction has to be made between family planning programme, fertility policy and population policy.

Once it is decided that government must go for reducing the fertility rates then they have three options:

- Use of coercion—making it compulsory to limit family size to one or two children through political, social and legal interventions

- Taking all necessary actions to promote knowledge and practice of family planning methods though voluntary means; and
- Focusing on those parameters of social and economic development which are known for having fertility depressing effects, such as raising age of marriage and educational standards among women.

All the above options have been exercised in different countries. China used coercion by going for one child policy, having legal restrictions on children, strong economic disincentives and through birth planning at the grassroots level. In democratic setups it is seldom the preferred or effective option. Indian political parties have learnt that even the indication of coercion in family planning is enough to bring about a change in the regimes. Initially, developing countries preferred the second option and those countries which went for population policy implemented family planning programme on voluntary basis. As time passed and evaluation reports of family planning programmes became available (and also with improved theorisation of mechanisms of fertility decline) the governments felt the need for beyond family planning measures.

Family Planning

Family planning measures refer to all those strategies which aim at promotion of contraception, sterilization and/or legitimate abortion as part of government policy. They include having a clear cut family planning policy and involvement of all government departments in implementing it, provision of resources, creation of facilities at the grassroots levels and launching awareness campaigns for building small family size norm. The state pursuing family planning programme has to take several decisions regarding quantum of resources to be pumped into various components of the programme; organization structures; family planning methods, supply and outlets; means of communication; and ways of monitoring and evaluation through which mid-term and end terms corrections may be made in different projects, launched as part of the family planning programme. Engineering demographic goals in a rather traditional society has been a very challenging task. In 1950s when family planning programmes were launched there was no help from the history. The developed countries rarely used family planning programme for reducing fertility levels. It was rather a strong motivation on the part of couples that caused a declining trend in fertility despite disapproval of contraception from the state and the church.

Beyond Family Planning Measures

Beyond family planning measures include all those policies which affect the value of children, sex preference, age of marriage, and women's reproductive decision making power. One reason behind high fertility in the developing countries has been the lack of old age security and dependence on son in the old age. If an effective old age security programme can be developed it will definitely reduce the need for having sons. Similarly, in multi-ethnic society like India alienation among certain groups may make them adopt a pronatalist stand. They can be brought into national mainstream by fighting inequalities and creating a more egalitarian society. Then they are likely to agree with government policies and their fertility levels are likely to change. Table 9.1 shows the various possible family planning and beyond family planning measures that governments can adopt to reduce fertility.

Table 9.1: Family Planning and Beyond Family Planning Measures to Reduce Fertility

Family planning measures	*Beyond family planning measures*
1. A clear policy and direction to different departments to promote contraceptive practices—targets, strategies, etc.	1. Improving literacy and secondary school enrolment rates among girls
2. Allocation of adequate resources for family planning programme	2. Raising age of marriage—through legal and other means
3. Effective organization—supervision, increased field visits of senior staff	3. Empowerment of women—promoting participation of women
4. Training	4. Providing effective reproductive health facilities
5. Sensitize political leaders and religious leaders to importance of family planning	5. Creation of social security, particularly old age security, and other welfare measures
6. Incentives and disincentives	6. Reducing child mortality
7. Information, education and communication activities involving multimedia approach—fighting rumours	7. Health insurance for children
8. Creation of facilities for abortion, sterilization, IUD insertion and other contraceptives at the lowest levels of health facilities	8. Schemes to affect sex preference such as insurance and other facilities for girl child
9. Creating trust	9. Fighting regional and social class disparities
10. Facilities for recanalization after sterilization	10. Welfare of minorities

The beyond family planning measures work in the following manner.

1. They subject the family size decisions to rational calculations based on knowledge, and minimize the importance of traditional, ethical, ethnic and emotional factors. This is achieved by providing various choices and opportunities to people and thus raising their aspirations level. They lead to individuation, modernization and Westernization.
2. They reduce the demand for children by providing functional alternatives to children such as pension schemes, insurance policies, and old age security.
3. They limit the reproductive span available for childbirth by raising age of marriage, and providing working opportunities for women.
4. They generate trust among people. Researchers have noticed that in absence of development works the governments lack the trust of people and whenever new programmes and schemes are launched (such as family planning) people do not come forward to avail the benefit of them. They may even reject them collectively.
5. Beyond family planning measures link the people to government health and family planning programmes. This leads to seeking information and eventually practice of birth control methods.

Advantages of Beyond Family Planning Measures

The advantages of beyond family planning methods are many. First of all, in general, the beyond family planning measures are acceptable to all sections of society. How can there be opposition to promoting education, reducing child mortality, extenuating regional inequalities, fighting domestic violence against women, empowering them and providing reproductive health facilities? They are on their own the major goals of social development. Whether they help in effective implementation of population policy or not they must be vigorously pursued. Secondly, the beyond family planning measures are the factors that will reduce the fertility levels on a sustained basis. Thirdly, they will also improve the quality of family planning acceptance and make it demand driven rather than enforced by the state policies. In the past stress on family planning has often resulted in alienation among masses, cooking up of data, forced sterilization and poor quality of acceptors (old, those who have already produced 6-7 children, those who are unlike to produce a child in the future for biological or social reasons, etc.). Stress on beyond family planning measures improves the participation of people in policy implementation. Fourthly, stress on the beyond family planning measures leads to better coordination between different government departments and more effective implementation of all programmes at the grassroots level.

Limitations of Beyond Family Planning Measures

Beyond family planning measures have certain limitations too. They have a long gestation period to yield any effect; it may not be advisable to wait for socio-economic development to take place so that fertility can decline. Waiting for this to happen would mean prolonging the period of demographic transition and raising the level of population at which it will ultimately stabilize. Beyond family planning measures involve huge monetary costs as well as trained manpower which may not be readily available. Sometimes putting a greater stress on them in the middle of family planning programme may leave the impression that government is not serious about population control.

Studies of implementation of National Rural Health Mission (NRHM) and Janani Suraksha Yojana (JSY) in India have revealed that monetary rewards for producing babies in health facilities have reportedly created an impression, in the rural and tribal districts, that government is no more serious about family planning, or wants to raise number of children. Thus the beyond family planning measures may in certain conditions boomerang.

CONCLUSION

In sum, it may be argued that the issue of implementing family planning programme and beyond family planning measures is not of choosing one approach over the other or of putting higher stress on one at the cost of other. If the goal is to reduce fertility both the approaches need to be used simultaneously. And this is precisely what the National Population Policy (NPP) 2000 aims to achieve in India.

QUESTIONS AND EXERCISES

1. What solution does McDonald offer for raising fertility in the developed countries?
2. What are the major factors that affect the effectiveness of the population policy?
3. What are different types of population policies in existence in different countries?
4. Distinguish between family planning and beyond family planning measures.
5. Select any two beyond family planning measures and argue that they can lead to decline in fertility levels in the developing countries.
6. Are the beyond family planning measures more acceptable to people?
7. Should the government target at reducing birth rate or total fertility rate or population growth rate?
8. What kind of data will be required to evaluate success of family planning programmes?
9. What are the sources of disagreements between religious leaders and government on the matters of population policy?
10. What will happen if a government does not have a population policy?

REFERENCES

International Institute for Population Sciences, 2010, *District Level Household and Facility Survey 2007-08*, Mumbai: IIPS.

Jain, Anrudh, 1998a, Population Policies that Matter. In Jain, Anrudh, 1998, *Do Population Policies Matter: Fertility and Politics in Egypt, India, Kenya, and Mexico*. New York: Population Council.

________, 1998b, The future of Population Policies. In Jain, Anrudh, 1998, *Do Population Policies Matter: Fertility and Politics in Egypt, India, Kenya, and Mexico*. New York: Population Council.

Keyfitz, Nathan, 1986, The Family that Does Not Reproduce itself, *Population and Development Review*, Vol. 12 (Supplement): 139-154.

McDonald, Peter, 2006, Low Fertility and the State: The Efficacy of Policy. *Population and Development Review*, Vol. 32, No. 3: 485-510.

United Nations, 2007, World Population Policies 2007: Government Views and Policies *http://www.un.org/csa/population/publications/wpp2007/Publication_index.htm* [assessed on 29th April 2011].

10

National Population Policy

FAMILY PLANNING PROGRAMME IN INDIA

Introduction

As mentioned earlier, India entered the second stage of demographic transition around 1921 after which its population started growing at rate more than 1 per cent a year. Nehru wrote extensively on falling birth and death rates in the West in *Discovery of India* and was a strong supporter of family planning programme. National Planning Committee of the Indian National Congress supported promotion of family planning as a state policy strongly. This explains how after independence, the Government of India recognized the vital role of population control in the overall development of national economy and in 1952 India became the first country of the world to launch an official family planning programme. Unrestricted population growth was viewed as a serious threat to all national developmental efforts. Over the years the planners have followed different approaches towards promoting family planning among the masses. These approaches are broadly grouped into Gandhian approach, clinical approach, extension approach, cafeteria approach, coercion and rights based approach (Table 10.1). While we started cautiously with Gandhian approach, after various experiments in this area, we have settled with a demand driven, rights based approach in which greater role is assigned to education, empowerment and meeting the unmet needs rather than attaining family planning targets. This chapter presents the three major policy statements issued by successive governments: a statement by Dr. Karan Singh in 1976, a statement by Janata Party Government in 1977, and the National Population Policy 2000 statement.

Gandhian Approach

Initially, the dominant thinking among the family planning experts in India was Gandhian. They held the view that abstinence or "the rhythm method" was the most suitable method in Indian programme, and the artificial methods of birth control were not only unpracticable, they were likely to be misused and result in moral degradation. Rajkumari Amrit Kaur, who was the Union Minister of Health at that time was a devoted disciple of Gandhi. Thus a beginning was made with the natural methods of family planning—rhythm and withdrawal.

Clinical Approach

With the Gandhian understanding of population control, clinical approach was followed. This approach included the natural methods of family planning and clinical methods. An allocation of Rs. 6500 lakh was made for family planning in the budget of the First Five Year Plan (1951-56) and a number of family planning clinics were established in the country to provide services to needy people. The same approach was further extended in the Second Five Year Plan period (1956-61). The budget allocation was raised to Rs. 49700 lakh and organizational structures were developed at the national and state levels. Posts of State Family Planning Officers were created in the States, and a Director of Family Planning at the Centre was appointed.

The pilot studies carried out in the First Plan period had shown that "the rhythm method" was not effective and people were not prepared for family planning. The main causes behind the failure of the clinical approach were: female bias; lack of general motivation; cultural obstacles and ignorance. Opening of a large number of birth control clinics at that time before educating the people and raising their level of consciousness was like putting the cart before the horse. Females who constituted the target population in the programme did not enjoy the same (equal) status in the family as in the West and the Westernized Indian planners did not see that in India family planning movement could not get momentum without men's support.

Extension Education

A large number of Knowledge, Attitude, and Practice (KAP) surveys were conducted in the first two Plan periods to help the planners to gather data on knowledge of family planning methods, attitude towards them and practices. The rising rather than falling growth rate of population created a panic among the planners. Thus the Third Five Year Plan stressed the role of "intensive education, provision of facilities and advice on the largest scale possible and widespread popular effort in every rural and urban community" as a matter of the greatest significance. This paved the way for extension education approach. Under the new approach the main burden of the programme was to educate the masses by appointing an army of extension educators or change agents.

IUCD and Mass Vasectomy Approach

In 1965 Intra Uterine Contraceptive Device (IUCD) was introduced in the programme which produced good results initially but gradually the number of acceptors of IUCD started declining. Bleeding and rumours were the main reasons behind its failure. Then during 1972-74 mass vasectomy camps were organized in different parts of the country and the incentive schemes whereby the couples were given incentive in cash and kind for adopting sterilization was adopted. A large number of males were sterilized in them. At some places the approach appeared to be quite successful in attracting couples to family planning as it used incentives as well as group approach to family planning. However, the family planning programme failed to make much headway and reduce the growth rate of population. There were several reasons: patriarchy because of which males were unwilling to bear the burden of family planning; rumours; failure of method in some cases; and fraudulent means to motivate people to adopt family planning.

Coercion

Family planning programme was given utmost importance during the Emergency time when the acceptors were drawn by a technique which was quite contrary to the basic philosophy of the extension approach. Use of coercion augmented the family planning achievements in all the states in India; and some states which were always behind the target, in fact, exceeded the targets. There was a talk of making sterilization compulsory after three children and some states had even passed legislation to this effect. Population growth was viewed as a national problem of urgency and the whole bureaucratic infrastructure was used to assist in the programme. The number of sterilizations increased to 2,669,000 in 1975-76, from only 942,000 in 1973-74, and further to 8,261,000 in 1976-77. At this stage two phenomena were marked: (a) the family planning programme degenerated into sterilization programme; and (b) population control became a political problem.

Cafeteria Approach

In the Third Plan period itself (1961-66) family planning was made a target oriented programme. It was proposed to reduce the birth rate in India to 25 births per 1000 population by 1973. The target was later modified to reduce birth rate to 25 as early as possible. A cafeteria approach was then adopted to provide a range of effective and approved family planning methods according to needs and preferences of the individuals, e.g., condoms, diaphragms, jelly, cream, foam tablets for newly married couples, IUCD for couples with one or two children, and sterilization for couples who have completed their desired family size.

By 1980 the term "cafeteria approach" became a buzzword in family planning programme and the influence of this approach continued. It may also be said that while we have more catchphrases in family planning today, the idea that the needy couples must be informed about all the methods of family planning and all methods of family planning must be accessible to them, so that they can practice one according to their own considerations continues. Broadly speaking, the different family planning methods are divided into two categories: terminal methods; and spacing methods. The former methods refer to methods which are used when couples have completed their desired family size and do not want to produce more children; they may go for male or female sterilization. The latter methods refer to those methods which are used to create gap between successive childbirths. For example, a young couple may produce a baby quickly after marriage but may like to have another child after four-five years. Then they may use condoms or IUCD. When they want a child they may discontinue the method and plan a baby. Under the cafeteria approach it was also thought that we should motivate younger couples to go for delayed childbirth and use spacing methods rather than focus on aged couples and motivate them to go for sterilization. In the context of high and natural fertility, the fertility impact of terminal methods may be much more than that of terminal methods.

The basic idea behind cafeteria approach still continues. It recognizes that different people have different needs, based on their religion, age, family size preferences, economic conditions and many other factors. The state policy should be to provide a method of their choice and not insist on any one method. Ironically, most users of family planning have gone for female sterilization. This is a situation that has not changed till now. This works against the policy of cafeteria approach and depicts male domination in society.

In India fertility has declined, partly due to family planning programme and partly due to development, but not to the desired level. The issue is: has family planning programme in India failed? One can argue both ways. In this context the views expressed by Dyson are worth consideration (Box 10.1).

Box 10.1: Family Planning Programme in India

The Indian family planning programme is often dismissed as a 'failure'. But in my view this is an unjust and rather too simple characterisation. Among other things, the programme's *proper* evaluation would need to take account of:

(i) the sheer size and complexity of the task which it has had to tackle, namely reducing the birth rate in a huge, poor, poorly educated, and largely rural population,

(ii) the aforementioned fact that in many respects India has been a *pioneer*; this is most commonly illustrated by the statement that it was the first country in the world to announce an official family planning programme (in 1952). But actually India has led the world in many other ways too (e.g. in the development of several methods of sterilisation). The main point I am making, however, is that it is particularly difficult to be a pioneer, and that pioneers inevitably tend to make more mistakes than those who follow and,

(iii) the fact that in the past some politicians have shied away from their duty of ensuring that Indian women, and men, have a real 'right to choose'. By this I mean their responsibility of making sure that everyone has access to safe, effective and affordable methods of contraception. Indeed there are still significant parts of the country where this 'right to choose' needs to be expanded. But this requires political backing and greater resources.

Of course, India's family planning programme has had its failings. For example, it has been much too 'target-bound', and for much too long it has badly neglected the promotion of *reversible* forms of contraception (today about eighty per cent of all married women who are currently using a modern method of contraception are relying upon sterilisation (i.e. tubectomy)).

Nevertheless, despite its problems, there can be little doubt that the Indian birth rate would be somewhat higher today, and the country's population would be larger still, if the family planning programme had not existed.

—From Dyson (2003)

Table 10.1: The Time Line of Family Planning Policy in India

Period	Approach
Before independence	**Factors behind general support for population control among the elite** • Lack of awareness among common people • Arguments in favour of population policy among the political and intellectual elites • Isolated efforts to establish clinics and inform people • Strong support for population control by Gandhi and Nehru despite difference in understanding of population dynamics and approaches to means of birth control
1952	**Family planning starts with Gandhian approach** • State sponsored family planning programme started • Gandhian approach with abstinence and rhythm as the main methods
1950-60	**Clinical approach** • Economic models suggesting a negative relationship between population growth and development • Estimation of demographic rates and ratios • Knowledge, Attitude and Practice (KAP) studies • Research in reproduction • Clinical approach
1960-70	**Extension approach and experimentations** • Extension programme • IUCD programme • Target orientation (Third Five Year Plan) • Organizational changes
1970-80	**Camp approach** • The concept of sustainable development • Mass vasectomy camps • National level studies in family planning • First population policy statement announced • Policy under Janata Govt. asserting voluntarism
1980-90	**Cafeteria approach** • Cafeteria approach and emphasis on limitation of family size rather than on contraception • Planning in terms of NRR (with the goal of achieving NRR of unity by 1996)
1990-2000	**Target free approach** • Collection of detailed national and regional level data on population, development and well-being • Abolition of targets • Shift from national to area specific approach
2000-	**National Population Policy 2000** • National Population Policy • Unmet needs concept • A rights based approach • HIV/AIDS • Participatory approach

POPULATION POLICY STATEMENT BY DR. KARAN SINGH

Introduction

By looking at increasing rate of population growth after independence and failure of various experiments in family planning the planners became a bit panicky. In April 1976, Dr. Karan Singh, the then Minister of Health and Family Planning, announced the National Population Policy of India. This became a landmark in population policy. The full text of the policy is given below.

First Policy Statement

The first population policy draft maintained that poverty is the real enemy of the country, and the Fifth Five Year Plan (1974-79) aimed to remove the widespread abject poverty by including Minimum Needs Programme with an integrated package of health, family planning and nutrition as components. The complete text of the statement by Dr. Karan Singh, released on 16th April, 1976 is as follows:

1. With 2.4 per cent of the world's land area, India has about 15 per cent of the world's people. It is estimated that our population as on 1st January, 1976 has crossed the 600 million mark, and is now rising at the rate of well over one million per month. Since Independence 250 millions have been added, equivalent to the entire population of the Soviet Union with six times the land area of India. The increase every year is now equal to the entire population of Australia which is 2½ times the size of our country. If the per cent rate of increase continues unchecked our population at the turn of the century may well reach the staggering figure of one billion. Indisputably we are facing a population explosion of crisis dimensions which has largely diluted the fruits of the remarkable economic progress that we have made over the last two decades. If the future of the nation is to be secured, and the goal of removing poverty to be attained, the population problem will have to be treated as a top national priority and commitment.
2. Our real enemy is poverty, and it is as a frontal assault on the

citadels of poverty that the Fifth Five Year Plan has included the Minimum Needs Programme. One of its five items is integrated package of health, family planning and nutrition. Far reaching steps have been initiated to reorient the thrust of medical education so as to strengthen the community medicine and rural health aspects, and to restructure the health care delivery system on a three-tier basis going down to the most far-flung rural areas where the majority of our people reside and where child mortality and morbidity are the highest. Similarly, ignorance, illiteracy and superstition have got to be fought and eliminated. In the ultimate analysis it is only when the underlying causes of poverty and disease are eliminated that the nation will be able to move forward to its desired ideals.

3. Nonetheless it is clear that simply to wait for education and economic development to bring about a drop in fertility is not a practical solution. The very increase in population makes economic development slow and more difficult of achievement. The time factor is so pressing, and the population growth so formidable, that we have to get out of the vicious circle through a direct assault upon this problem as a national commitment. The President in his address to the Joint Session of Parliament this year reiterated the importance of stepping up family planning efforts, and the Prime Minister has on several occasions laid stress upon the crucial role that population control has to play in the movement towards economic independence and social transformation, specially in the light of the 20-Point Economic Programme.

4. Considerable work has been done in our country in the field of family planning but clearly only the fringe of the problem has so far been touched. In this context, after a thorough and careful consideration of all the factors involved as well as the expression of a wide spectrum of public opinion, Government have decided on a series of fundamental measures detailed below which, it is hoped, will enable us to achieve the planned target of reducing the birth rate from an estimated 35 per thousand in the beginning of the Fifth Plan to 25 per thousand at the end of the Sixth. Allowing for the steady decline in the death rate that will continue due to the

improvement in our medical and public health services and the living standards of our people, this is expected to bring down the growth rate of population in our country to 1.4 per cent by 1984.

5. Raising the age of marriage will not only have a demonstrable demographic impact, but will also lead to more responsible parenthood and help to safeguard the health of the mother and the child. It is well known that very early pregnancy leads to higher maternal and infant mortality. Also, if the women of our country are to play their rightful role in its economic, social and intellectual life, the practice of early marriage will have to be severely discouraged. The present law has not been effectively or uniformly enforced. It has, therefore, been decided that the minimum age of marriage should be raised to 18 for girls and 21 for boys, and suitable legislation to this effect will be passed. Offences under this law will be cognizable by an officer not below the rank of Sub-Divisional Magistrate. The question of making registration of marriages compulsory is under active consideration.
6. It has been represented by some states that while on the one hand we are urging them to limit their population, those states which do well in this field face reduction of representation in Parliament while those with weak performance in family planning tend to get increasing representation. It is obviously necessary to remedy this situation. It has, therefore, been decided that the representation in the Lok Sabha and the State Legislatures will be frozen on the basis of the 1971 Census until the year 2001. This means in effect that the census counts of 1981 and 1991 will not be considered for purposes of adjustment of Lok Sabha Legislature Seats. Necessary constitutional amendment will be brought forward during the current year. Appropriate legislation for other elective bodies will also be undertaken.
7. In a federal system, the sharing of Central resources with the States is a matter of considerable importance. In all cases where population is a factor as in the allocation of Central assistance to State Plans, devolution of taxes and duties and grants-in-aid, the population figures of 1971 will continue to be followed till the year 2001. In the matter of Central

assistance to State Plans, eight per cent will be specifically earmarked against performance in family planning. The detailed procedures in this regard will be worked out by the Planning Commission.

8. While there is a direct correlation between illiteracy and fertility, this is particularly marked in the case of girls' education. Wherever female literacy improves, it has been seen that fertility drops almost automatically. It is, therefore, necessary that special measures be taken to raise the levels of female education, particularly above the middle level for girls as well as non-formal education plans for young women especially in certain backward States where the family planning performance so far has been unimpressive. The same is true with regard to child nutrition programmes, as high infant mortality and morbidity have a direct bearing on fertility. The Ministry of Education is urging, upon the State Governments the necessity to give these matters higher priority than has been accorded so far and fully earmarking adequate outlays both for girls' education up to the middle level and child nutrition.
9. My Ministry is also in close touch with the Education Ministry with regard to the introduction of population values in the educational system, and the NCERT has already made a beginning in bringing out some textbooks on these lines. It is essential that the younger generations should grow up with an adequate awareness of the population problem and a realization of their national responsibility in this regard. Indeed, if I may venture to say so, exhortations to plan families are more important for the younger generations than for those who have already made their contribution to our demographic profile.
10. The adoption of a small family norm is too important a matter to be considered the responsibility of only one Ministry. It is essential that all Ministries and Departments of the Government of India as well as the States should take up as an integral part of their normal programme and budgets the motivation of citizens to adopt responsible reproductive behaviour both in their own as well as the national interest. A directive to this effect is being issued by the Prime Minister to all Ministries of the Government of India, and a letter will

also be addressed by her to all Chief Ministers. The performance of family planning in the States will be more carefully and intensively monitored than in the past, and the Union Cabinet will review the situation in depth at least once a year.

11. Experience over the last 20 years has shown that monetary compensation does have a significant impact upon the acceptance of family planning, particularly among the poorer sections of society. In view of the desirability of limiting the family size to two or three it has been decided that monetary compensation for sterilization (both male and female) will be raised to Rs. 150 if performed with two living children or less, Rs. 100 if performed with three living children and Rs. 70 if performed with four or more children. This amount will include the money payble to individual acceptors as well as other charges such as drugs and dressings, etc, and will take effect from 1st May, 1976. Facilities for sterilization and MTP are being increasingly extended to cover rural areas.

12. In addition to individual compensation, government is of the view that group incentives should now be introduced in a bold and imaginative manner so as to make family planning a mass movement with greater community involvement. It has, therefore, been decided that suitable group incentives will be introduced for the medical profession, for Zila and Panchayat Samitis, for teachers at various levels, for cooperative societies and for labour in the organized sector through their respective representative national organizations. Details of these group incentives are being worked out in consultation with the concerned organizations.

13. Despite governmental efforts at Union, State and Municipal level, family planning cannot succeed unless voluntary organizations are drawn into its promotion in an increasing measure, particularly youth and women's organizations. There is already a scheme for aiding voluntary organizations, and it has been decided that this will be expanded. Also, full rebate will be allowed in the income tax assessment for amounts given as donations for family planning purposes to government, local bodies or any registered voluntary organization approved for this purpose by the Union Ministry of Health.

14. Research in reproductive biology and contraception is underway in several of our scientific institutions, and there are some very promising developments which, we hope, will lead to a major breakthrough before too long. This is a great challenge to our scientists, and efforts in this direction will receive special attention so that necessary research inputs are ensured on a long range and continuing basis.
15. The question of compulsory sterilization has been the subject of lively public debate over the last few months. It is clear that public opinion is now ready to accept much more stringent measures for famıly planning than before. However, the administrative and medical infrastructure in many parts of the country is still not adequate to cope with the vast implications of nation-wide compulsory sterilization. We do not, therefore, intend to bring in Central legislation for this purpose, at least for the time being some States feel that the facilities available with them are adequate to meet the requirements of compulsory sterilization. We are of the view that where a State Legislature, in the exercise of its own powers, decides that the time is ripe and it is necessary to pass legislation, for compulsory sterilization, it may do so, Our advice to the States in such cases will be to bring in the limitation after three children, and to make it uniformly applicable to all Indian citizens resident in that State without distinction of caste, creed or community.
16. Some States have also introduced a series of measures directed towards their employees and other citizens in the matter of preferential allotment of houses, loans, etc. for those who have accepted family planning. In this sphere also we have decided to leave it to each individual State to introduce such measures as they consider necessary and desirable. Employees of the Union Government will be expected to adopt the small family norm and necessary changes will be made in their service/conduct rules to ensure this.
17. In order to spread the message of family planning throughout the nation, a new multi-media motivational strategy is being evolved which will utilize all the available media channels including the radio, television (specially programmes aimed directly at rural audiences), the press, films, visual displays and also include traditional folk media such as the jatra,

puppet show, folk songs and folk dances. The attempt is to move from the somewhat urban-elitist approaches of the past into a much more imaginative and vigorous rural-oriented approach. In this context my Ministry is working in close coordination with the Ministry of Information and Broadcasting, and is also trying to draw the best media talent available in the country into the structuring of the new programme.

18. This package of measures will succeed in its objective only if it receives the full and active cooperation of the people at large. It is my sincere hope that the entire nation will strongly endorse the new population policy which, as part of a multi-faceted strategy for economic development and social emancipation, is directed towards building a strong and prosperous India in the years and decades to come.

The above statement shows that raising age of marriage and women's education were part of family planning policy since the beginning. However, too much stress on sterilization and targets proved to be counterproductive. There was no need to be panicky. Family planning programme would have been much more successful if the first policy statement did not stress on sterilization with involvement of all government departments (which include even the police department).

REVISION BY JANATA PARTY

Coercion in achieving the family planning targets led to defeat of Congress (I) in the General Parliamentary Elections, and the Janata Party which won the elections by mobilizing support of the masses to oppose "sterilization programme" declared a new population policy in June 1977. It was declared that the programme of family welfare (a new name for family planning) should be entirely voluntary. The statement of the population policy declared on 29th June, 1977 is given below:

1. The President in his address to Parliament on 28.3.1977, stated that "Family planning will be pursued vigorously as a wholly voluntary programme and as an integral part of a comprehensive policy covering education, health, maternity

and child care, family welfare, women's rights and nutrition". The Prime Minister has on a number of occasions underlined the vital importance of family planning as a means of individual and national development and well being. This government is totally committed to the Family Welfare Programme and will spare no efforts to motivate the people to accept it voluntarily in their own interest and in the interest of their children as well as in the larger interest of the nation.

2. Family planning has, however, to be lifted from its old and narrow concept and given its proper place in the overall philosophy of welfare. It must embrace all aspects of family welfare, particularly those which are designed to protect and promote the health of mothers and children. It must become a part of the total concept of positive health. At the same time, it must find meaningful integration with other welfare programmes, viz. nutrition, food, clothing, shelter, availability of safe drinking water, education, employment and women's welfare. It will be our endeavour to bring about this integration in a greater degree. We expect the state to do the same.
3. The change in the name of the programme from family planning to family welfare is a reflection of the government's anxiety to promote, through it, the total welfare of the family and the community. It is our intention to take the programme forward in the real sense as an investment in man. We wish to make it abundantly clear that in this task there is no room for compulsion, coercion or pressure of any sort. Compulsion, in the area of family welfare must be ruled out for all times to come. Our approach is educational and wholly voluntary. There will, however, be no slackening of our efforts in this direction.
4. The government attaches the highest importance to the dignity of the citizen and to his right to determine the size of his family. We have no doubt that by and large the people of India are conscious of the importance of responsible parenthood; given the necessary information and adequate services, they will accept the small family norms. We will promote all methods with equal emphasis and it will be left to every family to decide what method of contraception it will like to adopt. Employees of the Union Government, State Governments, autonomous bodies, local bodies, etc. will be

expected to set an example and to adopt the small family norm.

5. We are totally against any legislation for compulsory sterilization either at the Central level or by the States. Sterilization, both of male and female, is a terminal method and suitable for those couples who have reached the optimum family size. Services for sterilization will be offered free of cost to those who voluntarily wish to adopt this method. Similarly other services under the programme will be available to the people free of charge. The acceptance of voluntary sterilization and IUD involves to and fro travel to a clinic, a brief stay in the hospital resulting in possible loss of wages which the majority of our people cannot easily afford. In view of this, it has been decided to retain the provision for monetary compensation. Any medical complication resulting from a voluntary sterilization operation will be attended to free of cost; and if in an unfortunate case recanalization becomes necessary, this facility will also be offered to the individual concerned under the best possible professional care without any charge.
6. Nearly 80 per cent of our population lives in villages. Medical services are not able to reach them in an effective way. An integrated rural health scheme is on the anvil and will be implemented shortly. It is of the utmost importance that adequate antenatal, natal and postnatal care is made available to pregnant mothers. To this end a comprehensive scheme of training of indigenous mid-wives (dais) will be implemented. Under it maternity services will be made available to all mothers, who may need them. The programme of immunizing children against common disease such as a whooping cough, diphtheria and tetanus will be expanded further. We expect that the State Governments wiil give necessary cooperation and assistance in this direction.
7. The direct correlation between illiteracy and fertility and between infant/maternal mortality and the age at marriage is well established by demographic studies. While on the one hand the government will pursue its policy of according high priority to the improvement of women's educational level, both through formal and non-formal channels, it will also

bring legislation for raising the minimum age of marriage for girls to 18 and for boys to 21.

8. In a federal system, the sharing of Central resources with the States is a matter of considerable importance. In all cases where population is a factor as in the allocation of Central assistance to State plans, devolution of taxes and duties and grants-in-aid, the population figures of 1971 will continue to be followed till the year 2001. Family planning and population control is a subject in the Concurrent List, yet the implementation of the Family Welfare Programme is very much the responsibility of State Government. Assistance for the implementation of the Programme is provided by the Central Government to the States on cent-per-cent basis. In order to ensure a purposeful implementation of the Family Welfare Programme the principle of linking 8 per cent of Central Assistance to the State Plans with their performance and success in Family Welfare Programme will be continued.
9. Population education has so far not received the attention it deserves. The NCERT have developed some models for the introduction of population education in the school education system. These models have already been adopted by the Central School Organization. We would urge that the departments of education in the States should adopt these models, or their modified versions, in the syllabus in the schools. Forty-two per cent of our population is below the age of 15 years. It is this population which will soon be entering in the area of matrimony. We must take steps without any further delay to see that the youth receive population education as part of their normal courses of study.
10. The population of India has been increasing at the rate of about one million every month. It has increased by nearly 270 million since 1977 and is today estimated to be 615 million. If the present rate of growth continues, we will be touching the one-billion mark by the end of the century. This rate has to be arrested. The birth rate targets of 30 and 25 per thousand by the end of the Fifth and Sixth Plans, respectively can be achieved only with the total and willing participation of the community in the family welfare programme. For this purpose it is important that all media of publicity including motivation through the extension approach, should be utilized

fully by the Central and the State Governments. We should very much expect that just as at the Centre we have involved all media units of the Ministry of Information and Broadcasting in the motivational campaigns, in the States also the State Departments of Public Relations and other departments having their own publicity set-ups would be totally associated with the motivational efforts.

11. It is of equal importance that trade unions, chambers of commerce, cooperative societies, organizations of women, federations of teachers, village panchayats and all other institutions which can influence public opinion should be associated intimately with the educational campaigns. The village panchayats can play a significant role in this task. Their potential as change-agents needs to receive greater recognition and attention.
12. No programme will succeed unless voluntary organizations particularly youth and women's organizations participate in its implementation fully and extensively. So far this participation has been very limited. The government wishes to invite the suggestions of voluntary organizations and such public bodies as are engaged in the general task of Family Welfare for evolving suitable patterns of cooperation and assistance. Full rebate will be allowed in the income tax assessment for amounts given as donations for Family Welfare purposes to government, local bodies, or any registered voluntary organization approved for this purpose by the Union Ministry of Health.
13. While the existing methods of contraception will continue to be available to the people, it is important that the search for newer methods should be intensified. The government will give special attention to the necessary research inputs in the field of reproductive biology and contraception.
14. The programme and the approach for implementation of the Family Welfare Programme as outlined in the above paragraphs will succeed only if there is willing cooperation from all in full measure. The Family Welfare Programme embraces all the principal areas of human welfare. It will be wrong to leave it only to the Ministry of Health and Family Welfare in the Centre and their counterparts in the States. It is essential that all Ministries and Departments of the

> Government of India as well as of the States give due importance to this Programme and work for its furtherance. The performance of Family Welfare in the States will be intensively and carefully monitored and the Union Cabinet will review the situation in depth at least once a year. Suitable machinery for ensuring coordination with other connected programmes of welfare may be set up in States also.

As far as the major issues of population policy are concerned there was little change in the thinking except that it clarified that coercion would not be used for sterilization. Unfortunately, this created the impression that government was no more serious about family planning programme and for several years the statistics of achievement remained dismal. The family planning acceptance reduced to bottom line. The Indian case shows clearly that in democracy overenthusiasm in running a government programme can often boomerang. One has to go slowly and understand the grassroots processes and ideas of people. Even the large middle class did not appreciate coercion in family planning though it was all for promotion of small family size norm. It took many years before the politicians and bureaucrats could dare talk about importance of family planning programme in India again. It may be noted here that the above two statements were laid on the Table of the House in Parliament, but never discussed or adopted

NATIONAL POPULATION POLICY (NPP) 2000

In year 2000 Government of India passed the National Population Policy (NPP) 2000. It emphasized need for promotion of contraceptives once again but as a matter of choice, and in a target free environment. By this time planners had realized that target oriented approach leads to poor quality performance and cooking up of statistical data. It does not help. Those who want to limit family size are anyway doing this. Development aspirations have made people quite conscious about the need for limiting family size. The programme must particularly focus on meeting the unmet needs, i.e., providing services to those who do not want more children but have not found a suitable method. They must be provided required services. To quote:

> The National Population Policy, 2000 (NPP 2000) affirms the

commitment of government towards voluntary and informed choice and consent of citizens while availing of reproductive health care services, and continuation of the target free approach in administering family planning services. The NPP 2000 provides a policy framework for advancing goals and prioritizing strategies during the next decade, to meet the reproductive and child health needs of the people of India, and to achieve net replacement levels (TFR) by 2010. It is based upon the need to simultaneously address issues of child survival, maternal health, and contraception, while increasing outreach and coverage of a comprehensive package of reproductive and child heath services by government, industry and the voluntary non-government sector, working in partnership.

Box 10.2 presents the national socio-demographic goals for 2010.

Box 10.2: National Socio-Demographic Goals for 2010

- Address the unmet needs for basic reproductive and child health services, supplies and infrastructure.
- Make school education up to age 14 free and compulsory, and reduce drop outs at primary and secondary school levels to below 20 per cent for both boys and girls.
- Reduce infant mortality rate to below 30 per 1000 live births.
- Reduce maternal mortality ratio to below 100 per 100,000 live births.
- Achieve universal immunization of children against all vaccine preventable diseases.
- Promote delayed marriage for girls, not earlier than age 18 and preferably after 20 years of age.
- Achieve 80 per cent institutional deliveries and 100 per cent deliveries by trained persons.
- Achieve universal access to information/counselling, and services for fertility regulation and contraception with a wide basket of choices.
- Achieve 100 per cent registration of births, deaths, marriage and pregnancy.
- Contain the spread of Acquired Immuno Deficiency Syndrome (AIDS), and promote greater integration between the management of Reproductive Tract Infections (RTI) and Sexually Transmitted Infections (STI) and the National AIDS Control Organisation.
- Prevent and control communicable diseases.
- Integrate Indian Systems of Medicine (ISM) in the provision of reproductive and child health services, and in reaching out to households.
- Promote vigorously the small family norm to achieve replacement levels of TFR.
- Bring about convergence in implementation of related social sector programmes so that family welfare becomes a people centred programme.

In order to achieve the above goals Population Commission has identified 12 strategic themes. These are given below:

(i) Decentralised planning and programme implementation
(ii) Convergence of service delivery at village levels
(iii) Empowering women for improved health and nutrition
(iv) Child health and survival
(v) Meeting the unmet needs for family welfare services in urban and rural areas
(vi) Meeting the unmet needs for family welfare services specially among urban slums, tribal communities, hill area populations and displaced and migrant populations, and adolescents, and securing increased participation of men in planned parenthood
(vii) Diverse health care providers
(viii) Collaboration with and commitments from Non-Governmental Organisations and the private sector
(ix) Mainstreaming Indian systems of medicine and homeopathy
(x) Contraceptive technology and research on reproductive and child health
(xi) Contraceptive technology and research on reproductive and child health
(xii) Information, education, and communication.

It is clear that in 2000 there was a paradigm shift in population policy. The NPP 2000 has made family welfare a new responsibility of village panchayats. They are expected to develop area specific, needs based approaches to reproductive health services. It is believed that empowerment of women—political, economic and social—would strengthen this process further. The new policy suggests preparing need-based, demand driven, socio-demographic plans at the village level, aimed at identifying and providing responsive, people-centred and integrated, basic reproductive and child health care.

> The panchayats should seek the help of community opinion makers to communicate the benefits of smaller, healthier families, the significance of educating girls, and promoting female participation in paid employment. They should also involve civil society in monitoring the availability, accessibility and affordability of services and supplies.

NPP 2000 recognizes the importance of improving maternal mortality. It says:

> Maternal mortality is not merely a health disadvantage, it is a matter of social injustice. Low social and economic status of girls and women limits their access to education, good nutrition, as well as money to pay for health care and family planning services. The extent of maternal mortality is an indicator of disparity and inequity in access to appropriate health care and nutrition services throughout a lifetime, and particularly during pregnancy and child-birth, and is a crucial factor contributing to high maternal mortality.

NPP 2000 also recognizes the role of Ayurveda, Yoga, Unani, Siddh and Homeopathy systems of medicine (AYUSH) and the role of private practitioners and traditional healers though it is felt that "mobilising the private (profit and non-profit) sector to serve public health goals raises governance issues of contracting, accreditation, regulation, referral, besides the appropriate division of labour between the public and private health providers, all of which need to be addressed carefully". Ultimately the goal is to reach the people and promote low cost health care, specially the vulnerable sections of society such as urban slums, tribal communities, hill area populations and displaced and migrant populations, and adolescents.

The new policy also provides space to the conventional strategic themes dealing with contraception, and Information, Education and Communication (IEC) which are to play an important role in states where family planning acceptance is low and total fertility rate continues to be high.

Operational Strategies

To strengthen health services in the country Ministry of Health and Family Welfare has launched National Rural Health Mission 2005-12. The mission aims at providing improved health services by strengthening health facilities at various levels, creating Accredited Social Health Activists (ASHA) at the grassroots (village) level, providing untied funds to village panchayats, implementation of village health plan, and focusing on 18 special focus states. ASHAs have the following major responsibilities:

- Identify pregnant woman as a beneficiary of the scheme and report or facilitate registration for ANC
- Assist the pregnant woman to obtain necessary certifications wherever necessary,
- Provide and/or help the women in receiving at least three ANC checkups, TT injections, and IFA tablets
- Identify a functional Government health centre or an accredited private health institution for referral and delivery
- Counsel for institutional delivery
- Escort the beneficiary women to the pre-determined health centre and stay with her till the woman is discharged
- Arrange to immunize the newborn till the age of 14 weeks
- Inform about the birth or death of the child or mother to the ANM/MO
- Postnatal visit within 7 days of delivery to track mother's health after delivery and facilitate in obtaining care, wherever necessary
- Counsel for initiation of breastfeeding to the newborn within one-hour of delivery and its continuance till 3-6 months and promote family planning.

ASHAs are playing a vital role in improving institutional deliveries in rural areas. This should improve maternal health (particularly by reducing anaemia) and reduce maternal mortality ratio, infant mortality rate, child mortality rate and child morbidity. Yet fieldwork done by the author reveals that ASHAs are not happy with their role. In Vaishali and Muzaffarpur districts of Bihar they wanted to be identified as *Nirasha* (frustrated) rather than *Asha* (hope). There is a need to look into their problems.

Critical Evaluation of NPP

As said above, NPP 2000 has produced a paradigm shift in thinking on population issues. It has a rights based approach and aims at empowering women and vulnerable communities. Nobody has an issue with that. However, especially in the context of NRHM 2005-12, and Janani Suraksha Yojana, 2006 some believe that it has to some extent halted the declining trend in fertility in low performing states. The members of poor and vulnerable communities who get money for deliveries in the health facility are no more motivated to limit family size. To produce a baby is to get 1400 rupees in low performance states and 700 rupees (for BPL only) in high performing states plus money for transport which is much above the incentive or compensation for sterilization. Doctors at PHC say that people are more interested in producing babies than in family planning. Census of India 2001 figures suggest that this fear was not true.will tell whether these fears came true.

Increase in institutional deliveries has also put a lot of pressure on health officials and health facilities. Staff position and health infrastructure have not changed but number of deliveries has increased fast. This has led to deterioration in quality of services at most places. The staff is overworked, their number must be increased. More medicines, space, theatre facilities and equipment and materials need to be made available.

Lastly, it has to be stressed that so far all efforts have been made to reduce fertility. And this has certainly produced results. Several states have below or just replacement level fertility and others are experiencing declining fertility. If India also witnesses the second demographic transition and its fertility goes below the replacement level on a long term basis it will also suffer from aging, a risk afflicting the industrially advanced economies of the world. That means one has to think about achieving optimum levels of fertility rather than low fertility.

QUESTIONS AND EXERCISES

1. What is the history of family planning programme in India? Why did the planners start with Gandhian approach to family planning?
2. Distinguish between:
   a. clinical approach and extension education approach
   b. knowledge, attitude and practice of family planning
   c. target oriented approach and target free approach
   d. terminal and spacing methods
   e. the concepts of family planning and family welfare
3. Study the two population policy statements, one issued by Dr. Karan Singh, another by Janata Government. Identify major similarities and dissimilarities between the two.
4. Discuss the salient findings of National Population Policy 2000.

5. Why do some people who do not want another child are not using family planning methods?
6. Would you say that family planning programme in India has failed?
7. What are national socio-demographic goals for 2010? Are they achievable?
8. Should we plan for declining fertility only or start thinking about optimum fertility? What will happen if fertility continues to decline in all parts of India?
9. What was Dr. Karan Singh's position on making sterilization compulsory? What went wrong with that?
10. Define multi-media motivational strategy in family planning? How would that help?

REFERENCES

Dyson, Tim, 2003, India's Population: Past, Present and Future, The Pravin Visaria Public Lecture, delivered at Gujarat Institute of Development Research, Conference Hall of the Ahmedabad Management Association on March 4.

Government of India, 2009, Janani Suraksha Yojana, *http://mohfw.nic.in/dofw%20website/JSY_features_FAQ_Nov_2006.htm* [accessed on 24th December, 2009].

Government of India, 2009, National Rural Health Mission, *http://www.mohfw.nic.in/NRHM.htm*.

National Commission on Population, 2000, *National Population Policy 2000*, *http://populationcommission.nic.in/npp_intro.htm* [accessed on 19th November, 2009].

Sharma, A.K., 1985, *Social Inequality and Demographic Processes*. Delhi: Mittal Publications.

11

Ecological Degradation and Environmental Pollution

POPULATION AND SUSTAINABLE DEVELOPMENT

Introduction

Population has very close connection with environment. Experience shows that the relationship between population and environment is reciprocal: both population and environment affect each other. Yet it was in the second half of the twentieth century that the relationship between population and environment got serious attention of economists, sociologists and demographers who began exploring various linkages between population and environment. Earlier, population was linked more with economic development than with environment. In sociology the works on environment follow mostly one of the two lines of thought:

- Sociology of environment; and
- Environmental sociology

Sociologists of environment examine how social structure affects the environment, i.e., resource use, resource depletion, environmental pollution, climate change and access to various community resources. They also study environmental movements broadly covered under the aegis of neo-social movements. Their studies focus on local and global issues raised by the environmental movements and draw attention to the fact that all social classes participate in the movements. Sociologists of environment also look into organizational structure of the movements, motivation, successes and impact. On the other hand environmental sociologists took a neo-Durkheimian view of society and maintain that environment is a major factor in determing the social structure. This chapter attempts to expose students to certain basic concepts in environment studies in sociology such as the concept of sustainable development, population-environment link and environmental movements.

Complex Linkages

The two approaches mentioned above examine the same relationship but in the two the dependent and independent variables are interchanged. There are also some who do not accept separation between man and nature as logical categories. In their view, over centuries human ingenuity has constantly been working on nature, modifying it, assigning new meanings to nature, assigning new meanings to humanness itself, and redefining the relationship between man and nature. In the age of genetic engineering, use of techniques of molecular cloning and transformation to alter the structure and characteristics of genes directly how one can define the term natural? To quote:

> We inhabit a triangular world of society (including human biological existence), cultivated nature and non-cultivated nature. Interactions between them are also triangular. Impacts occur (in either direction) between non-cultivated nature and cultivated nature, between society (pollution, construction, irrigation) and non-cultivated nature (earthquakes, viruses and so on) and between human biological and social existence and both cultivated and non-cultivated nature (Harvey *et al.*, 2002,1).

Which view among the two is more conducive to study population-environment link?

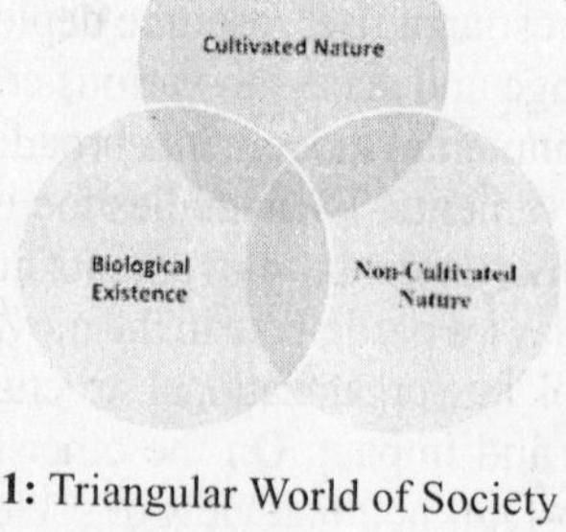

Figure 11.1: Triangular World of Society and Nature

At the empirical level linking population and environment is quite problematic because both population and environment refer to vectors of different conditions and complex processes. Population variables refer to size, growth rate, composition, structure, fertility, mortality, migration, etc. Environment factors refer to quality of air, water, soil, sound, minerals, agricultural and forest produce, and various types of pollutants with ill defined levels of permissible toxicity. Obviously, the effect of size of population on proximate variables of development may quantitatively and qualitatively differ from effect of aging on the same. Similarly the effect of climatic change on birth rate will be different from its effect on migration and occupational mobility.

In this section we focus more on the connection between population processes and sustainable development. It may be noted that the concept of sustainable development combines the concept of development as well as the concept of environmental quality.

What is Sustainable Development?

The idea of sustainable development is simple. All of us want development. There is no doubt about that. Yet, we also want that development should be sustained and the fruits of development should be available to all including the most vulnerable sections of society and the next generations. Development with benefits confined to some and to members of the present generation only may be called development but not sustainable development. In this framework, development needs to be subjected to the test of sustainability and sociologists have to go beyond the effect of population growth on savings, capital and growth rate of income. They must centre on social development.

Yet the term social development has been used in multivocal sense having multiple meanings. Sustainability has been conceptualized in several ways. The dictionary meaning of the word "sustainable" is that it is a thing that can be kept up, maintained or prolonged. Thus sustainable development may be defined as that process of development which can last. *The State of World Population 1992,* the report prepared by United Nations Population Fund quotes the following definitions of sustainable development:

(a) Sustainable development is development that meets the needs of the present without compromising the ability of future generations to meet their own needs.... Living standards that go beyond the basic minimum are sustainable only if consumption standards everywhere have regard for long-term sustainability (Brundtland Commission, 1987).

(b) Sustainable development.... involves providing a bequest to the next generation which is at least equal to that inherited by the current generation (*Blueprint for a Green Economy*, 1989).

(c) Development that distributes the benefits of economic progress more equitably, protects both local and global environments for future generations, and truly improves the quality of life (in *Our Own Agenda*, by Inter-American Development Bank, 1990).

(d) Sustainable development means improving the quality of human life while living within the carrying capacity of supporting ecosystems. A "sustainable economy" maintains its natural resource base. It can continue to develop by adapting and through improvements in knowledge, organization, technical efficiency, and wisdom (in *Caring for the Earth*, IUCN and WWF, 1991).

Beginning with the famous work of Meadows and others sponsored by the Club of Rome in 1972, entitled *The Limits to Growth,* among intellectuals and planners a feeling grew that the ongoing developmental processes are limited by their own results, and, therefore, the economic growth cannot be sustained for long. Before this, Forrester had argued how factors such as crowding, pollution, food supply, and natural resources cannot only bring the exponential population growth to halt but they can also lead to sudden and tragic collapse of population. This provided support to Malthusian credence and created the idea that development not accompanied by population control would threaten human survival in the long-run, both in the developed and developing countries. At this point natural resources (later called natural capital) rather than capital became central to environmental discourse. Studies established that development is neither a universal nor an irreversible process.

We need a type of development that does not lead to depletion of renewable resources, such as water and soil, forests and fisheries, and non-renewable resources, such as minerals. This raises a number of questions about:

- Values regarding desired levels and structure of development
- Welfare of future generations vs. welfare of present generation
- Relationship between man and environment
- Role and responsibility of science and technology
- Rising aspirations for development and modernization in the less developed countries
- Role of market in environmental degradation
- Notions of equality and justice
- Role of institutions in environmental protection.

For development to be sustainable there are three major options: (a) a check on the scale of living; (b) changeover from manufacturing to service as service sector consumes less natural resources than manufacturing; and (c) new technological developments to conserve resources, which raise their productivity and reduce pollution. Yet, some economists feel that the case of limits to growth is overstated and as such the possibility of extinction is remote. Culture and institutions can go a long way to protect environment. They can also contribute to disaster management and handling trauma caused by man made or natural disasters.

Divergent Views

There are very divergent views on environment, ranging from the view that development has not caused any threatening environment problem for humanity to the view that there is a need for urgent action. To quote Davis (1990) whose ideas reflect the first view:

> Thus the grizzly truth may turn out to be that limits are more prophetic than its detractors and even some of its defenders thought possible. In fact during the last three decades several basic developments have occurred that together amount to a revolution in environmental concerns. First, the sheer number of discoveries of environmental problems has increased precipitously; second, the long-term seriousness of the problems has been increasingly recognized as more of the consequences of growth are felt; third, many problems formerly thought to be local in character are in fact global or near-global in scope; fourth, the involvement of science in

> understanding the causes of environmental change has increased rapidly; and fifth, the international scope of environmental damages has led inevitably to strong demands for conservationist policies.

On the other extreme, Keyfitz (1991) stressed that now we have to recognize the ozone layer, carbon dioxide in the atmosphere, extinction of species, waste, and desertification. At high levels of income and technological development the effects of changes in economic and demographic variables on the ecosphere are great and cannot be neglected. Keyfitz (1990) articulates that the world is changing. "Communication, the conquest of space, computing, the new cellular biology, atomic physics, were indeed changing the world at exactly the time when economists discovered human capital". Yet, he differs frôm Davis on accounts of five factors: (a) non-linearity and non-substitutability of resources availability; (b) capital setting limits of economic progress; (c) structural bottlenecks in employment generation; (d) greater recognition of the fact that economy is set within the ecology; and (e) awareness of warming of the biosphere.

Differences in Perception between Developed and Developing Countries

There are serious differences in perception of sustainable development between developed and developing countries. Developing countries want to catch up with the developed countries. They too want high scale of living. They suspect that the very talk of environmental problems is essentially an instrument of debarring them from raising their standards to the level of developed countries. Developing countries like India feel that poverty rather than overdevelopment is the cause of environmental problems in the less developed countries. To quote:

> With the realization that poverty and the state of underdevelopment led to many of the environmental problems that confronted the nation, came the understanding that it was more rapid development that was the best approach. This development has to benefit people (and particularly the poor) by providing for their basic human needs and rising aspirations. Thus, many of the developmental programmes and …., could

indeed be termed as environmental management programmes (Govt. of India, 1985).

It has to be understood clearly that sustainable development is not a strategy of development. It is a goal or a vision. And this vision has been articulated differently in different contexts. To be of practical utility it has to be operationalized in specific contexts. It sensitizes us to the fact that the rich and the poor, the present and the future, cities and countryside, industry and agriculture, and man and nature are inseparable and they are linked with each other through complex socio-economic, cultural, biological and political chains. The concept of sustainable development stresses that the long-run welfare of a community depends heavily on the quality of surrounding environment and welfare of the other communities.

Strategies

Now you may ask: what are all the strategies possible if a country wants to go for sustainable development? The World Bank (1992) suggested a three-fold strategy for meeting the challenge of sustainable development. They are:

(a) Build on the positive links. Growth of income promotes efficient use of resources, technology transfer, market and investment in environment improvement. Poverty removal reduces population growth and provides resources and knowledge to enable the poor to take a long range view of development.

(b) Break the negative links. Incentives, environment policies and institutions building are necessary to guarantee sustainability. Mere improvement in income and capacity to solve environment problems are not sufficient.

(c) Clarify and manage the uncertain links. Knowledge generation is important to know new relationship between man and environment and effective management of resources.

The above description of strategies is useful but is abstract. It has to be operationalized in terms of indicators and processes, which will differ from country to country.

ROLE OF POPULATION IN MODELS OF SUSTAINABLE DEVELOPMENT

Effect of Population on Sustainable Development

Population size and demographic processes as intricately linked with sustainable development though population is not the only source of environmental crisis. Mode of social organization and technological development also affect a society's potential to develop in a sustainable manner. High rate of growth of population not only raises the demand for natural resources, it also affects most of those proximate variables which hamper the sustainability of development, e.g. organization of production, innovations, technological developments, politics, values and market forces. Population processes also affect the other indicators of sustainability such as equality, justice, absence of abject poverty, and greater participation of people in development.

In the less developed countries where population growth rates are high, and particularly in those countries where density of population is also high, the possibility of raising carrying capacities of scarce land resources (i.e. the maximum numbers that resources can support) is low, and alternative employment opportunities are limited, people would be forced to exploit natural resources without regard for future. Here people are forced to expand agricultural lands into unsuited areas, enlarge the size of their herds of livestock, and outmigrate to other areas. Ironically, the less developed countries also have low caring capacity, i.e., "the social, developmental and institutional variables that underpin the ability of institutions to cope with environmental stresses" (UNFPA, 2009).

Population growth leads to fragmentation of land, and causes low productivity, unemployment and reduced supply of fodder. People may respond to low farm productivity by increasing the number of livestock. Then the agricultural expansion and growth of livestock destroy the forests and pastures. They also cause soil erosion and thus ecological imbalance. As a matter of fact population growth, poor economic conditions, deforestation, soil desiccation and ecological imbalance tend to reinforce each other through dynamic multi-cyclic structures.

According to Demeny (1990), a significant change in the demographic parameters is found to cause shifts in relationships between population, income and resource-use intensity, sometimes compensating and sometimes reinforcing the environmental impact. To quote:

> In particular, over time non-linearties to scale may appear. Quantitative increases can generate qualitative changes; thresholds separating, for example, tolerable levels of pollution from levels that generate unacceptable risks for human health may be crossed. Up to a certain level, damage to a renewable resource such as a forest ecosystem, may be corrected by a spontaneous and relatively rapid biological process; beyond that level the damage may be irreparable, or the natural recovery or the human-engineered repair of the ecosystem in question may require a very long time or entail exorbitant cost.

In simple language, the relationship between population and environment is not amenable to one simple formulation. Population dynamics may offset or catalyze the effect of population size on environment. It depends on a number of socio-economic, political, cultural, technological and environmental factors. It also depends on whether we are focusing at micro level or macro level. Imagine that due to increase in family size in moderate fertility context there is a division of land, and in per capita terms the family becomes poorer. The family may respond by increasing fertility with the aim of diversification of economic activities and benefiting from division of labour and offset the negative effect of population growth on development. The family may also increase fertility without having the possibility of raising income and the negative impact of population may be reinforced. In the same way there are different possibilities for societies and nations. In absence of capital they may decide to substitute capital by labour and thus ignore or encourage high fertility. They may benefit from this strategy. They may simply increase fertility due to religious, cultural or political reasons. Then they suffer more. Ironically, some of the poorest countries of the world have high fertility levels though the consideration of externalities would suggest that they must limit family size.

Effect of Adopting Sustainable Development Strategies on Population

Sustainable development strategies too affect population growth. In literature on population role of demographic factors in development has been greatly explored, but the role of sustainable development in population management is less understood. In 1987 the World Commission on Environment and Development—the Brundtland Commission—urged that "all should keep in mind that sustainable economic growth and equitable access to resources are two of the most certain routes towards lower fertility rates." The State of World Population 1993 has clearly demonstrated that more often than not international migration has been caused by environmental disruption; sustainable development and environmental planning therefore needs control of migration.

Part of the difficulty in treating sustainable development as a determinant of demographic processes arises from the fact that there is no single blueprint of sustainability. Economic and social systems differ widely among countries. Thus although sustainable development has become a global objective, each nation will have to work out its own concrete policy. Also in the different regions of the world the nature of population problems is different. The developed countries are in general characterized by low death rates, low infant mortality rate, below replacement fertility, near zero or negative growth rate, high percentage urban and the problem of population implosion. The less developed countries are in general characterized by moderate but falling death rate, falling infant mortality rate, high growth rate, low percentage urban and the problem of population explosion. Several countries in both developed and less developed categories have unique demographic situation and they do not conform to the generalized pattern. Sustainable development policies may have both desirable and undesirable consequences in both developed and developing countries. Generalized connections may not exist. Each country requires its own response to population processes as well own strategies for sustainable development.

At the same time we may say that although there is a strong theoretical linkage between sustainable development and population, sustainable development is neither a necessary nor a sufficient condition for effective population management. The reverse is equally true. Falling birth rates have also not been associated with better environmental management. It may be emphasized that both the developed and the less developed countries will have to work on sustainable development and population simultaneously.

Total Environmental Impact

The total impact on the environment is determined by interaction of three factors: size of population, consumption standards, and wastages of resources for each unit of consumption (UNFPA, 1992).

$$\text{Impact} = \text{Population} \times \text{Consumption Per Person} \times \text{Technology Effect}$$

The above formula shows that the total impact on environment depends not only on population but also on consumption per capita and technology. Environment will be least disturbed if:

- Population is growing at a slower rather than a faster rate
- Consumption per capita is less, i.e., people exercise restraint on consumption
- Technology is environment saving rather than environment degrading

And environment will be most degraded if:

- Population is growing at a faster rather than a slower rate
- Consumption per capita is uncontrolled
- Technology is environment degrading rather than environment saving.

The above equation explains why the developed countries are more responsible for environmental damage despite the fact that they have lower population and more advanced (often environment friendly) technology. China, United States and European Union (EU) contribute to more than half of the carbon dioxide emission (56.25%) though their share in the would population is only around 30 per cent. United States has only 4.61 per cent of the world population but its contribution to cumulative carbon dioxide emissions from fossil fuels in year 2007 is 19.91 per cent. Same is the case with EU with 14.04 per cent contribution to carbon dioxide though it has only 7.3 per cent of the world population. India has 17.5 per cent of the world population but its contribution to cumulative carbon dioxide emissions from fossil fuels is only 5.24 per cent (CDIAC, 2008). It is notable that although the developing countries are far behind the developed countries in income and consumption but they are increasingly developing the philosophy of development based on the experience of the developed countries. Their population and consumption behaviour are changing fast and as they produced sudden population explosion in the second half of the last century they may cause a serious damage to the ecological system before developing the environmental consciousness.

Environment Impact Analysis

For legal and ethical reasons, now it has become quite common to go for environment impact analysis of a development project. The concept of environment impact analysis suggests that an economic project has a definite environmental impact and it is important to know what it is. Imagine that we establish a thermal power station in a tribal area. It certainly has economic benefits. But it also has some adverse impacts. Sometimes even desirable development projects such as dams and canals have impacts on population and society. Irrigation canals have helped in improving agricultural productivity and diversification and led to multiple cropping in several parts of Rajasthan but this has also created new problems. In the earlier days when they had water scarcity life was certainly difficult. Now threat to physical survival is reduced but risks have increased manifold. They include malaria, social conflicts, violence and dissatisfaction due to rising aspirations. It is important to know before establishing a project what its impacts are.

The impacts may be in various forms:

- Demographic impacts—measured in terms of population size, growth rate, density of population, birth rate, death rate, infant mortality rate, maternal mortality ratio, life expectancy, aging, sex ratio, etc.
- Economic impacts—measured in terms of employment and unemployment rate, per capita income, per capita expenditure, per cent expenditure on food items, per cent employed in the formal sector, per cent below poverty line, wealth index, per cent living in pucca house, etc.
- Social impacts—school enrolment rate, literacy rate, per cent migrants, ethnic diversity, degree of social integration, empowerment of women and other vulnerable groups, social capital or social support, trust, spirit of voluntarism, degree of alienation, etc.

- Political impact—political participation, political schisms, voting behaviour, etc.
- Governance—fairness in implementing various schemes, efficiency and effectiveness, transparency, etc.
- Quality of environment—measured in terms of presence of different types of toxic elements in air and water, noise, climatic changes, etc.

It may be noted that the above impacts do not exhaust the impacts of projects, some of which are positive, some negative. Impact assessment theories require improvement in measurements and data, and greater consensus regarding standards of toxic elements that are humanly safe, looking at both what the experts believe and what the people say.

ENVIRONMENTAL BELIEFS

Beliefs

Beliefs are by definition the assumptions regarding relationships between two things. Thus the term environmental beliefs refers to people's assumptions regarding causes and consequences of environmental problems and what strategies are going to succeed in short term and long term. It has been found that in polluted/contaminated environments people suffer not only from the physical effect of pollutants/contaminants but they also suffer from various misconceptions and stigma (Swarnakar and Sharma, 2009).

Study of beliefs is important for two reasons:

1. People may hold ecological (pro-environmental) beliefs and undertake action to prevent destruction of natural environment or they may hold an anthropocentric/instrumental belief that nature can be incessantly exploited for human ends. Some may hold a belief in between the two. The beliefs affect their action and, therefore, in the study of environmental action it is important to study belief systems.
2. In the risk areas where people suffer from the physical effects of environmental hazards the effects are socio-culturally interpreted. It is found that social stigmatization among the victims and discrimination against them can lead to extreme

instability in the social life and social harmony and social capital are eroded (Box 11.1). People tend to neglect the health problem until and unless it manifests visibly or becomes unbearable.

Box 11.1: Consequences of Arsenic Contamination

...people with arsenic suffer from stigma. Sometimes arsenic patients are identified as leprosy patients and are ostracized unkindly by society. The victims are abandoned not only by larger society but also by their relatives and family members. Children of arsenic patients are not allowed to attend social and religious functions as they are believed to have inherited a serious problem (something like leprosy) which might manifest anytime and may be transferred to others. This phenomenon is similar to that observed in cases of HIV positive people in various parts of the country.

(Quoted from Swarnakar and Sharma, 2009)

In India there is a dearth of studies on environmental beliefs. There is a need to explore environmental beliefs in diverse settings so that appropriate Information, Education and Communication (IEC) activities can be initiated. Social demographers with their competence to handle data in sociological frameworks can contribute a lot in this area. In one such effort, Swarnakar and Sharma (2011) have explored environmental beliefs in India using New Environmental Paradigm scale.

Sources of Beliefs

It is a truism that to protect the environment and also to save people from suffering the physical and cultural results of hazards it is important to change their belief systems. This is not an easy job. We have to learn about nature and sources of beliefs using both the textual view and the field view. There are many sources of beliefs in general and environmental beliefs in particular. They include:

- Folk wisdom, religious texts and religious organizations
- Education
- Media (newspapers, magazines, TV, radio, etc.)
- International and internal migration, increasing mobility of population and pilgrimage
- Market through advertisement, etc.
- Political parties and leaders who set political agendas

- Non-Governmental Organizations, community based organizations and other civil society actors.

All of them will have to be used to reverse the process, i.e., to change the anthropocentric beliefs to pro-environmental beliefs.

Today in developing countries there is a great hunger for development and very little environmental consciousness. Folk wisdom and traditions are reinterpreted to serve the goals of capitalism. During the independence struggle and in the post-independence period in India philosophers, leaders and intellectuals favoured synthesizing western materialism and eastern philosophy. It is difficult to convince the people of India that in the interest of survival of earth they must volunteer for the present low levels of consumption or surrender inessential needs when the developed countries (and also the elites in their own countries) have so much of wasteful consumption. Religion, the modern media, and political leaders are only promoting consumerism and commodification; with little interest in sustainability of ecological process. The result is strong anti-ecological belief system, maintained by social structure, capitalism, political leaders, and even religious leaders who denounce materialism.

In the above context a cynic may ask: what is the role of environmental consciousness or beliefs when all major decisions are taken by the economic elite (in connivance with political elite) and the ordinary citizens have virtually little role in saving environment. Change of beliefs and behaviours among the common people will be of little consequence unless it leads to mobilization of people to change the social structure of capitalism. Some people however think that the environment can be protected only when people at large develop strong pro-ecological worldview leading to philosophy of spiritualism, equality and simplicity. In a democratic society change in the belief systems of people would put strong pressure on political leaders to go for environmental action.

Environmental Movements

Environmental movements are mobilizations of people with the goal of protecting the environment or of fighting against the practices which are leading to any type of environmental degradation. In India they also refer to people's struggle to hold their traditional right to protect their natural habitats and resources. Often, they involve a new political struggle for safeguarding the interests and survival of the poor, and the marginalized, including women, tribals and poor peasants whose economic and political interests are closely associated with nature. In India these movements resulted from a deep agrarian unrest but in the post-independence period their nature has changed considerably. There has been a rapid growth of forest-based industries such as paper, plywood, rubber, soap, etc.

> This resulted in giving preference to large scale plantation of fast growing commercially viable species... Thus the organic and composite nature of forests with varied flora and fauna had been destroyed and thereby the people and the communities who were dependent on these forests were marginalized causing disenchantment among them. In this milieu the agrarian unrest continued after independence. (Augustine, 1995).

> Ecological degradation and economic deprivation generated by the resource insensitivity and intensity of the classical model of development have resulted in environmental conflicts... (Shiva, 1991).

Chipko movement of Tehri Garhwal, Kerala Sastra Sahitya Parishad's resistance to Silent Valley river project, people's protest against Narmada Sagar project and Appiko movement of Uttarkannada district of Karnataka are some of the most visible environment movements in India.

CONCLUSION

Environmental issues are some of the most important issues of our times. Apocalyptic talks about the end of earth caused by industrialization and insatiable human desire to attain higher and higher levels of material development have become common. Climate change is a high probability risk. Though this is true that the developed countries are more responsible for environmental degradation and climate change, the developing countries too have to accept their part in protecting environment. They also have a link between rapid population growth and climate change, worsened by increasing per capita income and environment degrading industry.

To quote from UNFPA's State of World Population 2009:

> Thirty-seven of the 41 National Adaptation Programmes of Action, or NAPAs, that developing-country Governments had submitted to the UNFCCC by May 2009 explicitly link climate change and population ard identify rapid population growth as a problem that either exacerbates the effects of climate change or hinders the ability of countries to adapt to it. Through the preparation of NAPAs, the least developed countries state their priorities and needs for adapting to climate change. The growth of population can contribute to freshwater scarcity or degradation of cropland, which may in turn exacerbate the impacts of climate change. So too can population growth make it more difficult for Governments to alleviate poverty and achieve the Millennium Development Goals.

Thus there is a need to explore the link between population and various facets of environmental issues. The major ones are: resource depletion, perception of risk, environmental beliefs, environmental action, and social organizations and institutions responsible for environmental management.

QUESTIONS AND EXERCISES

1. What is the role of population in environmental impact and climatic change? What other factors affect environment?
1. What are various views on population-environment links?
2. How can one assess the environmental impact of a proposed industrial project? What are major indicators?
3. Visit a tribal area where a big industry has come up during the last fifteen years. Talk to people and try to learn what has been the impact of industry on social and economic life of the people? What do they say about changes in agriculture and forest produce?
4. Define the following:
   a. sustainable development
   b. environmental conflicts between developed and developing countries
   c. sociology of environment

5. Why do the developed and developing countries have divergent views on sustainable development?
6. What is required to generate pro-environmental beliefs in India? Who has to play a leading role in this?
7. Examine the various definitions of sustainable development and develop your own definition for the use of policy makers in India.
8. Identify an environmental movement in India and write an essay on its history, successes and failures.
9. What are all the complexities involved in linking population with sustainable development?
10. Using internet resources collect data on carbon emissions for ten countries. Examine whether the carbon emission is in proportion to their population.

REFERENCES

Augustine, Clymes, 1995, *A Sociological Inquiry into the New Social Movements: A Study of Women, Ecology and Prohibition Movements in Kerala*, Unpublished Ph.D. thesis, IIT Kanpur.

Carbon Dioxide Information Analysis Center (CDIAC), 2008, *http://en.wikipeda.org/wiki/List of Countries_by_carbon_dioxide_emissions* [accessed on 29th April, 2011]

Davis, Kingsley, 1990, Population and Resources: Fact and Interpretation. In Davis, Kingsley and Bernstam, Mikhail, S. (eds.), *Resources, Environment and Population: Present Knowledge, Future Option*. New York: Population Council: 1-24.

Demeny, Paul, 1990, Tradeoffs between Human Numbers and Material Standards of Living. In Davis, Kingsley and Bernstam, Mikhail, S. (eds.), *Resources, Environment and Population: Present Knowledge, Future Option*. New York: Population Council: 408-421.

Harvey, Mark, Quilley, Steve and Beynon, Huw, 2002, *Exploring the Tomato*. Cheltenham, UK: Edward Elgar.

Keyfitz, Mathan, 1991, Population and Development within the Ecosphere: One View of the Literature. *Population Index*, Vol. 57, No. 1: 5-22.

_______, 1990, Towards a Theory of Population-Development Interaction. In Davis, Kingsley and Emstam, Mikhail, S., (eds.) *Resources, Environment and Population: Present Knowledge, Future Option*. New York: Population Council: 295-314.

Meadows, D.H., Meadows, J.R. and Behrens, W.W. III, 1972, *The Limits to Growth*. New York: Universe Books.

Shiva, Vandana, 1991, *Ecology and the Politics of Survival*. New Delhi: Sage Publications.

Swarnakar, Pradip and Sharma, A.K., 2009, People's Attitude towards Groundwater Arsenic Contamination in West Bengal, India. *The Eastern Anthropologist*, 62: 1, pp. 61-83.

________, 2011, Understanding Environmental Concern, In Lahiri, S., Paswan, B., and Das, K.C. (eds.), *Migration, Health and Development*. Jaipur: Rawat Publications.

The World Bank, 1992, *World Development Report 1992: Development and the Environment*. New York: Oxford University Press.

United Nations Population Fund, 1992, *The State of World Population*. New York: UNFPA, p. iii.

_______, 2009, *The State of World Population 2009*. New York: UNFPA, p. 8, *http://www.unfpa.org/swp/2009/en/pdf/EN_SOWP09.pdf* [accessed on 13th December, 2009].

United Nations, 1992, *Earth Summit in Focus*, No. 6, United Nations: United Nations Department of Public Information.

12

Emerging Issues in Sociology of Population

MILLENNIUM DEVELOPMENT GOALS

Introduction

All ideas belong to their age. Historical developments lead to new concerns among intellectuals and planners. In the twenty first century, sociologists of population are exploring new issues. Days are over when sociologists of population were involved primarily in model building or estimation of birth and death rates from incomplete or unreliable data. Enough data of acceptable quality on various aspects of population are now available. There are new experiences in implementing programmes and there are new discourses on development and population. This has produced new research initiatives and new ideas. Some of them are discussed here. One major factor that has changed the discourse on population in this century is the framework of Millennium Development Goals (MDGs). Therefore this chapter begins with the discussion of MDGs. There is a close resemblance in the MDGs framework and the National Population Policy 2000 and the discussion shows how MDGs and our population policy share the similar concerns.

Millennium Development Goals (MDGs)

MDGs are created by an international body of statesmen. In September 2000, 189 nations adopted Millennium Declaration. The declaration was signed by 147 heads of state and governments during the UN Millennium Summit. The Millennium Development Goals are drawn from the actions and targets contained in that declaration (UNDP, 2009). This includes eight goals to be achieved by 2015 that respond to the world's main development challenges. These eight goals are further divided into 21 quantifiable targets that are measured by 60 indicators.

- Goal 1: Eradicate extreme poverty and hunger
- Goal 2: Achieve universal primary education
- Goal 3: Promote gender equality and empower women
- Goal 4: Reduce child mortality
- Goal 5: Improve maternal health
- Goal 6: Combat HIV/AIDS, malaria and other diseases
- Goal 7: Ensure environmental sustainability
- Goal 8: Develop a global partnership for development.

India is a signatory to the above Declaration. A cursory reading of the goals shows that all the MDGs are of great relevance to population. The first goal aims at reduction in unemployment, poverty and malnutrition. The second goal aims at raising school enrolment rate and literacy rate, separately among men and women. The third goal aims at improving ratios of girls to boys in primary, secondary and tertiary education, share of women in wage employment in the non-agricultural sector, and proportion of seats held by women in National Parliament. The fourth goal is to reduce infant and child mortality and increase proportion of 1 year-old children immunized against measles. The fifth goal aims at improving maternal mortality ratio by reducing proportion of births as home delivery and lacking in emergency care, often leading to postpartum hemorrhage, which is the major cause of maternal deaths. The fifth goal also calls for universal access to reproductive health which implies:

- Increasing contraceptive prevalence rate
- Decreasing adolescent birth rate
- Improving antenatal care coverage (indicated by frequency of "at least one visit" and "at least four visits")
- Meeting unmet need for family planning

A. The sixth goal aims has several targets and indicators:
Halt and begin to reverse the spread of HIV/AIDS

The indicators are:

- HIV prevalence among population aged 15-24 years
- Condom use at last high-risk sex
- Proportion of population aged 15-24 years with comprehensive correct knowledge of HIV/AIDS
- Ratio of school attendance of orphans to school attendance of non-orphans aged 10-14 years

B. Achieve, by 2010, universal access to treatment for HIV/AIDS for all those who need it

The indicator is:

- Proportion of population with advanced HIV infection with access to antiretroviral drugs

C. Halt and begin to reverse the incidence of malaria and other major diseases

The indicators are:

- Incidence and death rates associated with malaria
- Proportion of children under 5 sleeping under insecticide-treated bednets
- Proportion of children under 5 with fever who are treated with appropriate anti-malarial drugs
- Incidence, prevalence and death rates associated with tuberculosis
- Proportion of tuberculosis cases detected and cured under directly observed treatment short course.

The seventh goal aims at sustainable development, pollution control, improving water and sanitation facilities and reduction in proportion of urban population living in slums. Finally, the eighth goal aims at changing international terms of trade in favour of developing countries, debt relief, access to affordable essential drugs on a sustainable basis, and improving information and communication facilities with the cooperation of private sector.

Millennium Development Goals in India

Table 12.1 reproduces Table 1 of *Millennium Development Goals: India Country Report 2005*, the report prepared by the present values and targets of various indicators as reported by Ministry of Statistics and Programme Evaluation, Central Statistical Organization, Government of India. It has a list of 16 indicators.

Table 12.1: Progress Towards Achieving MDGs In India

	Indicator	*Year*	*Value*	*Year*	*Value*	*MDG target value*
1.	Proportion of population below poverty line (%)	1990	37.5	1999-2000	26.1	18.75
2.	Undernourished people as % of total population	1990	62.2	1999-2000	53	31.1
3.	Proportion of under-nourished children	1990	54.8	1998	47	27.4
4.	Literacy rate of 15-24 year olds	1990	€4.3	2001	73.3	100
5.	Ratio of girls to boys in primary education	1990-91	0.71	2000-01	0.78	1
6.	Ratio of girls to boys in secondary education	1990-91	0.49	2000-01	0.63	1
7.	Under five mortality rate (per 1000 live births)	1988-92	125	1998-2002	98	41
8.	Infant Mortality rate (per 1000 live births)	1990	80	2003	60	27
9.	Maternal Mortality rate (per 1000 live births)	1991	437	1998	407	109
10.	Population with sustainable access to an improved water source, rural (%)	1991	55.54	2005	90	80.5
11.	Population with sustainable access to an improved water source, urban (%)	1991	81.38	2001	82.22	94
12.	Population with access to sanitation urban (%)	1991	47	2001	63	72
13.	Population with access to sanitation	1991	9.48	2005	32.36	72

The general thinking in India is that the MDGs are too ambitious. Looking at the available resources, state of governance in the country and the social environment, we may not be able to achieve the MDGs as fixed in the Millennium Declaration. Yet, one cannot deny the importance of the framework of MDGs. They have directed attention of the planners (and also of the researchers and NGOs) towards specific goals and targets. They have also influenced the perspective of Tenth and Eleventh Five Year Plans in the country. MDGs have put the development agenda on top of family planning. It has accorded special importance to women empowerment, reproductive and child health and fighting HIV epidemic.

PARADIGM SHIFT IN POPULATION POLICY

In India the National Population Policy 2000 has called for a more humane approach to population planning and for paying greater attention to social development with particular emphasis on improving education, reproductive health and unmet needs of slums and other special categories of population. One major factor of new thinking is the stress on three points: (a) importance of area specific approach about which some academicians were arguing for a long time (Misra, 1992); (b) a need to recognize the importance of reciprocal relationship between population and development; and (c) acceptance of the fact that there could be multiple perspectives on social and organizational issues (Riley and McCarthy, 2003). The goals of NPP 2000 are further operationalized in terms of facilities for people. For example, the goal of reducing maternal mortality ratio has been translated into increasing institutional deliveries under National Rural Health Mission (NHRM).

Box 12.1 shows the paradigm shift that began in the Ninth Five Year Plan of Government of India and became fully operationalized in the Tenth Five Year Plan.

A significant change in the National Population Policy 2000 has been the introduction of HIV/AIDS. Linking population dynamics to HIV/AIDS has generated whole lot of new issues in the area of reproductive health, sexuality, sexual networking, male involvement in reproductive health, mapping of high risk groups, awareness of risks, authority of women in decision making at family level, and the role of community support. It may be stressed that all these issues have led to disenchantment with positivism and scientism, and established

Box 12.1: Paradigm Shift in Population Policy in the Tenth Plan

- Demographic targets to focusing on enabling couples to achieve their reproductive goals;
- Method specific contraceptive targets to meeting all the unmet needs for contraception to reduce unwanted pregnancies;
- Numerous vertical programmes for family planning and maternal and child health to integrated health care for women and children;
- Centrally defined targets to community need assessment and decentralised area specific microplanning and implementation of programme for health care for women and children, to reduce infant mortality and reduce high desired fertility;
- Quantitative coverage to emphasis on quality and content of care;
- Predominantly women centred programmes to meeting the health care needs of the family with emphasis on involvement of men in planned parenthood;
- Supply driven service delivery to need and demand driven service; improved logistics for ensuring adequate and timely supplies to meet the needs;
- Service provision based on providers' perception to addressing choices and conveniences of the couples.

importance of social constructivism, yielding self-reports, qualitative studies, and discourse analysis as methodological tools. Situation analysis and mapping, with involvement of community members rather than trained researchers, have become the most important tools with donors and policy makers. Through situation analysis we can not only have the mapping of high risk groups we can also learn a lot about socio-cultural context of HIV transmission, sexuality, risk behaviour, comprehensive knowledge among people and the available support system from government and non-government sources.

MDGs debate and NPP 2000 have raised new issues. Some of them are discussed below.

Area Specific Approach

India is a vast country with diverse patterns of socio-economic development. As a result of that the demographic situation in India is highly fragmented. Lessons learnt from one setting cannot be used in other settings. After success of population control programme in Kerala many demographers and planners started talking about Kerala model in 1990s but it has now become clear that since the socio-economic, infrastructural, and geographical conditions of high fertility states (UP, Bihar, Rajasthan and Madhya Pradesh) are markedly different from those of Kerala, the Kerala model cannot be applied to all states mechanically. States with their specificities will have to develop their own models of action. Seemingly opposite factors such as affluence and poverty may produce the same result in the form of fertility transition; affluence through rational choice model; and poverty through Malthusian pressure. Of late Himachal Pradesh has emerged as one of the lowest fertility states. The case of Himachal Pradesh needs detailed examination.

In this context the following remarks of Prof. Ashish Bose (1991) are worth considering:

> The implication is that there is little scope for a uniform all-India population programme, whether in regard to actions which operate on the birth rate or in regard to actions which operate on the death rate. Yet, to a very large extent, our family planning programmes are more or less uniform throughout the country. Virtually the same package is delivered to the high population growth areas as to the low population growth areas.

There is now a general agreement among planners, coordinators of the programme and programme managers that this situation must change.

Social Class Differences

Population problems as well as the status of health in India have religious, regional, ethnic, social class and urban-rural dimensions. National Family Health Survey-3 (Das *et al.*, 2001), National Sample Survey Organization's survey on morbidity, health care and the condition of the aged (NSSO, 2006), and smaller surveys have established the nature of variation in population and health parameters according to socio-economic and cultural characteristics of people. Eleventh Five Year Plan has stressed the social class differences in economic conditions as well as demographic behaviour. These differences, their causes and consequences, need to be explored further.

Complex Linkages

Studies have consistently shown that the relationships between socio-economic factors and demographic factors do not have a fixed pattern. The relationships which exist at the micro level may be different from those existing at the macro level. One has to study the linkages between population and other factors at different levels. Yet, an overwhelming majority of people in both urban and rural areas want a small family. Some people may still want a large family (Mukherjee, 1983) but their number is very small and is falling. Some want large family because of high infant and child mortality. With time as mortality declines their number will decline further. Most people today have knowledge of traditional and modern contraceptive methods but there are some who do not have access to acceptable contraceptive methods. They have unmet need for family planning (National Commission on Population, 2004). As said earlier, in India the unmet need for contraception (i.e., percentage of couples who do not want more children but are not practicing family planning) is quite large. While NFHS-3 estimated it to be 12.8 per cent, DLHS-3 estimated it to be 21.3 per cent (age 15-44 years).

Demographic change has both positive and negative implications for human resource development. While the continuing high growth rate of population may be disadvantageous in macro economic terms, the country has the advantage of opening of demographic window for nearly twenty years.

If the growing proportion of young population can be supported with adequate resources and they have an encouraging atmosphere, they can exploit opportunities opening in the industrially advanced but aging economies as well as in new sectors in the national economy. In some smaller countries, (particularly in several of the gulf countries) sending and receiving large number of migrants every year the demographic window may open and close several times. One has to study cycles of opening and closing of demographic window and its impact on population and economy.

All developed countries are facing the problem of couples not having enough motivation to produce a baby. This is a very dangerous situation and in the future this may happen in India also.

We have to understand complex and symmetrical linkages between social structure and demographic factors at national, regional, village, household and individual levels. For example, a large number of couples in different parts of the country do not want a girl child. Social structure and difficulties associated with raising a girl child, protecting her honour, and arranging for her marriage are discouraging parents from producing a female child (Desai, 1994). There has been a worrisome decline in sex ratio in age group 0-6 in the period 1991-2011. This is the result of combination of modern technology and tradition of patriarchy. Affordable technical means to detect the sex of the baby during pregnancy and facilities to abort it and weaknesses in law enforcing agencies are as much responsible for this as tradition. Ironically, some of the regions where sex selective abortions are more prevalent are socio-economically and educationally the most developed regions of the country. The combination of sex preference, medical technology and economic development poses a very serious threat to social development and an effective strategy has to be developed to counter this pattern. In turn, declining child sex ratios are not going to remain inconsequential. They will have a definite impact on several institutions of society in short run and long run. There is a need to conduct studies of declining child sex ratios on marriage and kinship, religion and political institutions.

Sustainability and Survival

Ignoring the concept of sustainable development, i.e., the neglect of demography of environment will be perilous to society. Sociologists and demographers need:

- Recognition of "differences", i.e., the condition that there are no simple and universal solutions to problems faced by people in different settings;
- Linking local with global as one cannot anymore ignore the effects of global developments on local conditions or of local initiatives on global climate;
- Learning from local communities how they have dealt with climatic changes in the past;
- Need to combine demographic values with survival and progress, separately at micro, meso and macro levels;
- A strong commitment for empowerment and emancipation of the vulnerable groups; and
- Exploring the subjective meanings, favourable to or against sustainability, in the context of ethical and moral changes.

Socio-economic, cultural and demographic systems in India are highly diversified (Bose, 1991). In this milieu, the perceptions of effects of population growth on people are as much linked with culture as with natural resources. Studies have also shown that lay persons and experts do not share the same value systems or ideas about good life. Also the way lay persons define their problems is not the same as the way programme managers and NGOs define them. There are people in the country for whom survival is the highest value: even housing or shelter is of secondary importance to them. Among them the goal of intervention should be their emancipation and empowerment, not the reduction in family size or vaccination alone. Globalization and the resulting marginalization of classes, castes, tribes, and communities are producing uncertainties in demographic trends. In this milieu, sustainability and survival are the key issue to understanding of demographic and social action.

Issues Related to Population Policy

The most crucial problem of population policy in India at the moment is the problem of lack of understanding of reproductive decision making process. Reproductive rationality is a rather unexplored area. Linking personal choices with social ethics is one of the greatest challenges of our times. Traditional societies do not have this problem because individuals are closely tied to traditions and ego is only weakly developed. Modern societies too do not have this problem. They have replaced tradition by rationality but they have developed institutionalized ways of handing problems arising out of individuation and alienation. Of course, even modern societies have not so far been successful in changing attitudes of people in the interest of society. The micro level and subjective calculations are against the change. Otherwise they would not be facing the problems of fertility declining to below replacement level and the subsequent problem of ageing. Social scientists must address this problem.

A consensus seems to be emerging that population planning issues should form a part of empowerment and emancipation. The National Population Policy 2000 rightly gives importance to education, immunization, lowering infant mortality rate, raising marriage age, increasing institutional deliveries, information/counselling, containing spread of HIV/AIDS, promotion of Indian Systems of Medicine, and related social sectors programmes. Some of these issues were included in the earlier policies statements too but the shift of emphasis from national level to community level is the biggest achievement of the new policy. It is this framework of empowerment that should guide studies on and approaches to population policy and reproductive decision rationality. The issue is: how do individuals decide about family size or contraceptive uses so that the community supported ideas of well being are actualized by them? It is not an easy question to answer.

As early as 1994, ICPD held at Cairo, maintained that size, growth, age structure and rural-urban distribution of a country have critical impact on development prospects and called on countries to "fully integrate population concerns into development strategies, planning, decision-making and resource allocation at all levels."

The conference recognized that investing in people to broaden their potential as human beings is the key to sustained economic growth and sustainable development.

The ICPD Programme of Action fixed the following "mutually supportive" goals:

- Gender equality in education;
- Reduction in infant, child and maternal mortality (infant and child mortality to 35 and 45 and maternal mortality to below 60);
- Reproductive health services;
- Improvement in education so that at least 90 per cent of all children are in schools by 2010;
- Provision of wide range of reproductive health services (including family planning services, essential obstetric care, and prevention and management of reproductive tract infections in all health care facilities by 2015);
- Ensuring that by 2015, 90 per cent of all births are assisted by skilled attendants;
- Meeting unmet need for family planning; and
- Providing access to HIV/AIDS prevention methods, and voluntary testing, counselling and follow up services.

In the following year 4th conference on women was held in Beijing and it lent further support to the above goals. And these are the ICPD 1994 goals which further reverberate in the United Nations Millennium Development Goals (MDGs) 2000.

NEW ISSUES BEFORE THE SOCIOLOGISTS

Paradigm Shift in Population Research

There is a paradigm shift in population research. The shift is from estimation to explanation and from quantitative methods to qualitative methods. There is also a shift from study of demographic processes to heath and emancipation. This paradigm shift is caused by both improved data and by changes in intellectual climate. So far the emphasis was on exploring causal connections between different socio-economic and demographic processes but gradually the attention is shifted to understanding of complex relationships between demographic variables, culture, power, social reproduction, ethnicity and gender.

The above shift has several implications for the discourse in the broader field of population studies. It is not possible to address the new issues caused by shifting paradigm in the conservative framework of research. The paradigm shift needs a change in orientation and a change in research methodology. Table 12.2 presents the key aspects of the old approach and some suggestions for the future. It is proposed that what the population planning needs today is a participatory approach with the aim of empowering the community. The conservative approach was based on the neo-Malthusian theory that population growth has adverse effects on development and that it is of utmost importance to reach replacement level fertility as soon as possible. This was a wrong assumption. The relationship between population and development is dynamic, situational and symmetrical. Subjective understanding of population depends heavily on the history, culture, awareness, social structure and resource map of the people (Chambers, 1980; Chambers, 1997). To be effective population policy must address the issue of population in a holistic manner and community rather than regional and national level planning would offer the best solutions. Solutions should emerge from participatory exercises (Kumar, 2002) and not from the tool kits of experts.

MEANING OF PARTICIPATION

Participation is a key concept of development discourse today but it is often a misunderstood term. There is a need to define the term in the new paradigm. This is true that in some or other form the notion of participation has always been there in population policy but its meaning has changed. In the past also population policy suggested making family planning a people's movement but it was just a pretence to impose the elite perspective of population on people. Participation of people was seen either as *consultative participation*, in which people were supposed to come to clinics and get counselling and services, or *functional* in which participation was seen as a means to achieve the project goals. There is a need to go for *interactive participation* in which people participate in joint analysis, development of action plans, group decision making, and move towards self-mobilization (Jennings, 2004). This also entails understanding of social representations of family and health at the community level.

Table 12.2: Approaches to Population Studies: Old and New: Experts Driven to Participatory Approaches

	Old Approach	*New Approach*
1. Major assumptions	Population growth has adverse effect on development	The relationship between population and development is dynamic, situational and symmetric
2. Social theory	Positivism	Social constructivism
3. Approaches to reality	Analytical	Holistic
4. Methodology	Survey, fieldwork	Situation analysis and mapping (by the community members rather than trained researchers)
5. Level of analysis	National and regional	District and community (with special emphasis on SC/ST, OBC, and urban slums)
6. Concepts	Scientific, objective	Subjective and relative
7. Emphasis	National and regional plans	Community interventions
8. Major actors	Government (with or without involvement of NGOs)	Research groups and NGOs/CBOs
9. Goal of research	Objective knowledge	Enabling the community to analyse their problems and empowering people
10. Resources	Hard facts	Conceptual maps, social representations and networks
11. Goals of policy	Population stabilization through education and services	Participatory development involving community resources, public-private partnership

Under the aegis of participatory model social scientists must try to unearth the meanings and social representations of life and social processes and the role of family size (number of children) in this. Health psychologists have already done pioneering work in the field of social representations of health and social scientists working on population and development issues may benefit immensely from the works of such health psychologists (Murray *et al.* 2003; Herzlich, 1973; Herzlich and Pierret, 1987; Moscovici, 2000). These studies will show that social representations of reproductive health are fluid and are intertwined with social arrangements in society. For example, Bhatia and Cleland (2008) found that anxiety, stress and overwork may be associated with reported gynaecological morbidity among poor urban women. According to NSSO data (NSSO, 2006) as many as 50 per cent spells of ailments in urban areas remained untreated because they were not considered to be serious. Modernization and post-modernization have posed challenges to traditional culture and demographers need to understand their full implications for finding ways of development of various communities and classes.

Health as the Broader Issue

In the recent past, attention of sociologists has shifted away from purely demographic and reproductive health issues to broader health issues. Implementation of National Rural Health Mission and Janani Suraksha Yojana have raised new issues:

- Social representations of health
- Health choices, i.e., what combination of health facilities are used by people in different circumstances—Allopathic or bio-medical, Homeopathy, Ayurvedic, Yunani, Siddh, local herbal remedies, and magic and other traditional practices
- Quality of services
- Factors affecting institutional deliveries
- Postpartum haemorrhage and other determinants of maternal deaths such as transport facilities
- Access to and quality of services
- Government of India has gone for public-private-partnership in health in a big way. Public and private systems have their own strengths and weaknesses. Studies are needed to explore what combinations of the two are good for society and what

ways of delivering health services need to be developed to have optimal benefits.

Starting with the issue of estimation of birth and death rates in the second half of twentieth century population studies are shifting towards issues of empowerment and emancipation, particularly in the context of studies of reproductive behaviour and RTI/STI. Yet, there are other major issues which need proper attention.

HIV/AIDS and Sexuality

HIV is a high-consequence risk (Giddens, 2003) about which there is no historical precedent to call on in preventing its spread and whose origin is least understood, whether it has cropped up "naturally" or has been caused by technological or environmental changes. To quote (NACO, 2006):

> Scientists have different theories about the origin of HIV, but none have been proven. The earliest known case of HIV was from a blood sample collected in 1959 from a man in Kinshasha, Democratic Republic of Congo. (How he became infected is not known.) Genetic analysis of this blood sample suggests that HIV-1 may have stemmed from a single virus in the late 1940s or early 1950s.

We do know that the virus has existed in the United States since at least the mid-to late 1970s. From 1979-1981 rare types of pneumonia, cancer, and other illnesses were being reported by doctors in Los Angeles and New York among a number of gay male patients. These were conditions not usually found in people with healthy immune systems. In 1982 public health officials began to use the term "acquired immunodeficiency syndrome," or AIDS, to describe the occurrences of opportunistic infections, Kaposi's sarcoma, and Pneumocystis carinii pneumonia in previously healthy men. Formal tracking (surveillance) of AIDS cases began that year in the United States.

The cause of AIDS is believed to be a virus that scientists isolated in 1983. The virus was at first named HTLV-III/LAV (human T-cell lymphotropic virus-type III/lymphadenopathy-associated virus) by an international scientific committee. This name was later changed to HIV (human immunodeficiency virus). HIV is passed on from the infected person to another person through the contact of body fluids such as blood, semen, vaginal fluid, breast milk and other body fluids containing blood. In other words, the virus may be transmitted through blood to blood and sexual contact, and from pregnant women to baby during pregnancy, delivery or breast feeding. Among health workers it has also been acquired through contact of cerebrospinal fluid surrounding the brain and the spinal cord, synovial fluid surrounding bone joints, and amniotic fluid surrounding a fetus. The virus starts weakening the immune system of the body making it more and more susceptible to various types of infectious attacks. Since these infections can easily attack the body of the AIDS patient they are often called the "opportunistic" infections. The infected person ultimately succumbs to one or more of them and dies. Although, the relationship between HIV and AIDS is not fully understood, available evidence suggests that the HIV is the cause of AIDS: HIV may remain dormant for as many as 8-10 years and develop into AIDS after that (NACO, 2006).

HIV research has produced certain ideas: (a) transmission of HIV is complex and uncertain; (b) HIV risk is subjectively defined; (c) the focus has to be on risk behaviour rather than group; and (d) there is a need for a new sociological paradigm.

On the basis of various sources of data, Pandey *et al.* (2009) estimate:

> HIV prevalence among adults (15-49 yr) was 0.36 per cent (uncertainty bounds 0.29-0.46%) in 2006. Overall prevalence in the high prevalence States was 0.8 per cent and in low and moderate epidemic States was 0.2 per cent. Prevalence was highest in Manipur at 1.70 per cent followed by Nagaland at 1.41 per cent, and Andhra Pradesh at 1.04 per cent. The estimated number of PLHA in the population of all ages was 2.5 million (uncertainty bounds 2.0-3.1 million). The number of people living with HIV was highest in Andhra Pradesh at 525,560 (range 420,448-651,694) followed by Maharashtra at 495,488 (range 396,390-614,405), Karnataka at 276,129 (range 220,903-342,400) and Tamil Nadu at 246,473 (range 197,178-305,626).

HIV and AIDS epidemic has raised new issues in health research (Narain, 2004). The major ones are:

- Situation analysis of HIV/AIDS
- Knowledge and awareness of RTI/STI including HIV and AIDS
- Socio-psychological and other determinants of risk behaviour
- Sexuality.

HIV is a new risk without possibility of cure. In several countries youths and adults have a very high prevalence rate, even more than 20 per cent. There it spread very fast. In other countries also if timely action is not taken it can spread equally fast or even faster. Improvement in transport and communication, globalization, geographic and social mobility, changing norms and vulnerability of certain sections of society are leading to spread of "HIV epidemic". The biggest problem in fighting the HIV is that the positive people and the communities in which they are found are stigmatized. Therefore, the people will not come out and go for testing and treatment.

UNICEF has sponsored situation analysis of HIV/AIDS in different parts of the country. The main purpose of these studies is to examine risk of HIV, map the vulnerable groups and develop an inventory of resources for HIV/AIDS action. This has also called for identification of a large number of indicators at the district level in terms of which HIV action can be monitored and made more effective.

Sexuality research has opened many new areas for health researchers. Important among them are sexuality and sexual behaviour, brothels and their clients, men having sex with men and other high risk groups, non-marital sex, sex among adolescents and young adults, and determinant of condom use (Verma *et al.*, 2004). It has shown that the Indian masses know very little about RTI/STI and HIV, and cannot distinguish between HIV and AIDS.

Stigma and its Consequences

The recognition that to fight HIV is to fight stigma against HIV positive people has led to studies of stigma. Sociologically speaking, stigma implies devaluation. Stigmatized persons are targets of prejudice (attitudes), stereotypes (i.e., cognition as beliefs, knowledge and expectations of social groups) and discrimination. According to Goffman (1963), persons who possess an attribute that risks their full acceptance from others are said to possess a stigma. As a consequence of the stigma, such persons are reduced in people's minds from whole and usual persons to the tainted, discounted ones. For Goffman stigma is relational in nature, i.e., it is an attribute that is deeply discrediting within a particular social interaction.

Thus a stigma involves the public's attitude toward a person or group of persons who possesses an attribute that falls short of societal expectations in a given social context. To quote:

> ... we believe the person with a stigma is not quite human. On this assumption we exercise varieties of discrimination, through which we effectively, if often unthinkingly, reduce his life chances.

Goffman further explained that stigma falls into three categories:

1. *Abominations of the body*—various physical deformities.
2. *Blemishes of individual character*—weak will, domineering or unnatural passions, treacherous and rigid beliefs, or dishonesty. Blemishes of character are inferred from, for example, mental disorder, imprisonment, addiction, alcoholism, homosexuality, unemployment, suicidal attempts, or radical political behaviour.
3. *Tribal stigma of race, nation, and religion*—beliefs that are transmitted through lineages and equally contaminate all members of a family.

Stigmatising marks may be visible as physical disability or invisible as a social identity. Even membership of a vulnerable community or 'high risk group' is also stigmatised. For Goffman, race, ethnicity, religion, physical ability, appearance and gender are the common bases of stigma. Prostitutes, drug addicts, carnival workers, hobos, winos, show people, full time gamblers, beach dwellers, homosexuals and urban unrepentant poor are Goffman's examples of stigmatized persons. He further says that some terms used for stigmatized persons are cripple, bastard and moron. In case of HIV there is no visible mark. Yet, people have their own thinking of how a HIV infected person looks like.

In case of stigma against HIV too not only the HIV positive people but also the communities to which they perceivably belong are stigmatised. People lack comprehensive knowledge of transmission of HIV but a large majority of them think that HIV spreads through illegal sex. Then sex being central to morality, HIV positive people are most stigmatised; they suffer from double stigma, one from having HIV and another for violating the sexual mores of society. National surveys shows that there is very little knowledge that HIV can spread through non-sexual routes also (blood transmission, unsafe medical procedures, and mother to child). According to DLHS-3 only half of the women know about infected blood transfusion route and less than one-third about mother to child route. I believe that comprehensive knowledge, freeing HIV from sexual morality, will also help in reducing stigma. The problem of identifying and controlling HIV is further complicated by the fact that a single test of HIV is not enough to confirm the positive status.

Goffman divides all the stigmatized persons into four groups: in-group deviants, social deviants, minority members and lower class persons. In all cases, stigma leads to damage to self-concept and self-destruction. It may be stressed that people feel able to make guess about the characteristics of almost any defined social group on the basis of any information at their disposal though the social scientist would consider that information inadequate.

Stigma against HIV may be divided into the following categories:

- Instrumental stigma—a reflection of the fear and apprehension that are likely to be associated with HIV and AIDS
- Symbolic stigma—the use of emic concepts to express attitudes toward the social groups or "lifestyles" perceived to be associated with HIV and AIDS
- *Courtesy HIV-related stigma*—stigmatization of people connected to the issue of HIV/AIDS or HIV-positive people.

Among the above three types of stigmas the instrumental sigma seems to be of paramount importance. There is undoubtedly stigma against certain lifestyles such as homosexuals or drug users. In addition the fear that if they come in contact of HIV positive people they may catch a deadly and transmissible illness creates a great fear in people's mind. Stigma becomes more discriminatory when it occurs with domination, social discrimination and exploitation. Thus if a victim is also a member of socially disadvantaged groups, and is a woman, the HIV status has more negative implications.

International Migration

With increasing globalization and growth of world population growing migration has become an important issue. According to the assessments of The National Intelligence Council (2001) more than 140 million people live outside their countries of birth and migrants comprise more than 15 per cent of the population in over 50 countries. It is estimated that their numbers will grow further. Under certain conditions differences between migrants and natives are known to have produced stereotypes, discrimination and violent conflicts. Therefore, while migration may ameliorate the labour force shortfalls at the place of destination or relieve population pressure at the place of destination, it may evoke discrimination on the grounds of language, culture and religious practices. The most sufferers will be the migrants in those countries which receive a large number of illegal migrants.

Internal Migration

In case of India internal migration and its consequences are not less important than international migration. As discussed earlier in Chapter 6 on India's population, there is a need to study social responses to demographically induced migration from one region to another within the country. Due to socio-economic imbalances and demographic diversity and a strong link between the two a significant shift is taking place in spatial distribution of population. Strong push factors of insecurity and unemployment are causing migration of people from states like Bihar to Maharashtra, Delhi, Gujarat, Punjab and Haryana where they can find employment in industry or agriculture. As the economic conditions are becoming harsher everywhere the local people are resenting. They want more jobs for the "sons of the soil." This leads to conflict. This also has implications for national integration. The major migration issues are:

- Volume and pattern of inter-district and inter-state migration caused by unemployment and climate change
- Social causes and consequences of internal migration
- Vulnerability of migrants to various types of risks at the place of destination

While lot of data are now available on volume and pattern of migration as well as the causes and consequences of migration there is less information on vulnerability of migrants at place of destination. For several countries, including India, internal migration, is already a burning political issue. In the future it would become a more important issue than fertility and mortality. If the regional inequalities—economic, political and social—increase further, as there seems to be the case, more people will be forced to migrate from one region to another. In several cases this will involve migration of a large number of people and significantly affect the composition of population at the place of destination. Usually when size of migrants is small the stream of migration is followed by absorption and assimilation but when a large number of people migrate they have a tendency to form a distinctive ethnic identity at the place of destination and that may result in ethnic conflicts caused by economic conflicts and increasing misery. There are already signs of such conflicts in several cities of India.

Disabled Population

Apart from the regional, sex and social class differences there are special problems of the physically challenged people who have been made the part of horizontal reservation policy in the country. There is a need to estimate their population, understand the various problems they face, and how disability is intertwined with religion, sex, class and caste. Census 2001 provided data on disabled population. It revealed that over 21 million people in India are suffering from some or other disability. They constitute about 2.1 per cent of the population of India. Sex wise break up shows that among the 21 million disabled people 12.6 million are males and 9.3 million are females. The disability rate (number of disabled per 100,000 population) for the country as whole comes out to be 2,130; 2,369 in the case of males and 1,874 in the case of females. Here one may also ask: why the disability rate among females is lower than among males? Is it due to underreporting or due to higher death rates among the disabled females as compared to disabled males? We require elaborate data to have an understanding of this issue. Further, the census data (Census of India, 2009) shows:

> Among the five types of disabilities on which data has been collected, disability. In seeing at 48.5 per cent emerges as the top category. Others in sequence are: In movement

(27.9%), Mental (10.3%), In speech (7.5%), and In hearing (5.8%). The disabled by sex follow a similar pattern except for that the proportion of disabled females is higher in the category In seeing and In hearing.

Across the country, the highest number of disabled has been reported from the state of Uttar Pradesh (3.6 million). Significant numbers of disabled have also been reported from the state like Bihar (1.9 million), West Bengal (1.8million), Tamil Nadu and Maharashtra (1.6 million each). Tamil Nadu is the only state, which has a higher number of disabled females than males. Among the states, Arunachal Pradesh has the highest proportion of disabled males (66.6%) and lowest proportion of female disabled.

Table 6.6: Number of Disabled Population and Type of Disability

	Population	*Percentage*
Total population	1,028,610,328	100.0
Total disabled population	21,906,769	2.1
Disability rate (per lakh population)	2,130	–
Type of disability		
(a) In seeing	10,634,881	1.0
(b) In speech	1,640,868	0.2
(c) In hearing	1,261,722	0.1
(d) In movement	6,105,477	0.6
(e) Mental	2,263,821	0.2

CONCLUSION

To conclude, there is a need for micro and participatory studies of population linking the global imbalance between population and resources with the local solutions acceptable to people in different social milieus. Let us learn from the people how they decide what is best for them and how they evolve sustainable models of development in the value framework of their culture, keeping in view their limited resources. In these studies social scientists would act as facilitators, helpful to the communities and people, in arriving at more optimal solutions. Econometric and statistical models have certainly played a role in the past in estimating the unknowns and in suggesting macro level solutions but when it comes to developing effective intervention strategies they have been found to be of limited application: the abstractions on which they are based are far away from reality. Voluntary action groups, research

NGOs, and those receptive to idea of multiplicity of perspectives are the most suited people to evolve the workable development plans in the fragmented society of India in our times. Time has come to learn about possible emancipatory strategies and empower communities and people to manage common and limited resources.

QUESTIONS AND EXERCISES

1. What are the major differences between old and new approaches to population policy in India? Critically examine the old approach and suggest how the new approach addresses the weaknesses of the old approach.
2. What are MDGs? Is there any link between MDGs and population policy?
3. Identify some major issues in population studies.
4. Write short notes on the following:
   a. area specific approach
   b. participatory approach
   c. relationship between gender gap and high fertility.
5. What are the major pitfalls of the new approach to population?
6. Why is the study of internal migration important?
7. What is HIV? Which countries are affected by HIV epidemic most? What can be done to arrest spread of HIV?
8. What is the relationship between HIV and sexuality? Why is the issue of stigma so important in dealing with HIV?
9. Write a short note on the extent of disability in India?
10. Collect data on prevalence of HIV in different countries from the net? Which countries have high or low rates of HIV? What could be the reasons for high rate of HIV in the former?

REFERENCES

Bhatia, J.C. and Cleland, John C., 2008, Perceived Gynaecological Morbidity: Health Seeking Behaviour and Expenditure in Karnataka. In Koenig, M.A., Shireen Jejebhoy, John C. Cleland, and Bela Ganatra (eds.), *Reproductive Health in India: New Evidence.* Jaipur: Rawat Publications, 266-282.

Bose, Ashish, 1991, *Demographic Diversity of India: 1991 Census*. Delhi: B.R. Publishing Corporation.

Census of India, 2009, *http://www.censusindia.gov.in/Census_And_You/disabled_population.aspx* [access on 19th January, 2010).

Chambers, Robert, 1980, *Rural Development: Putting the Last First.* Harlow: Longman.

Chambers, Robert, 1997, *Whose Reality Counts? Putting the First Last.* London: Intermediate Technology Publications.

Das, N.P., Misra, Vinod K. and Saha, P.K., 2001, Does Community Access Affect the Use of Health and Family Welfare Services in Rural India? *National Family Health Survey Subject Reports*, No. 18. Mumbai: International Institute for Population Sciences.

Desai, Sonalde,1994, *Gender Inequalities and Demographic Behaviour*. New York: The Population Council.

Giddens, Anthony, 2003, Modernity under a Negative Sign: Ecological Issues and Life Politics. In Pepper, David, Webster, Frank and Revill, George (eds.), *Environmentalism: Critical Concepts.*, London: Routledge, 267-291.

Goffman, E., 1963, *Stigma: Notes on the Management of Spoiled Identities.* Englewood Cliffs, NJ: Prentice-Hall.

Government of India, 2005, *Millenium Development Goals: India Country Report 2005.* New Delhi: Ministry of Statistics and Programme Evaluation, Central Statistical Organization. Available at *http://www.unicef.org/india/ssd04_2005_final.pdf* [accessed on 20th November, 2009].

Herzlich, C. (1973). *Health and Illness: A Social Psychological Analysis.* London: Academic Press.

Herzlich, C. and Pierret J., 1987, *Illness and Self in Society.* Baltimore: John Hopkins University Press.

Kumar, Somesh, 2002, *Methods for Community Participation: A Complete Guide for Practitioners.* New Delhi: Vistaar Publications.

Misra, B.D., 1992, *Area-specific Approach in Health and Family Welfare-Uttar Pradesh.* Lucknow: State Institute of Health and Family Welfare, U.P.

Moscovici, S., 2000, *Social Representations: Explorations in Social Psychology.* Cambridge: Polity Press.

Mukherjee, Ramakrishna, 1983, Population and Social System. In Narain, Vatsala, and Prakasham, C.P. (eds.), *Population Policy Perspectives in Developing Countries*, Bombay: Himalaya Publishing Company, 18-33.

Murray, Michael, Pullman, Daryl and Rodgers, Theresa Heath, 2003, Social Representations of Health and Illness among 'Baby-boomers' in Eastern Canada, *Journal of Health Psychology*, Vol. 8, No.5: 485-499.

Narain, J.P. (eds.), 2004, *AIDS in Asia: The Challenge Ahead.* New Delhi: Sage.

National AIDS Control Organization (NACO), 2006, FAQs on AIDS, *http://www.nacoonline.org/events_events.htm* [accessed on 3rd May, 2009].

National Commission on Population, Found at *http://www.populationcommission.nic.in/npp_obj.htm*, 19th March, 2004.

National Sample Survey Organisation, *Morbidity, Health Care and the Condition of the Aged*, NSS 60th round, January-June 2004, National Sample Survey

Organisation, Ministry of Statistics and Programme Implementation, Government of India, 2006.

Pandey, Arvind, Reddy, Dandu C.S., Ghys, Peter D., Thomas, Mariamma, Sahu, Damodar, Bhattacharya, Madhulekha, Maiti, Kanchan D., Arnold, Fred, Kant, Shashi, Khera, Ajay and Garg, Renu, 2009, Improved estimates of India's HIV burden in 2006. *Indian Journal of Medical Research*, Vol. 129: 50-58.

Poston Jr., Dudley L., Micklin, Michael and Baumle, Amanda K., 2007, Demography. In Bryant, Clifton D. and Peck, Dennis L. (eds.), *21st Century Sociology: A Reference Handbook.* Thousand Oaks: Sage Publications, 508-517.

Premi, M.K., 1991, *India's Population: Heading Towards a Billion.* New Delhi: B.R. Publishing Corporation.

Ray, Jennings, Participatory Development as New Paradigm: The Transition of Development Professionalism. Found at *http://www.usaid.gov/hum_response/oti/pubs/pbdv1000.pdf,* April 2004.

Riley Nancy E., and McCarthy, James, 2003, *Demography in the Age of the Postmodern*, Cambridge: Cambridge University Press.

UNDP, 2009, *http://www.undp.org.in/index.php?option=com_content&task=view&id=11&Itemid=44* [accessed on 20th November, 2009].

United Nations Population Fund (UNFPA), *State of World Population 2004: The Cairo Consensus at Ten: Population, Reproductive Health and the Global Effort to End Poverty,* UNFPA, 2004:.2-12.

United Nations, 1999, Below Replacement Fertility, *Population Bulletin of the United Nations*, Special Issue Nos. 40/41.

Verma, Ravi K., Pelto, P.J., Schensul, S.L. and Joshi, Archana (eds.), *Sexuality in the Time of AIDS: Contemporary Perspectives from Communities in India*. New Delhi: Sage Publications.

Visaria, Leela, and Pravin Visaria (1998). "India's Population in Transition", In Singh, J.P. (ed.), *Studies in Social Demography,.*, New Delhi: M.D. Publications Pvt. Ltd, 1-66.

Index